GRILL THIS NOT THAT!™

BACKYARD SURVIVAL GUIDE

BY DAVID ZINCZENKO
AND MATT GOULDING

RODALE.

Rodale books may be purchased for business or promotional use or for special sales.
For information, please write to:
Special Markets Department, Rodale, Inc., 733 Third Avenue, New York, NY 10017

Men's Health is a registered trademark of Rodale Inc.

Printed in the United States of America

Rodale Inc. makes every effort to use acid-free ♾, recycled paper ♻.

Book design by George Karabotsos

Photo direction by Tara Long

Cover photos by Jeff Harris / Cover prop styling by Roscoe Betsill
Hand modeling by Ashly Covington

All interior photos by Thomas MacDonald and Mitch Mandel/Rodale Images

Food styling by Diane Simone Vezza and Melissa Reiss

Illustrations on pages 129, 164, and 166 by Harry Campbell

Library of Congress Cataloging-in-Publication Data is on file with the publisher

ISBN-13: 978-1-60961-822-3 trade paperback
ISBN-13: 978-1-60961-934-3 direct mail hardcover

Trade paperback and exclusive direct mail edition published simultaneously in May 2012

Distributed to the trade by Macmillan

2 4 6 8 10 9 7 5 3 1   paperback
2 4 6 8 10 9 7 5 3 1   direct-mail hardcover

We inspire and enable people to improve their lives and the world around them.

www.rodalebooks.com

Dedication

To all the men and women who have
ever set fire to something, intentionally or not.
Here's how to harness your power
for the best purposes possible.
And to all of America's brave firefighters.
We're really, really sorry.

ACKNOWLEDGMENTS

Plenty of sizzling steaks and singed arm hairs went into making this book. So did a lot of long days and nights spent designing pages, checking facts, correcting punctuation, buying ingredients, crunching numbers, grating cheese, taking photos, and countless other efforts, both big and small. This book is the product of all those efforts—and all those people behind them that make this team the finest in the publishing industry. Thanks to all of you who were a part of this project, especially:

To Maria Rodale and the Rodale family, who have done as much to improve the way Americans eat as any other family in this country.

To George Karabotsos, whose vision and creativity continue to take these books in amazing new directions. And to his crew of rock star designers, including Laura White, Mark Michaelson, Courtney Eltringham, and Elizabeth Neal. If this series has proved anything, it's that this design team has no equal.

To Laura Perez, the world's most amazing sous chef. And to Clint Carter, Hannah McWilliams, and Cathyrne Keller, three individuals who make everything we do better.

To Debbie McHugh and Erin Williams, you two are the glue that holds these pages together.

To Tara Long, who has tamed many a fire to perform her acts of alchemy. And to the rest of the team that brings this food to life, including Diane Vezza, (Smokin') Joan Parkin, Tom MacDonald, Mitch Mandel, Troy Schnyder, Nikki Weber, and Melissa Reiss. No appetite is safe when you guys are at work.

To the talented and dedicated Rodale book team: Steve Perrine, Chris Krogermeier, Sara Cox, Jennifer Giandomenico, Wendy Gable, Keith Biery, Liz Krenos, Brooke Myers, Sean Sabo, Deri Reed, Sonya Vogel, and Jodi Schaffer. These books could not succeed without your incredible efforts.

And to our friends, family, and loved ones: There's no one we'd rather cook for.

—Dave and Matt

Check out the other bestselling books in the **EAT THIS, NOT THAT!**® and **COOK THIS, NOT THAT!**® series:

Eat This, Not That! for Kids! (2008)

Cook This, Not That! 350-Calorie Meals (2010)

Eat This, Not That! No-Diet Diet (2011)

Eat This, Not That! (2011)

Eat This, Not That! Supermarket Survival Guide (2012)

CONTENTS

"Feel the Burn"

You've heard it said hundreds of times, in spin classes and workout DVDs and gyms of every kind. If you want to lose weight, get in shape, and feel your best, you've got to "feel the burn." You have to "burn off calories," and "maximize your burn rate."

Well, that's all well and good, but it's not always fun. Wouldn't it be easier if, instead of feeling the burn, you could melt off pounds by applying the burn? And rather than burning off the calories from the foods you eat, what if you could burn the calories off before you eat them? And what if the only burn rates you had to worry about involved making sure you brought enough sunscreen?

Wouldn't that be a heck of a lot more fun?

It is. And that's what this book is all about. In the following pages, you're going to learn how to save hundreds, if not thousands, of calories at each meal, simply by using the easiest, most enjoyable, most tasty cooking method ever invented. You'll eat great, you'll look great—and you'll have a great time doing it.

Ready to get started?

In the beginning, there was fire.

Paleolithic man wouldn't have survived without it. He used it to heat his home, light his way, mold his tools. But most important of all, he used it to cook. The open flame tenderized his food, made it more appetizing, and even made it more delicious.

And if you've ever tried Woolly Mammoth Tartare...not good.

But besides making his food more palatable, the open flame made it healthier by melting off unwanted fat and making nutrients more accessible. Primitive man worshipped fire and kept it constantly burning, feeding it kindling and tending to it the way Taylor Lautner tends to his abs. And when wood wasn't plentiful, our ancestors used alternative fuels like weeds, moss, and even animal dung.

Nowadays, we're lucky enough not to have to cook with animal dung (although if we could actually harness all the animal dung tossed around in election campaigns, we'd have enough energy to power all of the Kardashian family hair dryers into eternity). Instead, we have grills: Eighty-two percent of American households own a grill, whether it's a propane-fueled combustion machine eating up a parking space in the garage or just a little bucket of charcoal hanging out on the terrace. And if you can learn to fire it up right, you'll discover that it just might be the most effective weight-loss tool in your arsenal. In fact, our research shows that you can save, in some instances, as many as 1,500 calories per meal just by choosing to grill dinner instead of driving to the local restaurant.

How's that, you ask? Isn't the backyard barbecue the sort of place for *King of the Hill*–type potbellied dads to gather 'round like priests worshipping at the altar of beer and hot dogs? Sure, it can be. But it can also be a perfect place to start stripping pounds from your body. When you drop a piece of meat on your grill, much of the fat bubbles out and burns up on the coals below. A study in the journal *Meat Science* found that grilling a pork chop could actually decrease its fat content by nearly a third!

Okay, sure, but there are plenty of "grilled" foods available at the chain restaurants that anchor your local mall. Why not just swing by one of those? Well, here's where things get tricky. In many cases, restaurant "grills"

are actually grill plates, or hot slabs of flat metal that lock fat in instead of cooking it out. Plus, restaurants routinely paint their meats with hot oil and clarified butter, effectively ramping up the fat count to flab-inducing levels. In fact, a USDA study found that people eat about 107 more calories each time they choose to eat out instead of eating at home.

But often, the reality is much worse. For instance, let's say you're hankering for a nice, meaty dinner—but you want to make sure you're eating healthy. So you'd naturally opt for chicken over red meat— if it's white meat, it's light meat, right? Well, in some cases that's true. But take a close look at some of those "healthier" alternative dishes out there. Outback's Alice Springs Chicken entrée might sound like a healthy choice, but wherever Alice Springs is, we think it's probably polluted with runoff from a lard factory. For the $14.49 you'll spend for that "healthy" option, you'll be getting 1,468 calories and a heart-stopping 2,220 milligrams of sodium— nearly two whole days' worth of salt! If you ask them to hold the Aussie fries, you're still getting 784 calories and a day's allotment of sodium. By comparison, you'll find a recipe on page 136 for something very similar: We call it Prosciutto Pesto Chicken. It comes in at only 230 calories, and has less than one-third the sodium. (And the ingredients will cost you about $1.83 a serving.) If you stayed home and grilled just once a week, a swap like this would save you 18 pounds this year alone! Just by eating the same food from your own backyard grill!

Oh, and did we mention you'll save a ton of time, money, and stress?

Beyond rescuing you from more than 18 pounds of flab every year, that chicken swap would also save you $12.66 per person. For a family of four making a swap like that just once a week, you're talking about putting—this sounds incredible, but it's true—an additional $2,633.28 in your pocket this year. Just by grilling once a week!

And that's before you factor in the hassle of loading everybody into the car, finding a parking spot, waiting out in the vestibule for that creepy little vibrator thing to light up, and then trying to feign interest in a restaurant you've probably been to a hundred times before—because all of these chains look exactly alike, whether you're dining in Austin or Augusta, Akron or Albany. So, instead of all the restaurant hassle and having to entertain the kids when they get fidgety, all you need to do is open the back door, arm the kids with some Super Soakers or a football, and call them when dinner's ready. Plus, there's no limited menu.

We've packed this book with 150 super-easy, super-delicious recipes so you can grill almost every night of the week.

And each one of these new foods will be something you selected yourself. You'll know exactly what's in it—something that can't be said about a plate from your local restaurant chain. Isn't it better to toss some fresh mushrooms on the grill and watch them sizzle, especially when you know that the canned kind often used in restaurants can legally contain up to 19 maggots and 74 mites in every 3.5-ounce can? Yikes! And wouldn't you rather be able to check the ingredients of your burger buns to make sure they're free of a dough strengthener called L-cysteine—a non-essential amino acid most often made from dissolved duck feathers or, sometimes, human hair? Blech! (Bet the waitress at your local diner can't tell you whether your entrée comes with a side of L-cysteine or not, huh?)

Is this book the best investment you've ever made, or what?

But you'll not only get leaner and richer—you'll get healthier, too!

New research has discovered that of all cooking methods, grilling is clearly the healthiest—better than frying (obviously), baking (hmm), and even nuking (really?). Consider what researchers are now saying about the magic of the grill:

You'll ingest less fat and calories.
A 2011 study looked at how one kind of fish stacked up nutritionally depending on whether it was baked, fried, microwaved, or grilled. It was discovered that the lowest levels of fat and calories were found in the grilled fish.

You'll build more lean muscle. In the same study, researchers studied the amount of muscle-maintaining protein found in the fish. They found that the grilled fish actually had higher levels of protein than fish cooked by other methods! A second study, published in the *Journal of Medicinal Food*, looked at different ways of cooking five types of fish: In each species, the highest levels of essential amino acids—the building blocks of muscle—were found in the grilled samples.

You'll shrink your belly. The foods we recommend in *Grill This, Not That!* are designed predominantly to target belly fat—by keeping your belly full of smart, healthy choices that keep your resting metabolism revving and never let you go hungry. That means you'll be at the top of your game and burning fat all day, every day.

You'll boost your brain power. In a 2009 study from the journal *Food Chemistry*, researchers looked at the vitamin and mineral content in meat that was baked, grilled, microwaved, and fried. It found that grilling alone seemed to significantly increase the levels of vitamin B2, which is essential to a healthy nervous system.

You'll protect your heart. Grilling also increases levels of niacin, the researchers said. Niacin has been found to boost HDL, the "good" cholesterol that keeps arteries clear. And, in another shocker, all cooking methods significantly decreased the meat's level of vitamin B6—all except for grilling! By retaining the food's levels of B6, grilling helps to maintain normal levels of homocysteine, an amino acid in the blood. High levels of homocysteine have been linked to heart disease.

Okay, so let's be clear here: By grilling at home just once a week, you could strip more than 18 pounds off your belly; build lean, healthy muscle; and reduce your risk of heart disease. And you could do it all while saving enough money to buy four round-trip tickets to Paris.

Makes you think that maybe the backyard barbecue has gotten a bad rap, huh? Well that's about to change. It's time to forget about *King of the Hill*.

It's time to become *King of the Grill!*

How to lose weight with this book

If you want to shed belly fat, there's only one formula you need to know, and, luckily for you, it's easier than anything you encountered in ninth-grade algebra.

The magic formula is this: Calories in – calories out = total weight loss or gain. This is the equation that determines whether your body will shape up to look more like a slender 1 or a paunchy 0, a flat-bellied yardstick or a pot-bellied protractor. That's why it's critical that you understand what sort of numbers you're plugging into this formula.

On the "calories out" side, we have your daily activities: cleaning house, lining up at the post office, hauling in groceries, and so on. Often when people discover extra flab hanging around their midsections, they assume there's something wrong with this side of the equation. Maybe so, but more likely it's the front end of the equation—the "calories in" side—that's tipping the scale. That side keeps track of all the fast-food value meals, Chinese buffets, and stuffed-crust pizzas you eat every day.

In order to maintain a healthy body weight, a moderately active female between the ages of 20 and 50 needs only 2,000 to 2,200 calories per day. A male fitting the same profile needs 2,400 to 2,600. Those numbers can fluctuate depending on height, age, and activity level, but they're reasonable estimations for most people. (For a more accurate assessment, use the calorie calculator at mayoclinic.com.)

Let's take a closer look at the numbers: It takes 3,500 calories to create a pound of body fat. So if you eat an extra 500 calories per day—the amount you'd take in by eating T.G.I. Friday's Pulled Pork Sandwich instead of the Spicy Asian Pork Burger in this book—then you'll earn 1 new pound of body fat each week. But here's the silver lining: If you currently make a habit of eating out at restaurants, and you start grilling in your backyard instead, then you can drop 52 pounds—or more—this year!

That's where this book comes in. Within these pages are nearly 150 flavorful recipes that save you as many as 1,500 calories over similar dishes constructed in the grease-stained restaurant kitchens of America. The more often you fire up your grill, the quicker you'll notice layers of fat melting away from your body! Check this out:

• **CHILI'S SMOKEHOUSE BURGERS** have more than 2,000 calories each! Our version—covered with bacon, dripping with sauce—still saves you 1,830 calories! (Check it out on page 90.)

• Despite the healthy-sounding name, **APPLEBEE'S ORANGE GLAZED SALMON** delivers 730 calories. Switch to the **CEDAR PLANK SALMON** on page 222 and save 490 calories. Make this or similar swaps a couple times a week and you'll shed 15 pounds this year.

• **ON THE BORDER'S DOS XX FISH TACOS WITH CHILI SAUCE** has 1,670 calories—before adding sides. Switch to our **GRILLED FISH TACOS WITH PICO DE GALLO** and you'll save an astonishing 1,350 calories a week. That's enough to burn off 9 pounds of flab in 6 months!

And here's the best news of all: While cooking on your grill shrinks your waistline, it also fattens your bank account. The food prepared by restaurants uses cheaper ingredients, yet it regularly costs two to four times as much as the meals you can prepare at home. So by making food yourself, you're saving both money and calories, and the more you fire up the grill, the more dramatic the savings. So go ahead: Get grilling!

America's
WORST
Grilled Foods

At the heart of the grill lies the key to a powerful convergence of flavor and nutrition, a fire that melts fat and delivers heaping quantities of smoke and sizzle, the world's greatest zero-calorie ingredients.

But a scorching Weber isn't always the weight-loss weapon we want it to be. Consider this: We've found dozens of grilled dishes in the restaurant world with more than 1,000 calories per serving, from salads with nutritional numbers that make double cheeseburgers seem healthy, to racks of ribs that pack more calories than 11 Krispy Kreme Original Doughnuts. Yes, it is possible to screw up food on the grill, as the biggest restaurants in the country continue to prove every day by choosing bad cuts of meat, coating them with sugary sauces, and serving them with a lousy supporting cast of side dishes—all tactics that compromise the inherent goodness of the grill.

To keep you from getting scorched next time you head out to dinner, we've identified the 20 worst flame-broiled foods in America. But it's not all bad news: We offer delicious alternatives that you can make at home for a fraction of the cost and calories, a strong reminder that the grill, when used responsibly, is a world-class weight-loss weapon.

695 calories

Five Guys makes America's most dangerous dog.

WORST GRILLED HOT DOG

20 Five Guys' Bacon Cheese Dog

695 calories
48 g fat (22 g saturated)
1,700 mg sodium

Price: $4.75

Five Guys doesn't give you many options. Not in the mood for a burger? There's grilled cheese, a 1,474-calorie bag of French fries, or a hot dog with more than a full day's worth of saturated fat. You could eat two fully loaded dogs from a New York street vendor and still take in fewer calories and fat. Our favorite dog, a bacon-wrapped, teriyaki-glazed beauty, made with the high-quality, low-calorie franks from Applegate Farms, gives you all the decadence you need for less than half the calories.

Grill This Instead!
Teriyaki Dogs with Grilled Pineapple (page 98)
270 calories
9 g fat (3 g saturated)
880 mg sodium

**Cost per serving: $1.65
Save 425 calories and $3.10!**

WORST GRILLED WHITE FISH

19 IHOP's Grilled Tilapia Hollandaise

810 calories
46 g fat (13 g saturated)
1,890 mg sodium

Price: $9.99

An 8-ounce fillet of grilled tilapia contains just 6 grams of fat, so you know the calories in this dish aren't coming from the fish. For a better explanation of how one of the leanest pieces of protein ends up with more calories than a Wendy's Baconator, look no further than the sauce. Hollandaise is a butter- and egg yolk-based emulsion that clings to food like a blanket of molten fat. Along with packing an astounding 40 grams of fat, it also has the unique ability to make all food taste exactly the same.

Grill This Instead!
Swordfish with Smoky Aioli (page 242)
280 calories
14 g fat (2.5 g saturated)
490 mg sodium

**Cost per serving: $4.04
Save 530 calories and $5.95!**

WORST GRILLED LAMB

18 Outback Steakhouse's New Zealand Rack of Lamb

910 calories
56 g fat (29 g saturated)
2,197 mg sodium

Price: $19.99

We applaud Outback for being one of the only chain restaurants to serve lamb. In its best iteration, lamb is a lean, tender, tasty alternative to a steak. The rack is normally among the healthiest cuts of lamb, too—yet still, somehow, Outback manages to get this dish wrong, injecting their version with more than a full day's worth of saturated fat. Don't blame it on the lamb; blame it on the huge portion size and the rich red wine sauce poured liberally over the top.

Grill This Instead!
Balsamic Lamb Chops (page 184)
280 calories
21 g fat (8 g saturated)
435 mg sodium

**Cost per serving: $3.66
Save 630 calories and $16.33!**

810 calories

Order tilapia at IHOP and you'll find yourself in troubled waters.

WORST GRILLED STEAK

17 Ruby Tuesday's Rib Eye (no sides)

912 calories
71 g fat
1,040 mg sodium

Price: $16.99

When it comes to a grilled steak, the cut of meat is everything. Opt for a sirloin, flank, or skirt steak and you're looking at a piece of beef that is predominantly protein, buffered by just enough fat to keep things interesting. On the flip side of the coin, rib eyes come from the most heavily marbled part of the cow, which means that along with rivers of fat, you also get a steak dense with calories. We're not sure where Ruby Tuesday gets its beef from, but its rib eye easily qualifies as the worst steak in the business.

Grill This Instead!
The Perfect Grilled Steak (page 168)

230 calories
7 g fat (2.5 g saturated)
620 mg sodium

Cost per serving: $2.61
Save 682 calories and $14.38!

WORST GRILLED FISH TACOS

16 Chevys Fresh Mex's Mesquite Grilled Fresh Fish Tacos

920 calories
27 g fat (8 g saturated)
2,400 mg sodium

Price: $10.89

There are tacos that are worse than these (though not many), but these land on the list by virtue of the gaping chasm between perception and reality. "Grilled fresh fish"—three healthier words have never lived together in the same menu blurb, and yet, Chevys nevertheless finds a way to deliver a plate that provides more than half of your day's calories and fat and nearly two full days' worth of sodium. It's a troubling turn of events to which we have only one response: Time to fire up the grill out back.

Grill This Instead!
Grilled Fish Tacos (page 238)

320 calories
13 g fat (2 g saturated)
490 mg sodium

Cost per serving: $2.89
Save 600 calories and $8!

WORST TURKEY BURGER

15 Ruby Tuesday's Avocado Turkey Burger

968 calories
61 g fat
1,601 mg sodium

Price: $8.99

This burger may sound like a nutritionist's dream dinner, but the truth is that it packs more calories than Ruby Tuesday's Classic Cheeseburger. Why? Because turkey alone does not a healthy burger make, especially when you consider that ground dark-meat turkey can contain as many calories as ground beef. Add to that the aggressive condiment treatment turkey burgers tend to receive and you start to see why it's not always the healthy alternative it pretends to be.

Grill This Instead!
Stuffed Meat Loaf Burgers (page 94)

460 calories
20 g fat (8 g saturated)
965 mg sodium

Cost per serving: $1.83
Save 508 calories and $7.16!

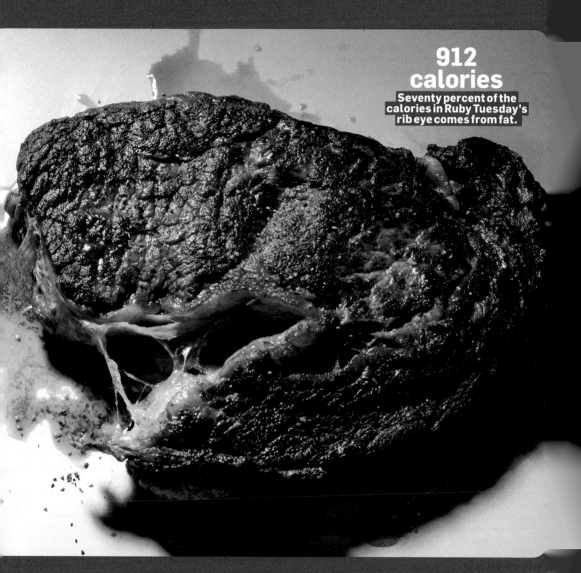

912
calories

Seventy percent of the calories in Ruby Tuesday's rib eye comes from fat.

WORST DRESSED-UP GRILLED STEAK

14 Outback's New York Strip (14 oz) with Blue Cheese Crumb Crust

989 calories
70 g fat (34 g saturated)
857 mg sodium

Price: $21.98

In an effort to squeeze a few extra bucks out of its customers, Outback offers diners the option of adding items like sautéed mushrooms, grilled scallops, and, worst of all, this blanket of bread crumbs and blue cheese. It turns an already hefty steak into a punishing proposition. Outback does offer a number of lean beef options (the small Outback Special and the 6-ounce Victoria's Filet are two excellent options), so go in with a game plan and you'll escape relatively unscathed.

Grill This Instead!
Strip Steaks with Blue Cheese Butter (page 196)
300 calories
20 g fat (10 g saturated)
510 mg sodium

Cost per serving: $2.92
Save 689 calories and $19.06!

WORST BARBECUE

13 T.G.I. Friday's Jack Daniel's Pulled Pork Sandwich

990 calories
35 g fat (11 g saturated)
2,710 mg sodium

Price: $7.89

A real pulled pork sandwich, like the kind they dish out in the barbecue shacks of eastern North Carolina, is a simple construction: steamed bun, a splash of vinegar-based sauce, maybe a bit of coleslaw. Friday's defies that formula by starting with a butter-packed brioche, then drowning the pork in sugary barbecue sauce and topping it all with fried onion strings. Somewhere out there a pitmaster is shuddering at the thought of this bastardized barbecue.

Grill This Instead!
Carolina Pulled Pork, Two Ways (page 186)
350 calories
16 g fat (5 g saturated)
650 mg sodium

Cost per serving: $1.31
Save 640 calories and $6.58!

WORST GRILLED SALMON

12 Red Lobster's Cedar Plank Salmon

1,050 calories
40 g fat (9 g saturated fat)
1,780 mg sodium

Price: $19.50

Red Lobster's fresh fish menu is one of the most admirable menu sections in the country: dozens of different types of seasonal fish, cooked over an open flame and served with an admirable selection of healthy sides. With that in mind, it's hard to figure out how they got this one so wrong. Sure, salmon is naturally loaded with health-boosting omega-3 fatty acids, but with a quadruple-digit calorie count and a full day's worth of sodium, you'd find a leaner meal in a 20-pack of Chicken McNuggets.

Grill This Instead!
Cedar Plank Salmon (page 222)
240 calories
9 g fat (1.5 g saturated)
470 mg sodium

Cost per serving: $2.91
Save 810 calories and $16.59!

**990
calories**

Friday's pulled
pork gives barbecue
a bad name.

WORST GRILLED CHICKEN SANDWICH

11 T.G.I. Friday's Jack Daniel's Chicken Sandwich

1,140 calories
58 g fat (18 g saturated)
2,780 mg sodium

Price: $9.09

Jack Daniel's real name was Jasper Newton Daniel and he was a 5-foot, 2-inch pioneer of American distillery. He made a mean whiskey, but it's hard to imagine ol' Jasper being excited to know that his creation adorns some of America's worst grilled dishes, from steak to pork to chicken. He'd probably go on a bender if he ever found out that the Jack Daniel's Chicken Sandwich packs more calories than 17 shots of Jack Daniel's Tennessee Whiskey.

Grill This Instead!
Grilled Chicken & Pineapple Sandwich (page 88)

400 calories
11 g fat (6 g saturated)
640 mg sodium

Cost per serving: $2.64
Save 740 calories and $6.45!

WORST GRILLED CHICKEN

10 Romano's Macaroni Grill's Chicken Under a Brick

1,180 calories
18 g saturated fat
2,590 mg sodium

Price: $16

Macaroni Grill was smart to bring the long-held Tuscan tradition of cooking chicken under a brick to the shores of America. Unfortunately, the chicken put on about 700 calories, 10 grams of fat, and 2,000 milligrams of sodium on the journey. Save this one for the backyard, where the birds are lean, the bricks are abundant, and the beers are cheap.

Grill This Instead!
Chicken Under a Brick (page 158)

470 calories
28 g fat (8 g saturated)
780 mg sodium

Cost per serving: $2.83
Save 710 calories and $13.17!

WORST GRILLED SALAD

9 Chevys Fresh Mex's Grilled Chicken Fajita Salad

1,220 calories
90 g fat (23 g saturated)
1,480 mg sodium

Price: $12.19

Mexican-style salads are invariably clobbered with a blizzard of high-calorie add-ons such as sour cream and grated cheese. Don't be distracted by the words "grilled chicken" —this baby packs as much fat as 18 scoops of Breyers Original Strawberry ice cream. But the Mexican pantry has plenty of excellent ingredients to fill out a salad bowl that are both lean and deeply delicious. Don't believe us? Try our Blackened Chicken and Mango Salad.

Grill This Instead!
Blackened Chicken & Mango Salad (page 298)

440 calories
22 g fat (2.5 g saturated)
490 mg sodium

Cost per serving: $3.69
Save 780 calories and $8.50!

1,440
calories
Friday's Fusion Skewers turn a lean grilling vessel into a weapon.

WORST GRILLED SAUSAGE
8 Olive Garden's Grilled Sausage and Peppers Rustica
1,320 calories
80 g fat (30 g saturated)
2,860 mg sodium
Price: $11.75

Olive Garden normally opts for the stovetop over the grill to concoct its line of pseudo-Italian fare, but here the chain proves that it's just as dangerous with a spatula as it is with a sauté pan. This dish boasts a solid foundation of grilled meat, fresh veggies, and antioxidant-rich marinara, but a huge pile of carb-heavy penne and an indecent amount of fatty pork sausage sabotage any shot for nutritional prudence. If it's sausage you seek, make sure it's chicken or turkey.

Grill This Instead!
Sausage & Peppers with Orecchiette (page 122)
520 calories
22 g fat (6 g saturated)
670 mg sodium

Cost per serving: $2.23
Save 800 calories and $9.52!

WORST FAJITAS
7 Applebee's Sizzling Steak Fajitas
1,410 calories
55 g fat (25 g saturated)
5,630 mg sodium
Price: $13.79

Picking this loser was no easy task; there are at least half a dozen viable candidates for the title of Worst Fajitas (Chili's, Chevys, and Baja Fresh among them), a reflection of just how easily corrupted an inherently good recipe can be when placed in the wrong hands. Applebee's comes out at the bottom of the pack not just because its sizzling platter edges out the others in the calorie department, but because it contains more salt than you'd find in 33 small bags of Lay's Potato Chips.

Grill This Instead!
Grilled Steak Fajitas (page 180)
430 calories
16 g fat (7 g saturated)
810 mg sodium

Cost per serving: $3.86
Save 980 calories and $9.93!

WORST SKEWERS
6 T.G.I. Friday's Mediterranean Black Angus Sirloin Fusion Skewers
1,440 calories
77 g fat (19 g saturated)
3,220 mg sodium
Price: $10.89

As you'll find in the pages to come, we're huge fans of the skewer. Just load one up with protein and vegetables and you're all but assured of a lean, tasty meal. Unfortunately, that equation only applies at home; in the bizarro restaurant world, a skewer more closely resembles a weapon than the means to a healthy dinner. Friday's Fusion Skewers are wrong for so many reasons, but most of all because they make a mockery of one of our favorite grilling vessels.

Grill This Instead!
Steak-and-Potato Skewers with Horseradish Steak Sauce (page 198)
440 calories
15 g fat (6 g saturated)
710 mg sodium

Cost per serving: $2.74
Save 1,000 calories and $8.15!

1,500 calories

Pig out on Cheesecake Factory's pork chops and you'll gain nearly half a pound before you pay the bill.

WORST GRILLED PORK
5 Cheesecake Factory's Grilled Pork Chops

1,500 calories
52 g saturated fat
2,441 mg sodium
Price: $18.95

Pork chops rule. Just ask Homer Simpson. Besides being drool-inducingly delicious, a loin chop can be surprisingly lean, containing a modest 5 grams of saturated fat per average serving. Unfortunately, Cheesecake Factory's servings are anything but average; they tend to feed their diners as if they were on the eve of a hunger strike. Through the combination of elephantine portion sizes and reckless cooking habits, this plate ends up with more than six times the saturated fat of our decadent goat cheese—stuffed chops.

Grill This Instead!
Stuffed Pork Chops (page 178)
410 calories
19 g fat (8 g saturated)
460 mg sodium

Cost per serving: $2.28
Save 1,090 calories and $16.67!

WORST GRILLED SHRIMP
4 Cheesecake Factory's Grilled Shrimp and Bacon Club Sandwich

1,740 calories
22 g saturated fat
2,608 mg sodium
Price: $13.95

Not only is this the worst shrimp dish we've seen, it's also America's worst sandwich. You'd think the latter would be reserved for a hulking cheese-steak or a foot-long submarine of sinful excess, but the diabolical minds responsible for Cheesecake Factory's menu manage to put two slices of bread around one of the world's leanest proteins and create a sandwich that contains as many calories as you'd find in nearly 4 pounds of cocktail shrimp.

Grill This Instead!
Shrimp Po' Boys (page 82)
370 calories
5 g fat (1 g saturated)
860 mg sodium

Cost per serving: $3.17
Save 1,370 calories and $10.78!

WORST GRILLED APPETIZER
3 Baja Fresh's Charbroiled Steak Nachos

2,120 calories
118 g fat (44 g saturated)
2,990 mg sodium
Price: $7.25

People don't always look to the grill when they think about appetizers, but as a toaster of bread, a melter of cheese, and a crisper of lean proteins, it is well suited for the task of kicking off a meal. But even genius devices can be used for dubious ends when left in the wrong hands. Baja Fresh, for all of its talk about fresh ingredients, is responsible for some of America's most caloric Mexican food: bulging burritos, catastrophic salads and fajitas, and nacho platters that would be dangerous if shared among an entire room full of eaters.

Grill This Instead!
Ham and Pineapple Quesadillas (page 260)
370 calories
18 g fat (10 g saturated)
620 mg sodium

Cost per serving: $1.77
Save 1,750 calories and $5.48!

2,290 calories
You could eat nearly five of our bacon cheeseburgers for the caloric cost of this sinister Chili's creation.

2 Chili's Southern Smokehouse Burger with Ancho Chile BBQ

2,290 calories
139 g fat (46 g saturated)
6,500 mg sodium
Price: $9.69

The average American eats 150 burgers a year. That's an eye-popping reminder that for most people, burgers aren't an occasional indulgence, but a lifestyle. We stand by America's love affair with the burger, just as long as most of those burgers are coming from your backyard and not some dubious restaurant griddle glazed in a sea of molten beef fat. Unfortunately, we're afraid more burgers are consumed at places like Chili's than they are around the family dinner table, and that's a frightening prospect, because there is no worse place in America to eat a burger. Even the most basic Chili's option—the plain Oldtimer—will saddle you with more than 1,300 calories. What's most shocking about

the Southern Smokehouse, America's worst burger by a long shot, isn't that it alone will add two-thirds of a pound of pure body fat to anyone crazy enough to eat it, it's that you can have a burger with the exact same flavors (bacon, cheddar, sweet onions, barbecue sauce) at home for a fifth of the caloric cost.

Grill This Instead!
Cowboy Burgers (page 90)

460 calories
22 g fat (11 g saturated)
850 mg sodium

Cost per serving: $2.62
Save 1,830 calories and $7.07!

WORST GRILLED DISH IN AMERICA
1 Chili's Shiner Bock Ribs

2,310 calories
123 g fat (44 g saturated)
6,340 mg sodium
Price: $17.99

Eating ribs at a sit-down restaurant is risky business no matter where you've chosen to eat. The problem begins with the fact that baby back ribs are a naturally fatty cut. The danger

is only compounded by portion distortion and reckless sauce application, a killer combination that leaves even the "leanest" ribs packing quadruple-digit calorie counts. That's why the biggest restaurants in America—Applebee's, Friday's, Outback—all serve ribs with more than 1,500 calories per serving. Chili's adds insult to injury by rubbing their rendition with enough salt to preserve an entire hog. Even at home, there are only two ways to avoid the wrath of the ribs: Control your portion size (no more than half a rack per person) and keep the sauce slathering to a minimum.

Grill This Instead!
Classic Baby Back Ribs (page 182)

370 calories
15 g fat (4.5 g saturated)
870 mg sodium

Cost per serving: $2.93
Save 1,940 calories and $15.06!

2,310 calories

Chili's baby back ribs: The song sticks in your head, the ribs stick to your gut.

THE BACKYARD BASICS

POP QUIZ:

What do these three things have in common?

Lil Wayne's dental work

Every single episode of *Law & Order*

Super-easy weight loss

ANSWER: They all involve grills!

Of course, the part that's relevant to you—the weight-loss part—doesn't involve sweating out a confession from a perp or adding diamonds to a rapper's teeth. (Although both would seem to make overeating pretty impossible.) But a grill is the place where you can make healthy foods even healthier—and help those less-than-lean indulgences shed some of their sin. (In fact, a study in the journal *Meat Science* found that grilling a pork chop by conventional methods could actually decrease its fat content by nearly a third.)

That said, the starting line for any healthy diet is healthy ingredients. Yes, a cheeseburger is better for you when it's grilled rather than fried, but you can't turn a nutritional Paula Deen into a tasty Paula Patton just by tossing it on the grill. Using simple swaps that up your nutrition intake will make stripping away pounds easier.

Here's why: When you eat a meal packed with nutrients, your body doesn't send you out searching for MIA vitamins and minerals, driving you to eat more and more. In fact, the more healthy food you eat, the less food you'll eat overall: In a 2006 study published in the *European Journal of Clinical Nutrition,* researchers found that participants who had fish for lunch ate 11 percent fewer calories at dinner than participants who had beef for lunch.

So, to make sure your pantry, fridge, and freezer are stocked with only the healthiest ingredients, we've broken down every major fire-friendly food brand in the supermarket, compared them all, and found the foods that should be picked for the grill—and some that should be kicked in the grill.

The BEST & WORST Foods for the Grill

The path to healthy grilling starts off in the supermarket. Fill your cart with starch-riddled buns, sugary condiments, and calorie-dense dogs and sausages and you're undermining one of the world's greatest weight-loss weapons. To make sure your pantry is stocked with the best possible building blocks, we've raided the aisles and identified the most dangerous waistline saboteurs in the supermarket. More importantly, we've picked out 24 first-rate staples that no smart griller should be without.

BEEF HOT DOG

Eat This

Applegate The Super Natural Beef Hot Dogs
(one frank)
70 calories
6 g fat (2 g saturated)
6 g protein
330 mg sodium

Applegate Farms uses lean, preservative-free meat, so you get real beef flavor minus the hefty saturated-fat load found in other franks.

Not That!

Oscar Mayer Selects Angus Beef Hot Dogs
(one frank)
180 calories
17 g fat (7 g saturated)
6 g protein
420 mg sodium

Angus beef is no leaner— and arguably no tastier— than regular beef, and these franks pack nearly three times the fat found with Applegate Farms.

LIGHT HOT DOG

Eat This

Hebrew National 97% Fat Free Beef Franks
(one frank)
40 calories
1 g fat (0 g saturated)
6 g protein
520 mg sodium

With no fillers and an impressively low calorie count, these uber-lean dogs are a nutritious, protein-packed addition to your cookout.

Not That!

Oscar Mayer Classic Light Beef Franks
(one frank)
90 calories
7 g fat (3 g saturated)
5 g protein
380 mg sodium

"Light" is a relative term when it comes to shopping for franks. Just one of these low-cal dogs has more fat than half a dozen of the Hebrew Nationals.

PORK SAUSAGE

Eat This

Aidells Cajun Style Andouille
(one link)
160 calories
11 g fat (4 g saturated)
15 g protein
600 mg sodium

Aidells uses quality lean pork in its sausages, which translates into better flavor, more protein, and less fat.

Not That!

Hillshire Farm Smoked Bratwurst
(one link)
240 calories
22 g fat (8 g saturated)
8 g protein
780 mg sodium

Fat crowds out protein in these brats, accounting for 83 percent of the calories. We'll take Aidells all summer long.

SPICY SAUSAGE

Eat This

Al Fresco Chipotle Chorizo Chicken Sausage (one link)
140 calories
7 g fat (2 g saturated)
15 g protein
420 mg sodium

These lean chicken links— like all of Al Fresco's sausage selections—pack tons of flavor and a generous portion of protein.

Not That!

Hillshire Farm Hot & Spicy Italian Style Smoked Sausage
(one link)
250 calories
22 g fat (8 g saturated)
8 g protein
670 mg sodium

To justify these sky-high calorie and fat counts, this link would need to pack triple the protein.

The Best & Worst Foods

CHEESY SAUSAGE

Eat This

Johnsonville Chicken Sausage Chipotle Monterey Jack Cheese
(per link)
170 calories
12 g fat (4 g saturated)
13 g protein
770 mg sodium

Because this sausage is made with lean chicken, adding cheese doesn't take it over the calorie edge.

Not That!

Johnsonville Beddar with Cheddar
(per link)
200 calories
17 g fat (6 g saturated)
8 g protein
620 mg sodium

There's nothing better about these links: Extra calories, more fat, but only half the protein of the Johnsonville sausage.

VEGGIE BURGER

Eat This

Boca Bruschetta
(per patty)
90 calories
2 g fat (0.5 g saturated)
13 g protein
440 mg sodium

Plenty of protein and low calories—exactly what you want in a meat substitute. Try a double stack for a more powerful protein punch.

Not That!

Amy's All American Veggie Burger
(per patty)
140 calories
3.5 g fat (0 g saturated)
13 g protein
390 mg sodium

Amy's patties pack 50 extra calories without providing any extra protein in return.

GUACAMOLE

Eat This

Wholly Guacamole
(per 2 Tbsp)
60 calories
5 g fat (1 g saturated)
1 g protein
90 mg sodium

With nothing but avocados and seven other simple ingredients, this dip's the closest you'll find to homemade guac at the supermarket.

Not That!

Mission Guacamole Flavored Dip (per 2 Tbsp)
40 calories
3 g fat (0 g saturated)
0 g protein
150 mg sodium

Oil, cornstarch, and "avocado powder" replace real avocados in this guacamole imposter.

HOT DOG BUN

Eat This

Martin's Famous Long Potato Rolls
(per bun)
130 calories
1.5 g fat (0 g saturated)
26 g carbohydrates
4 g fiber
200 mg sodium

Martin's mines the humble spud to pack these rolls with as much fiber and protein as you'll find in any hot dog buns on the market.

Not That!

Pepperidge Farm Classic Hot Dog Buns
(per bun)
140 calories
2.5 g fat (0.5 g saturated)
26 g carbohydrates
<1 g fiber
180 mg sodium

Bread products should have at least 2 grams of fiber per serving.

for the Grill

HAMBURGER BUN

Eat This

Martin's Potato Rolls
(per roll)
130 calories
1.5 g fat (0 g saturated)
25 g carbohydrates
3 g fiber
200 mg sodium

This isn't just one of the lightest, most fiber- and protein-rich buns on the shelves, it's also the tastiest.

Not That!

Arnold Select White Hamburger Rolls
(per roll)
150 calories
2 g fat (0.5 g saturated)
30 g carbohydrates
1 g fiber
350 mg sodium

These refined buns give you 15 percent more calories and 67 percent less fiber than the Martin's rolls.

TRADITIONAL BBQ SAUCE

Eat This

Stubb's Original Bar-B-Q Sauce
(per 2 Tbsp)
30 calories
6 g carbohydrates
220 mg sodium

Robust flavor without a ton of sugar or salt. What more could you ask for in a barbecue sauce?

Not That!

Kraft Original Barbecue Sauce
(per 2 Tbsp)
60 calories
15 g carbohydrates
450 mg sodium

High-fructose corn syrup is this sauce's primary ingredient, which is why it packs twice as many calories as the bottle of Stubb's.

SWEET BARBECUE SAUCE

Eat This

Jack Daniel's Honey Smokehouse
(per 2 Tbsp)
45 calories
11 g carbohydrates
280 mg sodium

One of the few "honey" sauces that won't put you in a sugar coma.

Not That!

Famous Dave's Sweet & Zesty
(per 2 Tbsp)
70 calories
17 g carbohydrates
320 mg sodium

With more than 3 teaspoons of sugar per serving, this condiment is better suited for an ice cream sundae than a rack of ribs.

ALL-PURPOSE MARINADE

Eat This

Lawry's 30 Minute Marinade Steak & Chop
(per 2 Tbsp)
10 calories
0 g fat
1 g carbohydrates
780 mg sodium

The lemon juice and vinegar base of this marinade will tenderize your meat and poultry without adding a ton of sugar.

Not That!

KC Masterpiece Steakhouse
(per 2 Tbsp)
60 Calories
2 g fat
7 g carbohydrates
660 mg sodium

KC Masterpiece goes heavy on the high-fructose corn syrup, which adds unnecessary calories. Sugars also convert to bitter-tasting carbon when they hit the grill.

The Best & Worst Foods

DRY RUB

Eat This

McCormick Grill Mates Applewood Rub
(per 2 tsp)
15 calories
350 mg sodium
McCormick's line of rubs is relatively low in sodium, and this Applewood option adds smoky flavor and a hint of sweetness to chops, chicken, and steak.

Not That!

Emeril's All Natural Steak Rub
(per 2 tsp)
0 calories
1,680 mg sodium
Would you like some steak with your salt?

TERIYAKI SAUCE AND MARINADE

Eat This

La Choy Stir Fry Teriyaki
(per Tbsp)
10 calories
3 g carbohydrates
105 mg sodium
This bottle is low in both sugar and salt—a rare find in the world of store-bought teriyaki sauces.

Not That!

La Choy Teriyaki
(per Tbsp)
40 calories
10 g carbohydrates
570 mg sodium
Each tablespoon has almost as much sugar as two Oreo cookies and more salt than three small bags of Lay's Classic potato chips!

KETCHUP

Eat This

Heinz Organic Tomato Ketchup
(per Tbsp)
20 calories
5 g carbohydrates
190 mg sodium
A study from the *Journal of Agricultural and Food Chemistry* found that organic ketchup has nearly three times the amount of lycopene, a cancer-fighting antioxidant, as conventional ketchup.

Not That!

Heinz Tomato Ketchup
(per Tbsp)
20 calories
5 g carbohydrates
160 mg sodium
This iconic condiment from Heinz placed dead last in a blind ketchup taste test conducted for *Eat This, Not That! All-New Supermarket Survival Guide*.

HONEY MUSTARD

Eat This

Grey Poupon Savory Honey Mustard
(per Tbsp)
30 calories
3 g carbohydrates
15 mg sodium
Heart-healthy mustard seeds are this bottle's primary ingredient, and unlike other brands, Grey Poupon doesn't use "honey" as an excuse to load its mustard with sugar.

Not That!

Inglehoffer Sweet Honey Mustard
(per Tbsp)
45 calories
6 g carbohydrates
135 mg sodium
When sugar and water show up before mustard seeds on the ingredients list, should it really be labeled mustard?

DIPPING SAUCE

Eat This

Peter Luger Steak Sauce
(per 2 Tbsp)
60 calories
0 g fat
g carbohydrates
250 mg sodium

sauce is the perfect
w-calorie meat
diment, and this
avored option from
ooklyn's famed
ouse can't be beat.

Not That!

Kraft Buttermilk Ranch Dressing & Dip
(per 2 Tbsp)
120 calories
12 g fat (2 saturated)
2 g carbohydrates
290 mg sodium

It's unfortunate ranch
has become a default dip
and sauce for so many;
few condiments
pack more calories and fat.

CHUTNEY

Eat This

Wild Thymes Mango Papaya Chutney
(per Tbsp)
15 calories
0 g fat
3.5 g carbohydrates
0 mg sodium

This jar contains
only fruit, spices, and
a touch of sugar.
Perfect for pork, chicken,
and lamb dishes.

Not That!

Kitchens of India Shredded Mango Chutney
(per Tbsp)
80 calories
0 g fat
18 g carbohydrates
50 mg sodium

Sugar's the first
ingredient in this jar.

BEER

at This

ss Draught
r bottle)
calories
tbohydrates
ent alcohol

e lightest
around, and it
s nicely
illed meat.

Not That!

Guinness Extra Stout
(per bottle)
153 calories
18 g carbohydrates
4.3 percent alcohol

Extra stout means
extra calories. This beer's
packed with flavor,
but it'll add too much weight
to your meal, especially
if you have more than one.

LIGHT BEER

Eat This

Amstel Light
(per bottle)
95 calories
5 g carbohydrates
3.5 percent alcohol

Under 100 calories
and refreshing,
not watery—everything a
light beer should be.

Not That!

Michelob Light
(per bottle)
123 calories
8.8 g carbohydrates
4.3 percent alcohol

This brew has far too many
calories and carbs
to bear the "light" label.

for the Grill

Eat This

**Kraft Reduced Fat
Mayonnaise
with Olive Oil
(per Tbsp)**
45 calories
4 g fat (0 g saturated)
95 mg sodium

By slashing the calories in
half and adding heart-
healthy monounsaturated
fats, Kraft gives mayo
a much-needed makeover.

Not That!

**Hellmann's
Real Mayonnaise
(per Tbsp)**
90 calories
10 g fat (1.5 g saturated)
90 mg sodium

"Real" mayonnaise is
one of the heaviest
condiments around.
One hundred percent
of this bottle's
calories come from fat.

Eat This

**Sargento
Reduced Fat Swiss
(per slice)**
60 calories
4 g fat (2 g saturated)
7 g protein
30 mg sodium

Low-fat cheese will lighten
your burger's calorie load,
and Swiss has a fraction
of the sodium of
most other popular cheese

14

Steak
lo
con
full-fl
Br
choph

Eat This

**Kraft Singles 2% Milk
Sharp Cheddar
(per slice)**
45 calories
3 g fat (1.5 g saturated)
4 g protein
250 mg sodium

You'd be hard-pressed
to find a cheese slice with
fewer calories.
Plus, it melts like a dream.

Not That!

**Kraft Deli Deluxe
Sharp Cheddar Slices
(per slice)**
110 calories
9 g fat (5 g saturated)
6 g protein
450 mg sodium

These slices are labeled
"Deluxe," but there's nothing
superior about them:
More calories, three times
the fat, same flavor.

Eat This

**Vlasic
Reduced Sodi
Kosher Dill Sp
(per 2 spears**
0 calories
0 g carbohydr
450 mg sodi

Great straight
the jar or a
burger topper, th
are crispy, cal
and not too

E

**Guinn
(pe
127
10 g ca
4.2 per

It's t
dark brew
pai
with g

3 Grilling Buzzkills

It may be an inherently healthy cooking method, but grilling is not without its hazards. Here are three of the biggest health concerns that come with cooking over an open fire, along with strategies for cutting back on the risk.

1. Heterocyclic amines (HCAs)

What they are: Carcinogens that develop when the creatine, sugars, and amino acids in meat react to your grill's high temperatures.

Why they're bad: Several studies have linked HCAs with cancer development in animals, and a growing body of research supports a connection between HCA exposure and increased risk of colorectal, pancreatic, and prostate cancers in humans.

Chop your risk: *SPICE IT UP!* A 2011 study published in the *Journal of Food Science* revealed that adding antioxidant-rich spices like rosemary to beef patties before grilling can slash the production of HCAs up to 39 percent. Another way to reduce your risk? Turn down the heat—burnt meat contains higher concentrations of HCAs.

2. Advanced glycation end products (AGEs)

What they are: Toxic compounds that develop when animal proteins are heated at high temperatures. Grilled beef has been shown to contain the highest levels of AGEs.

Why they're bad: AGEs can increase oxidative stress and have been linked to the development of chronic diseases like diabetes and heart disease.

Chop your risk: *SOAK BEFORE YOU SEAR.* A 2010 study from the American Dietetic Association found that marinating meat in lemon juice or vinegar for 1 hour cuts AGE production in half.

3. Polycyclic aromatic hydrocarbons (PAHs)

What they are: Carcinogens that form when fat drippings burn at the bottom of your grill. The burnt fat produces PAH-rich smoke, which then penetrates whatever food you're grilling.

Why they're bad: Recent research has linked PAHs to an increased risk of a variety of cancers, including prostate cancer and renal cell carcinoma. A 2011 Polish study also found a correlation between prenatal PAH exposure and lower birth weight.

Chop your risk: *CUT THE FAT.* Lean meats produce less drippings and, therefore, less PAHs. Choosing propane over charcoal may also limit your PHA exposure, as charcoal grilling creates more smoke.

The GRILL
Glossary

To conquer the backyard, you'll first need to decode the loaded language of fire and smoke.

Barbecue

A style of cooking distinguished by indirect heat and low temperatures. Barbecuing typically takes place between 200 and 250°F, which is less than half the temperature reached with direct heat. At this low, steady temperature, tough muscle fibers break down and collagen slowly melts, giving you the rich taste and luscious mouthfeel characteristic of awesome barbecue. Barbecue sauce, while common, is not the defining characteristic of barbecue, and it often buries delicious smoke flavors under unnecessary sugars.

Beef, Prime

Only 2 percent of beef is rated Prime by the USDA, and most of that goes to restaurants willing to pay the premium. But let the restaurants have it; the rating system is based largely on marbling—i.e., fat—and Prime is the fattiest of all the grades. Falling just below Prime is Choice, and just below that is Select. Lower grades are considered less flavorful, but they're also cheaper and less caloric.

Caramelization

A reaction in which sugar browns and develops delightfully bitter flavors. A similar reaction is known as the Maillard reaction, and it occurs when small quantities of sugars or carbohydrates are cooked alongside proteins. In most cases, it's the Maillard reaction—not caramelization—that's responsible for the flavorful crust created when you sear meat.

Dry Rub

Similar to a marinade, a dry rub utilizes seasonings, spices, and other adjuncts to add flavor to food. Since it contains no liquid, it has to be rubbed onto the meat. Whereas marinades are great for softening muscle tissue, rubs are better for creating complex and flavorful crusts.

Grilling, Direct

Cooking directly over flame. This is the simplest and most common type of grilling, and it's best for thin and fast-cooking pieces like steaks, burgers, vegetables, and individual cuts of chicken.

Grilling, Indirect

A technique that moves food away from the flame, allowing it to cook slowly, as in an oven. The easiest method for the home griller is banking, which means heaping charcoal along one side of the grill, placing the food on the opposite side, and closing the lid. You should also slide in a small pot of water to keep the meat from drying out. Indirect grilling is ideal for large or tough cuts of meat like ribs, briskets, and whole chickens.

Grilling, Plank

A faster and simpler variant of smoking that places the meat directly on a flat piece of wet wood, and then places the plank directly above the flame.

Marinade

Liquid used to add flavor to and help tenderize meat before cooking. The best marinades pair big-flavor ingredients with some sort of acid like vinegar or citrus, which breaks down tissues for more tender meat.

Searing

Cooking meat over high heat to create a thick and flavorful external crust. (However, as we discuss on the next page, searing does not "seal in the juices.") With thinner pieces of meat, the inside can reach doneness while the outside sears, but with thicker cuts, you'll want to finish cooking over low heat after the crust forms. For the best possible crust, pat your protein dry before cooking.

Smoking

A type of indirect grilling that infuses meats, fish, and vegetables with the roasted notes of woods like oak, mesquite, and hickory. Smoked foods can be cooked entirely over wood, or a combination of charcoal or gas and wet wood chips.

7 Grill Myths DEBUNKED

These popular beliefs may be making your food worse. We hope to relieve you of them once and for all.

MYTH 1

Searing locks in the juices.

This may be the most persistent cooking myth of all time, propagated at every opportunity by self-anointed grill masters and television "chefs" alike. Amazingly enough, research has been out for many years disproving this theory, particularly by the king of all kitchen scientists, Harold McGee, author of *On Food and Cooking*. McGee's studies have shown that, if anything, searing actually decreases the amount of moisture in the end product.

Searing still has its place on the grill: High heat causes rapid browning, which amplifies the flavor and texture on the surface of your meat or fish. But for the best of all worlds (i.e., moist, tender meat inside paired with a deeply browned, almost-crunchy exterior), turn the process on its head, starting first with a low, steady flame, then finishing with serious heat. By reversing the order of operations, the browning will occur more rapidly (since the surface of the meat will already be quite warm after time on the grill), resulting in juicier, more evenly cooked meat inside.

MYTH 2

Flip your meat once and only once.

This is another misguided maxim that holds a lot of currency with the talking heads on the Food Network. Research done by Harold McGee found that flipping meat frequently helps meat cook both more evenly and more rapidly, cutting cooking time by as much as 40 percent overall. McGee recommends flipping every 15 seconds, but even flipping the meat once every minute could help improve the quality of your food.

That being said, there is a fine line between careful flipping and destructive manipulating. Grilling is still mainly a spectator sport, an exchange between meat and fire that demands minimal human interference. Get too aggressive with the food on the grill and you can puncture your meat, sacrificing all of those precious juices to the fire below.

MYTH 3
Hotter is better.

Not necessarily. While grill marks and deeply browned crusts on meat, fish, and vegetables are attractive to the eye and tasty to the palate, high-heat cooking isn't always the path to grilling enlightenment. Try a fillet of salmon cooked over a low, steady flame—taste how the fish gently flakes and melts like warm butter across your palate—and you'll see the other side of the coin.

As a general rule for choosing the heat of your grill, think about the size of what you're cooking: For a thin cut of steak like flank or skirt, you'll need high heat if you want to develop a crust on the meat without overcooking the inside. But try to cook a big piece of meat—a brisket, a leg of lamb, a tri-tip—over high heat and you'll end up with a burnt exterior and a cold center—not exactly good eats.

As for chicken with the skin on, cooking over high heat is an invitation for flare-ups, those aggressive fire spikes that will char your chicken to smithereens before the meat closest to the bone is fully cooked. Medium-low should be your go-to temperature.

MYTH 4
All of that grill buildup is extra flavor for your food.

That crusty stuff clinging to your grate? That's not flavor; that's dirt. Carbonized fat and protein, to be specific, and not only does it add an unpleasant bitter note to your food, it can also be a health hazard, since these burnt particles have been shown to be carcinogenic.

Always keep a wire grill brush beside your grill. The best time to clean the grate is when it's hot, so just before you load up the grill with goodies, take 30 seconds to scrape it clean.

MYTH 5
Thermometers are for suckers.

Know what's really for suckers? Cutting into a piece of meat to see if it's done and losing all the delicious juices. Do what the pros do and keep a thermometer close at hand for careful monitoring of your food's internal temperature.

Still, thermometers can provide escape routes for swirling juices, too, so don't go poking holes in that nice steak as if it were a voodoo doll. Better to wait until the meat looks close to being done, then insert the thermometer in the thickest part of the cut and leave it there until you hit your target temperature. With time and practice, you can learn when a steak or a burger is done by touch, but better to be safe than to eat a piece of raw—or scorched—meat.

MYTH 6
Food is best hot off the grill.

That first juicy bite is the stuff food dreams are made of, but if you cut into a piece of protein directly off the grill, every bite that follows will be drier and more disappointing than the last. When meat and fish are hot, the muscle fibers contract, leaving all those savory, swirling juices with no way to be reabsorbed into the flesh. Cut into meat or fish too soon and those juices go leaking out onto your plate or cutting board. By waiting for the temperature of the meat to cool, you allow the muscle fibers to reabsorb all of those juices, which ensures a moist, flavorful steak, chop, chicken breast, or fish fillet.

So, how long do you have to wait before diving in? Depends on how thick the food is. Think 5 to 7 minutes for burgers, chicken breasts, and pork chops, 10 minutes for a thick steak, and at least 15 minutes (and up to 30) for whole chickens, turkey breasts, and large cuts of meat like pork shoulder and brisket.

MYTH 7
Grilling is a warm-weather pastime.

Unless you live in northern Minnesota, grilling can be a year-round affair. According to a 2008 study conducted by Weber, 57 percent of grill owners grill all year round. One major benefit of uncooperative weather is that it teaches you to work more efficiently. Here's the best way to grill when you don't feel like lingering outside: Fire up the grill, return to the kitchen to do prep work while the heat builds, then return with everything you need for the grill on a cutting board or baking sheet. Be sure to keep the lid closed to speed up the cooking.

If you do happen to live in northern Minnesota, or if you just don't feel like going outside on a frosty January evening, a grill pan provides many of the same advantages of the real thing (high heat, nice grill marks) without the need to leave your kitchen.

8 Ways to Up Your Grill Game

From professional tricks to overarching outdoor techniques, these savvy strategies will produce healthier, more delicious results every time you fire up the grill.

Cook Food Perfectly Every Time.

Everything else is just frosting on the cake. Your steaks can come from pampered bovine royalty and be showered with black truffles and molten foie gras, but if they're not properly cooked, then they're barely worth eating. People have their own tastes and should grill accordingly, but for us perfect means a rosy medium-rare with burgers and steaks, a hair beyond medium for pork and salmon, and until that last bit of pink disappears from the chicken and not a minute more.

More than anything, this book is about teaching you how to cook food simply, but expertly. We try to highlight as often as possible the tricks and tips—big and small—that will help you turn something as basic as a chicken breast or sirloin steak into something memorable. For more on how to cook every type of protein to your desired level of doneness, see "Is It Done Yet?" on page 70.

Adopt a New Salt Strategy.

A great marinade is a marvelous thing, and we discuss the technique at length later in Chapter 6, but there is an even simpler way to instantly improve your grilling: salting. Salt is the single most important ingredient in the kitchen, yet we give so little thought to how best to employ it. A shower of salt right before grilling is the default approach we all use, but that means only the surface of the meat or fish is seasoned. There are two simple techniques you can employ to make sure your food is seasoned all the way through.

The first is called curing, which is a term normally reserved to describe the process of seasoning and drying hams or sausages. Salt will slowly, steadily extract water from meat, both preserving it and concentrating its flavors. For something like prosciutto, the curing process might last 18 months, but try salting a whole chicken the night before you cook it, or a handful of pork chops a few hours ahead, and you'll be amazed at how juicy and flavorful they emerge from the grill.

The second is brining, a tactic used everywhere in the food industry—from the greatest high-end restaurants to the largest cold-cut manufacturers—to impart moisture and flavor to meat, particularly pork and poultry, before cooking. Despite its ubiquity outside of the home, few cooks ever use it in their kitchen. But try it once and we promise you'll be convinced.

HERE'S A BASIC BRINE RECIPE:

Combine 8 cups of water with ½ cup kosher salt and ½ cup light brown sugar. Heat just enough to dissolve the salt and sugar, then cool completely before using. Working with this as your base, you can flavor the brine in dozens of different ways: Apple juice, honey, chile peppers, whole garlic cloves, bay leaves, orange peels, peppercorns, rosemary, and many more flavor builders are common additions to brines.

Immerse the food in the brine and refrigerate. Remember that size and brining time are directly related. Shell-on shrimp can be brined for 30 minutes, pork chops and chicken parts for an hour or two, and whole chickens, turkeys, and pork shoulders can soak overnight.

Go High and Low.

Whether gas or charcoal is your fuel of choice, there's a huge strategic advantage to having more than one temperature zone on your grill. Having hotter and cooler sides of your grill allows you to sear and to slow cook over the same surface. It also allows you to cook big, tough pieces of meat via indirect heat (try cooking a pork shoulder or a brisket over a direct flame and you'll need jaw replacement surgery when you're finally done chewing). Here's how to set up your grill to maximize its potential.

For a charcoal griller, it means banking: Build your charcoal fire (for the easiest, safest way to do that, see page 35), and when the coals have burned down and are ready for grilling, use a long metal spatula to "bank" your charcoal against one side of the grill, leaving the other side either empty, or with a few scattered lumps to maintain a low heat. When cooking big cuts of meat, place them on the cool side of the grill and close the top.

If gas is your weapon of choice, then a two-fire zone is simple: Turn one or two of the burners on high and leave one on low— or, if you're cooking something for a long time, leave the burner off entirely.

Bring Smoke to the Fire.

Few home cooks have the time and patience to smoke a brisket, pork shoulder, or rack of ribs over hardwood for 8 hours, but by using a small wood-chip tray or even a foil packet with a normal grill setup, you can infuse your foods with that rich barbecue flavor with minimal effort.

Choose the right wood for your meal in the same way you'd choose a wine: The stronger the dish, the more intense the wood flavor can be. Here's a rundown of the most common woods used for smoking:

HICKORY: Well-loved among barbecue barons for its assertive aroma, hickory is the chip of choice for pulled pork and baby back ribs.

MESQUITE: Another intense wood, mesquite works best with pork chops, chicken wings, and burgers.

OAK: The preferred wood of the beef masters of Texas is oak, used to smoke brisket and sausages.

APPLE AND ALDER: These lighter-scented woods are best used for more delicate proteins like chicken breast and salmon fillets, or when you only want the faintest whisper of smoke in your finished product.

HERBS: Spiking your fire with fresh and dried herbs can add an extra layer of complexity to your grillables. Rosemary creates an intense aroma best for beef and lamb. Thyme gives off a moderate smoke well suited for pork chops and grilled chicken. For fish, try a handful of tarragon.

Soak the chips in hot water: The heat opens up the wood fibers, helping the water penetrate more deeply, which in turn creates more smoke for your grill.

Wet wood can go directly onto a charcoal fire. For a gas grill, use a small wood-chip box, like the one we recommend on page 69. Or make a smoker packet by wrapping the soaked chips in a foil packet poked with holes all over so that the smoke can escape. Whether using the box or the packet, it goes directly over the fire just before you begin cooking.

Become a Spice Master.

There is no faster, healthier, cheaper way to bring flavor to your food than a skillfully deployed spice rub. A few pinches can transform a chicken breast from boring to brilliant. And given that most common spices are essentially calorie-free vessels for powerful antioxidants, it's a markedly more nutritious way to season your food than relying on heavy sauces and dressings.

A true grill master develops his or her own specific spice blends and you should, too. Salt (kosher), sugar (light brown), and black pepper (fresh cracked, please!) are good starting points, but from there you can tweak however you see fit. Cumin, chili powder, and cayenne pepper have become common constituents in the American spice rack, but to really turn up the heat on your food, try out new grill-friendly spices: crushed fennel seed for pork; cracked coriander on meaty fish fillets like mahi-mahi; ground chipotle or ancho powder for steaks. Make big batches of spice rubs to have on hand at all times; covered, they keep in your cabinet for up to 3 months. (Check out a few of our favorite rubs at the end of this chapter.)

Over time, spices' essential oils fade, and with them goes the flavor you're looking (and paying) for. To avoid the outrageous markup on bottled spices, refresh your rack at stores like Whole Foods and ethnic markets where you can buy spices from bulk containers that allow you to control for quantity. Fifteen grams of cardamom or cumin or coriander will cost you about a quarter of what a normal supermarket charges for a small bottle and will last for months. Plus, high turnover ensures you're getting potent spices—not something that's been sitting on a shelf since the Reagan era.

Create Your Own Sauces.

Sauces are kitchen game-changers, capable of lifting mediocre meals to heroic heights.

But why pay $5 for a bottled sauce made primarily with high-fructose corn syrup when high-quality sauces can be improvised on the spot from common pantry items? The important thing is to always think about balance when making a sauce: If it's too spicy, a hit of sweetness will help cool things off; if it's too salty, a splash of acid from vinegar or citrus will cut through the sodium and liven the sauce up. Mix and match members from each major flavor group below and it's hard to go wrong.

SWEET: Ketchup, honey, brown sugar, molasses, maple syrup, hoisin

SALTY: Soy sauce, Worcestershire, fish sauce, miso paste, peanut butter

SOUR: Vinegar (red or white wine, balsamic, rice wine, or apple cider are your best bets), lemon, lime, orange

SPICY: Dijon mustard, chipotle peppers, cayenne pepper, Tabasco, chili sauces like sriracha

Thickness is paramount. You want a sauce that's substantial enough to cling to meat and fish but not so thick that it's gloppy or smothering. Shoot for the consistency of ranch dressing. Keep in mind when applying sauces that sugars burn quickly, so if you have a particularly sweet sauce, or a large piece of meat that will take time to cook, don't apply the sauce until the final stage of cooking. For more on improvising first-rate sauces, check out the Sauce Matrix on page 218.

Mop Up the Competition.

This one comes straight from the competitive barbecue circuit, where pitmasters are desperate for tricks and techniques that will help them stand out in a crowded field. Mopping is essentially basting over an open flame, the constant application of liquid helping to soften tough connective tissue as well as adding a layer of flavor to the final product.

Mops can be made from just about any liquid imaginable—beer, booze, vinegar, oil, juice—usually accompanied by a few supporting cast members to help build flavor. You can buy a special mopping tool from barbecue stores, but save your money and just use a brush instead. Generally speaking, mops are best reserved for bigger cuts of meat like whole chickens, brisket, and pork shoulder, but that doesn't mean individual servings of meat and fish wouldn't also benefit from the same treatment. Here are a few of our favorite mops:

FOR BEEF: 1 (12 oz) Guinness draught, 2 Tbsp Worcestershire sauce, 2 Tbsp honey

FOR PORK: 1 cup cider vinegar, ½ cup vegetable or canola oil, Tabasco to taste

FOR CHICKEN: 1 cup orange juice, ½ cup vegetable or canola oil, 2 cloves minced garlic, 2 Tbsp chipotle pepper puree, 1 Tbsp dried oregano

Grill This *and* That!

If all you're cooking on that big, hot surface are a couple of steaks or chicken breasts, then you're wasting a lot of heat—and an easy opportunity to cook the rest of your meal at the same time. It's a time-crunching, money-saving measure that will not only help lower your monthly gas or electric bills, but also open up your grill repertoire to a world of new flavors.

Next time you have a pork chop or sirloin or salmon fillet to cook, plan at least one other element of your meal around the grill. Skewers of mixed vegetables are just a starting point: You can also sear lettuce for salads (yes, firm heads of lettuce like romaine love a bit of face time with the grill—check out the Sizzling Caesar Salad on page 286), roast oysters for appetizers, or grill fruit for dessert. With a bit of practice, the only time you'll need to head inside is to fetch another drink.

The Backyard BUILDING BLOCKS

Use these versatile sauces, salsas, dressings, and rubs to instantly elevate your grilling game.

Classic Barbecue Sauce

Forget the high-fructose corn syrup–laden supermarket sauces: You have everything you need for a killer batch of homemade sauce in your pantry. Consider this your barbecue-sauce blueprint; from here, you can adjust with ingredients like molasses, honey, beer, hot sauce, or anything else that excites your taste buds.

You'll Need:
2 Tbsp butter
1 small onion, minced
1 cup ketchup
2 Tbsp brown sugar
2 Tbsp apple cider vinegar
1 Tbsp Worcestershire sauce
½ Tbsp dry mustard
½ tsp paprika (preferably smoked)
½ tsp garlic powder
⅛ tsp cayenne
Black pepper to taste

How to Make It:

In a medium saucepan, melt the butter over low heat. Add the onion and sauté until soft and translucent. Stir in the ketchup, brown sugar, vinegar, Worcestershire, mustard, paprika, garlic powder, cayenne, and a few pinches of black pepper. Simmer over low heat for 15 minutes until you have a thick, uniform sauce.

Makes about 1½ cups; keeps in the refrigerator for up to 2 weeks.

Grill This!

NC Vinegar Sauce

In eastern North Carolina, barbecue means finely chopped whole hog dressed in a spicy vinegar-based sauce. It's a distinctive flavor used to cut through the intensity of the smoked pork without masking its flavor the way thicker barbecue sauces do. It's our favorite way to eat pulled pork.

You'll Need:

2 cups apple cider vinegar
½ Tbsp red pepper flakes
1 Tbsp sugar
1 Tbsp hot sauce
Salt and black pepper to taste

How to Make It:

Combine all of the ingredients in a sauce pan over low heat. Heat until the sugar dissolves. (You can also heat this in the microwave for 30 seconds.) Cool completely before using.

Makes about 2 cups; keeps for 2 weeks in the refrigerator.

SC Mustard Sauce

Cross the border into South Carolina and suddenly pulled pork is served with a mustard sheen. Barbecue hounds will debate which is better until pigs fly, but there's only one person's opinion that matters: yours. This sharp sauce also goes well on grilled chicken and smoked baby back ribs.

You'll Need:

1 cup yellow mustard
  cup ketchup
¼ cup light brown sugar
2 Tbsp apple cider vinegar
Pinch cayenne pepper
Black pepper to taste

How to Make It:

Combine the ingredients in a sauce pan over low heat. Heat until the sugar dissolves. (You can also heat this in the microwave for 30 seconds.) Cool completely before using.

Makes about 1 cup; keeps for 2 weeks in the refrigerator.

Pico de Gallo

This chunky, fresh tomato salsa comes together with about 3 minutes' worth of knife work, yet it adds a complex trio of sweet, heat, and acid to everything from sandwiches to grilled fish.

You'll Need:

2 lb Roma tomatoes, seeded and chopped
1 small red onion, diced
1 jalapeño pepper, seeded and minced
½ cup chopped cilantro
Juice of 1 lime
Salt to taste

How to Make It:

Combine the tomatoes, onion, jalapeño, cilantro, and lime juice in a mixing bowl. Season with salt.

Makes about 3 cups; keeps for 3 days in the refrigerator.

Grilled Chipotle-Lime Salsa

This is a smoky, spicy, all-purpose salsa, great on any of the Mexican-inspired recipes in the book (fish tacos, fajitas, etc.) or, of course, with a bag of tortilla chips.

You'll Need:

1½ lb Roma tomatoes, halved and seeded

2 (¼"-thick) slices from a medium red onion, skewered with a toothpick

Juice of 1 lime

1 clove garlic, minced

1 chipotle pepper

½ cup chopped cilantro

Salt to taste

How to Make It:

Preheat a grill or grill pan over high heat. When hot, grill the tomatoes and onion, turning, for about 10 minutes, until both are lightly charred and the tomato skins are blistered. Combine the tomatoes and onion in a blender or food processor along with the lime juice, garlic, and chipotle pepper and pulse for 10 seconds, until pureed but not perfectly smooth. Stir in the cilantro and season with salt.

Makes about 2 cups;
keeps in the refrigerator for
up to 10 days.

Mango Salsa

This is deceptively simple to make for something that tastes so good. Especially awesome with blackened fish and chicken. Try folding in a cubed avocado for a tasty, creamy-sweet dynamic.

You'll Need:

2 fresh mangoes, peeled, seeded, and diced

1 small red onion, minced

½ cup chopped cilantro

1 jalapeño pepper, seeded and minced

Juice of 1 lime

Salt to taste

How to Make It:

Combine the mangoes, onion, cilantro, jalapeño, and lime juice in a mixing bowl. Season with salt.

Makes about 2 cups;
keeps in the refrigerator for
up to 3 days.

Chimichurri

Chimichurri, an herb-based sauce from Argentina, is used to adorn and enhance a variety of different dishes—grilled meats and fish above all. After some careful reflection, we've decided that chimi is pretty much the world's greatest condiment, turning mediocre food good and making good food great. Once you make it, you'll have a hard time not painting it on everything you come across: sandwiches, grilled vegetables, eggs.

You'll Need:

2 Tbsp water

½ tsp salt

1 cup fresh parsley leaves, finely chopped

3 Tbsp red wine vinegar

2 cloves garlic, minced

Pinch red pepper flakes

3 Tbsp olive oil

How to Make It:

Combine the water and salt in a bowl and microwave for 30 seconds. Stir until the salt thoroughly dissolves, then mix in the parsley, vinegar, garlic, and pepper flakes. Slowly drizzle in the olive oil, whisking to incorporate. You can use the chimichurri now, but it's best to let the flavors marry for 20 minutes or more.

Makes about 1 cup;
keeps in the fridge for 3 days.

Grill This!

Peanut Sauce

Spicy peanut sauce is a vital grill staple throughout Southeast Asia. Classically, it doubles as a marinade and a dip for skewers of grilled chicken—but beef, pork, and shrimp all take well to its rich, spicy embrace.

You'll Need:

1 can (13.5 oz) light coconut milk
¾ cup creamy peanut butter
¾ cup sugar
2 Tbsp Thai red curry paste
2 Tbsp apple cider vinegar or white vinegar
1 Tbsp soy sauce
1 Tbsp minced fresh ginger
½ cup water
Juice of 1 lime

How to Make It:

Combine the coconut milk, peanut butter, sugar, curry paste, vinegar, soy sauce, ginger, and water in a medium saucepan. Simmer over low heat, stirring occasionally, for 10 minutes. Remove from heat and add the lime juice. Allow to cool completely before using.

Makes about 2 cups; keeps in the fridge for up to 1 week.

Green Sauce

Inspired by the epic Peruvian chicken restaurants of Northern Virginia, this all-purpose sauce is good slathered on sandwiches, drizzled over thick-sliced tomatoes, and used as a dip for grilled shrimp. And, of course, served alongside pieces of juicy grilled chicken.

You'll Need:

1 cup cilantro
Juice of 2 limes
¼ cup mayonnaise
¼ cup plain Greek yogurt
1 jalapeño pepper, stem removed (if you want a less incendiary sauce, remove the seeds as well)
2 cloves garlic, chopped

How to Make It:

Combine the cilantro, lime juice, mayonnaise, yogurt, jalapeño, and garlic in a food processor. Pulse until the ingredients form a smooth, light green puree.

Makes about 1½ cups; keeps in the fridge for up to 1 week.

Tzatziki

Though this Greek-style yogurt sauce matches perfectly with a charred lamb chop, it also can— and should—be applied to grilled chicken, pork, and fish on a regular basis.

You'll Need:

1 cucumber, peeled, halved, and seeded
1 cup plain Greek yogurt (we like Fage)
Juice of 1 lemon
2 Tbsp olive oil
2 cloves garlic, finely minced
2 tsp minced fresh dill
Salt and black pepper to taste

How to Make It:

Grate the cucumber with a cheese grater, then use your (clean!) hands to wring out all the excess water. Combine the cucumber with the yogurt, lemon juice, olive oil, garlic, dill, and a good pinch each of salt and pepper.

Makes about 1½ cups; keeps in the fridge for 5 days.

Honey-Dijon Vinaigrette

This is not just a great all-purpose salad dressing, it's also an easy way to brighten up slices of grilled chicken or a plate of asparagus.

You'll Need:

1 shallot, minced
¼ cup red or white wine vinegar
½ Tbsp Dijon mustard
½ Tbsp honey
½ cup olive oil
Salt and black pepper to taste

How to Make It:

Combine the shallot and vinegar in a mixing bowl and let sit for 10 minutes. Stir in the Dijon and honey, then slowly drizzle in the olive oil, whisking to fully blend the oil and vinegar into a uniform dressing. Season with salt and pepper.

Makes about 1 cup; keeps in the refrigerator for up to 1 week.

Pesto

You can buy perfectly fine pesto in the refrigerated section of most supermarkets (we like Cibo), but it will never taste as good as a homemade batch—which, by the way, takes all of 3 minutes to make. It works equally well as a marinade as it does for a post-grill dipping sauce. To keep it extra fresh and green, float a thin layer of oil on top of the pesto before refrigerating—the oil will keep the basil from oxidizing and turning dark. Try substituting arugula for the basil for a peppery alternative.

You'll Need:

2 cloves garlic, chopped
2 Tbsp pine nuts
3 cups fresh basil leaves
¼ cup grated Parmesan
Salt and black pepper to taste
½ cup olive oil

How to Make It:

Place the garlic, pine nuts, basil, and Parmesan, plus a few pinches of salt and pepper, in a food processor. Pulse until the basil is chopped. With the motor running, slowly drizzle in the olive oil until fully incorporated and a paste forms.

Makes about 1 cup; keeps for 2 weeks in the refrigerator.

Guacamole

Many American versions of guacamole include ingredients like cumin, sour cream, and (gasp!) mayo. But guac is really at its best with just a few carefully balanced ingredients: garlic (preferably chopped into an oily paste), a good pinch of salt, and a squeeze of lemon or lime. And of course, perfectly ripe Hass avocados. Use that as your base; everything else—onion, jalapeño, cilantro, tomato—is just a bonus.

You'll Need:

2 cloves garlic, peeled
Kosher salt to taste
¼ cup minced red onion
1 Tbsp minced jalapeño
2 ripe avocados, pitted and peeled
Juice of 1 lemon or lime
Chopped fresh cilantro (optional)

How to Make It:

Use the side of a knife to smash the garlic against the cutting board. Finely mince the cloves, then apply a pinch of salt to the garlic and use the side of your knife to work the garlic into a paste (the salt will act as an abrasive). Scoop the garlic into a bowl, then add the onion, jalapeño, and avocado and mash until the avocado is pureed, but still slightly chunky. Stir in the lemon juice, cilantro (if using), and salt to taste.

Makes about 2 cups; keeps in the refrigerator for 2 days.

Grilled Garlic

Raw garlic can be harsh and overpowering. Overcooked garlic can be acrid and off-putting. But slow-cooked garlic, roasted over the open flame of the grill, is like savory candy—sweet and inviting with its mellow garlic flavor. Fold into sauces or salad dressings (especially Caesar), or simply spread on slices of grilled bread, perhaps with a bit of crumbled goat cheese and a drizzle of olive oil.

You'll Need:

1 head garlic
Olive oil for coating

How to Make It:

Preheat a grill over medium heat. Use a sharp knife to cut off the very top of the garlic head, revealing just the tips of the individual garlic cloves. Place the head in the center of a piece of aluminum foil, drizzle with a bit of oil, then fold the foil to enclose the garlic. Place on the grill and cook, lid closed, for about 30 minutes, until the cloves are very soft and lightly caramelized.

To use the garlic, simply squeeze the bottom of the bulb until the soft individual cloves pop out.

Keeps in the refrigerator for up to 1 week.

Romesco

This Catalan condiment is used throughout Spain as a dip for vegetables and a sauce for grilled meats and fish. It's at its best when served alongside lightly charred asparagus spears, tuna steaks, or a few slices of sirloin.

You'll Need:

3 Tbsp olive oil
2 slices bread, torn into small pieces
2 Tbsp chopped almonds
2 cloves garlic, chopped
1 tsp smoked paprika
½ (12 oz) jar roasted red peppers
1 Tbsp red wine vinegar or sherry vinegar
Salt and black pepper to taste

How to Make It:

Heat 1 tablespoon of the olive oil in a medium sauté pan set over medium heat. Add the bread crumbs, almonds, garlic, and paprika and sauté for about 5 minutes, until the bread is lightly golden and crunchy. Transfer to a blender and add the remaining 2 tablespoons olive oil, the red peppers, vinegar, and a sprinkle of salt and pepper; puree until smooth. The romesco should have the texture of apple sauce; if you need to thin it out, stir in a tablespoon or two of water.

Makes about 1½ cups; keeps in the refrigerator for up to 1 week.

All-Purpose Barbecue Rub

Nearly all competitive barbecue teams have their own special spice blend, used for smoked chickens and racks of ribs and whole pork shoulders. This one is ours.

You'll Need:

¼ cup brown sugar
¼ cup salt
2 Tbsp paprika (preferably smoked paprika)
2 Tbsp black pepper
1 Tbsp garlic powder
1 Tbsp cumin
1 tsp cayenne

How to Make It:

Mix all of the spices together in a bowl or plastic storage container.

Makes about ¾ cup; keeps in your spice cabinet for up to 2 months.

Southwestern Rub

Smoke and fire combine in this Tex-Mex-style spice blend, a perfect one-two punch for pork tenderloins, chicken legs, and skirt steak. Use about 1 tablespoon for every pound of meat (the same ratio functions for the other rubs here as well).

You'll Need:

1 Tbsp salt
1 Tbsp black pepper
1 Tbsp smoked paprika
1 Tbsp ancho or chipotle chile powder
½ Tbsp ground cumin
½ Tbsp garlic powder
½ tsp cayenne pepper

How to Make It:

Mix all of the spices together in a bowl or plastic storage container.

Makes about 6 tablespoons; keeps in your spice cabinet for up to 2 months.

Moroccan Spice Rub

Rub this on a leg of lamb and grill it until it's tender and juicy and you'll be transported to the markets of Marrakesh. Or coat a fillet of salmon or halibut with this blend and serve it over a heap of steamed couscous.

You'll Need:

1 Tbsp paprika
1 Tbsp cumin seeds, roughly chopped, or 1 Tbsp ground cumin
1 Tbsp coriander seeds, roughly chopped, or 1 Tbsp ground coriander
½ Tbsp black peppercorns
1 tsp cinnamon
1 tsp ground nutmeg
¼ tsp cayenne pepper

How to Make It:

Mix all of the spices together in a bowl or plastic storage container.

Makes about ¼ cup; keeps in your spice cabinet for up to 2 months.

Magic Blackening Rub

Coat meat, fish, or vegetables with this potent blend of seasonings and cook over high heat until it transforms into a dark, savory crust.

You'll Need:

1 Tbsp paprika
1 Tbsp salt
2 tsp black pepper
2 tsp ground cumin
2 tsp garlic powder
2 tsp onion powder
1 tsp dried oregano
½ tsp cayenne pepper

How to Make It:

Mix all of the spices together in a bowl or plastic storage container.

Makes about ⅓ cup; keeps in your spice cabinet for up to 2 months.

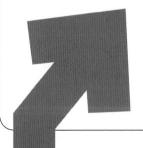

THE GRILL MASTER'S GEAR GUIDE

CHAPTER **2**

GRILL
THIS
NOT
THAT!

The Grill Master's GEAR GUIDE

Imagine going in for heart surgery and discovering once you're on the table that there are none of those precise scalpels and flashy medical tools on hand; all the doctor has to work with is a dull pocketknife and a bottle of whiskey to ease the pain (his).

Or imagine you've been invited to a rock concert, only to discover that there are no Marshall amps or Stratocasters to be found; the only instruments the band has are a half-dozen kazoos, a rusty cowbell, and a gallon drum of Justin Bieber's hair gel.

Not good, right?

It doesn't matter if your heart's in the hands of Dr. Oz or if your ears are in the hands of Ozzy Osbourne—without the right tools, even the most skilled medicine man can't heal; without the right instruments, even the wildest rocker can't rock.

And even the best chef can't cook.

It doesn't matter if you're some wild genetic mix of Mario Batali, Julia Child, and the Hamburglar; you're not going to be able to whip up a great meal—and strip away a great deal of calories—without the right tools.

Fortunately, we've tried, tested, and accidentally tipped over just about every kind of grill on the planet, as well as the myriad accoutrements of the grill game. So whether you're a weeknight warrior or a total grill geek, this comprehensive guide highlights the best equipment for every type of cook.

SEAR Factor

Whether you're a weeknight warrior or a fair-weather griller, this comprehensive guide highlights the best equipment for every type of cook.

If you've spent any time shopping for grills, then you understand the frustration. What was once little more than a metal clamshell with gridiron teeth has grown to resemble a Michael Bay creation outfitted with multiple burners, drawers, knobs, and levers. Some of those accessories might serve you well, but they can just as easily blind you from the basic goal of finding a grill that cooks honest food without bleeding your bank account dry. Ultimately the grill you buy should fit your needs and lifestyle, and this guide is designed to help you match your personality to your equipment. With the right grill, you'll be more likely to cook the recipes in this book, and that's your first step toward a leaner, tastier lifestyle.

30
Percentage of grillers who own more than one grill

53
Percentage of grill owners who cook out at least a few times per week during the grilling season

31
Percentage of grill owners who cook out more than they did the previous year because "they're trying to eat healthier"

You don't mind getting your hands dirty, and when you go camping, you're the one tossing logs on the fire. Your pantry contains no pre-sweetened oatmeal packages, and you'd rather eat beans from a can than microwave a frozen dinner. For you, grilling is an art and, for the most part, you'd rather invest a little extra time than risk a subpar meal.

The Grill Type: CHARCOAL

Charcoal grills have three things going for them: They're cheap, they generate high heat, and they give your food a more pronounced smoky flavor. The downsides are that charcoal is messy and you have to factor in 20 minutes to heat the grill. What's more, studies indicate that by burning fat, charcoal grills are responsible for creating more carcinogenic polycyclic aromatic hydrocarbons (PAHs). You can reduce your risk by trimming fat and marinating (the acids in marinade further reduce carcinogens).

Make the Most of It: When building a charcoal fire, always have a hot zone and a cool zone. The hot zone should have 75 to 100 percent of the charcoal collected on its side of the grill. And the zone should occupy the same space on the grill every time, that way you know instinctually where you can sear steaks and where you can move a chicken leg that's burning because of flare-ups.

 OUR PICKS

WEBER ONE-TOUCH SILVER 18.5"
$79, Weber.com
A prize-worthy dinner is made from proper technique, not fancy equipment, and no grill proves that better than the classic model that's probably been behind more burgers and steaks than any other cooking vessel in America.

CHAR-GRILLER OUTLAW
$159, CharGriller.com
More than 1,000 square inches of hot gridiron spread over two shelves makes this the best value for high-volume grilling. Plus the elongated barrel makes it easy to bank coals for indirect cooking.

To you, grilling should be every bit as convenient as other methods of cooking. Sure you enjoy the sizzle of a steak against hot iron, but you have no intention of planning your day around a meal. You want to cook, eat, and get on with life.

The Grill Type: GAS

Barbecue buffs often belittle gas grills for producing food they deem inferior. They argue that gas doesn't generate smoky flavors, and that the grates of the gridiron rarely get hot enough for a proper sear. But today's gas grills are more powerful, versatile, and affordable than ever, capable of charring a chicken breast and slow-cooking a pork shoulder with nearly equal ease. Cooking on a gas grill is quicker and cleaner than the charcoal alternative, and if that's what it takes to keep you grilling, then by all means crank the propane.

Make the Most of It: There's no smoke better than that from wood chips, and you don't need charcoal for that. Wood-chip boxes and planks are both viable options (see pages 68 and 69), but for something even more low-tech, wrap a handful of soaked wood chips in aluminum foil and puncture it several times with a fork (to let the smoke escape). Place it over the flame before you cook and you'll notice a serious upgrade in the flavor of your food.

OUR PICKS

CHARBROIL K6B 6-BURNER GAS GRILL (with side burner)
$375, Charbroil.com
You won't find another grill with this combination of power and surface area for under $500.

DUCANE AFFINITY 4100
$410, Ducane.com
In a *Men's Health* field test, the Affinity 4100 heated twice as quickly as more expensive propane grills. Credit the burners' 48,000 BTUs of heating power.

THE GRILL GEEK

The perfect caramel-colored shell of a steakhouse rib eye gives you goose bumps, but you're equally impressed by the fall-from-the bone tenderness of slow-cooked ribs. In general you leave little to chance, and you approach grilling as equal parts science and art.

The Grill Type: CERAMIC

The hefty price tag keeps most people away from a ceramic grill—especially considering that most of the models appear to be little more than rudimentary orbs with vents at top. But don't be misled: These grills provide optimal control over cooking temperature, capable of holding a sirloin-searing 700°F heat just as steadily as a pulled-pork-perfect 250°F. They're also more efficient and durable than steel grills, and because they lock in heat so well, the outer surface remains cooler to the touch.

Make the Most of It: Stick with natural lump charcoal. Fumes from lighter fluid—soaked briquettes can linger and give subsequent meals a chemical-like aftertaste. And once the coals are lit, use the top and bottom vents to control temperature. Wide-open vents increase airflow for a warmer fire, while barely open vents create the lower temperatures necessary for slow-cooking barbecue.

OUR PICKS

BIG GREEN EGG
$750 for a medium model with stand
($633.29 for the egg, $121.95 for the stand), BigGreenEgg.com
Egg Heads worship at the altar of this funky green grill, swearing by its ability to do it all, from searing to smoking. The medium-size model offers 177 square inches of cooking space, while the pricier extra-large model goes up to 452 inches.

PRIMO OVAL XL
$1,099, PrimoGrill.com
It's the only ceramic charcoal grill made entirely in America, and it features a massive 680-square-inch cooking surface.

"The more, the merrier" is an expression you use often, and when you grill, you expect neighbors, family, and friends to swing by. You think food should be the main attraction at a good party, and you're entirely comfortable commanding a grill with a beer in one hand and an 18-inch spatula in the other.

The Grill Type:
MULTI-FUNCTION

This is the Swiss Army knife of grills, complete with multiple burners and all the gadgetry necessary to prep sides and appetizers. If you're willing to invest the money, the drawbacks here are few— many multi-function grills provide all the amenities of a kitchen aside from the sink and dishwasher. But here's our advice for shopping on a budget: Don't sacrifice quality for extra bells and whistles. You're better with one really strong burner than half a dozen weak ones.

Make the Most of It: Don't neglect the side burner. Use it to warm beans, roast brussels sprouts, or fry bacon. Keep a sauce on simmer and it will thicken while your steak cooks, or sauté onions and peppers for instant fajitas. Think of the extra hot pad as the ideal alternative for anything that doesn't cook well on the grill.

OUR PICKS

VERMONT CASTINGS 501 SIGNATURE SERIES GRILL
$2,199, VermontCastings.com

You can buy bigger, brasher, pricier grills, but with Vermont Castings' combination of power, versatility, and special features, we're not sure why you would want to. High-quality cast-iron grates, a built-in smoker box, and a 20,000-BTU rotisserie burner make this one of the best grills on the market today.

WEBER GENESIS E-330
$819, Weber.com

The porcelain-enameled cast-iron grates create even distribution for the 38,000 BTUs of heat coming off the main burners and 12,000 BTUs on the side.

THE GRILL DISCIPLE

You bow down at the altar of barbecue. Your fixation on smoky, tender meat borders on religious, and more than once you've traveled out of your way in pursuit of perfect barbecue. You are patient about grilling—perhaps even Zen-like—and you're willing to rise before the sun to begin prepping an evening feast with friends.

The Grill Type: SMOKER

A smoker is easily the best option for daylong cooking projects, and the meat it produces is more tender than anything you'll cook on a traditional grill. That said, if you're not committed to planning entire days—and sometimes weekends— around a cookout, then you're probably better off with a basic gas or charcoal grill.
Make the Most of It: The low, slow heat of the smoker works best on large pieces of meat—think ribs, brisket, pork shoulder, a whole chicken. But when you go to purchase wood, beware of the price gouge. Many stores will charge you a few bucks for a couple handfuls of wood chips, and you'll probably need a couple bags just for one big job. Look for better prices at your local lumberyard. If they don't sell wood chips in bulk, save some cash by purchasing untreated cedar and chopping or slicing it into chunks.

OUR PICKS

BRINKMANN PROFESSIONAL CHARCOAL GRILL
$380, Brinkmann.net
Constructed entirely of steel, the Brinkmann Pro is a tank among grills, and it's the best solution for grillers who want to dabble with smoke. The side-mounted chamber functions as a smoker box, but also works to cook smaller meals while using less charcoal or wood.

WEBER SMOKEY MOUNTAIN COOKER
$299, Weber.com
Smoking made simple: The Smokey's bullet-shaped housing holds two 18.5-inch gridirons, a top mounted thermostat, and an easy-access door for adding water and wood chips without letting all that precious heat escape.

THE TRAVELER

Your Coleman cooler gets more use than your DVD player, and your weekends are reserved for camping, tailgating, and family gatherings in the park. You're not fussy about food, but when it comes down to it, you'd much rather eat a hand-pressed burger hot off the grill than a prefab factory burger coming at you through a drive-thru window.

The Grill Type: PORTABLE

The upside is obvious: These grills go wherever you want them to. They also store easily in the closet, so they're great for people who don't have dedicated outdoor space for grill storage. That said, a grill that's built to travel is certainly not going to provide the biggest cooking area, and you won't find one that gets as hot as a well-built standing model.

Make the Most of It: Find the grill that best suits your needs. If it's too small you won't be able to use it, and if it's too big you won't want to lug it around. Our favorite models are those that maximize gridiron surface area without being overly bulky, and we appreciate firmly attaching lids that make them easy to carry.

OUR PICKS

LODGE LOGIC SPORTSMAN GRILL
$140, Lodgemfg.com
This throwback hibachi-style grill sports thick cast-iron grates that can sear a steak better than most full-size grills. It's heavy, but also small enough to fit in your fireplace for rainy-day grilling.

WEBER GO-ANYWHERE CHARCOAL GRILL
$50, Weber.com
The rectangular design makes good use of surface area, and when you travel, the grill's legs fold over the lid to hold it firmly in place. It's available in both charcoal and gas models.

THE WEEKN1GHT WARRIOR

Sure, you'd grill outside every day if you could. But that's not happening with your schedule. You barely have time to cook, let alone keep a grill clean and shuffle food in and out of the house as you slog over to the Weber. You're okay sacrificing barbecue's smoky flavor so long as you can still preserve some of the magic of the grill.

The Grill Type: GRILL PAN

Technically it's not a grill, but it does mimic some of the effects. The grill pan's running grooves create authentic-looking grill marks, and they allow some fat to drip out. That's ideal for thin cuts of steak, burgers, and pork chops, but it's useless if you're tying to obtain the indirect heat needed for ribs or brisket.

Make the Most of It: A panini press goes for about $150, but a good grill pan can produce the same crispy, melty sandwiches for no extra cost to speak off. Set the grill pan over medium heat, stack your bread with meat, cheese, and vegetables (we suggest grilled chicken, roasted peppers, and fresh mozzarella for your maiden panini voyage), then use a light weight to press the sandwiches down; a pot filled with a bit of water works perfectly. Once the first side is crisp, flip the sandwiches and repeat.

OUR PICK

LODGE LOGIC SQUARE GRILL PAN
$30.95, Lodgemfg.com
There are plenty of nonstick grill pans on the market, but nothing handles high temperature as well as cast iron. And nobody makes cast iron as well as Lodge. Consider this the closest thing to a grill that fits into your cupboard.

USE THIS, NotThat!

The essential tool kit for the savvy griller

To test your grill heat, place your hand 3 inches above the grilling surface and count, "One Mississippi, two Mississippi…" until you have to pull away. Less than 3 Mississippis is high heat; 5 to 6 is medium; 10 to 12 is low.

To Build the Fire

Use This!

NATURAL LUMP CHARCOAL

OUR PICK

Not That!

BRIQUETTES (like from Kingsford)

BIG GREEN EGG NATURAL LUMP CHARCOAL
$27.99 for a 20-lb bag, bbqislandinc.com

Lump charcoal is a simple product created by burning wood in the absence of oxygen. Briquettes, on the other hand, are bound together with starch, laced with lime, and often soaked in lighter fluid. Lump coal may cost a little more, but for our dollar, it's worth the extra money. Among the many reasons the world's greatest pitmasters choose lumps over briquettes: They light faster, provide better temperature control, and produce less ash to clean.

To Light the Grill

Use This!   *Not That!*

CHIMNEY   LIGHTER FLUID

> **OUR PICK**
> **WEBER RAPIDFIRE CHIMNEY STARTER**
> $17.99, Weber.com

Lighter fluid is a petroleum-derived chemical, but if that alone doesn't freak you out, pay close attention next time you eat food that was cooked over lighter fluid–soaked coals. Notice the tinge of a metallic, chemical aftertaste? That's the result of lighter fluid. No thanks. The speed, ease, and purity of chimney starters is slowly making lighter fluid a thing of the past, and we couldn't be happier. Pick one up on weber.com for $18.

Stuff wadded paper—old newspaper is perfect—in the bottom of the chimney, and fill the top half with coals. Light the paper, and as it burns it will ignite the coals above. When they begin to glow, slowly lift the chimney off the grill. Angle the mouth of the chimney down toward the grill, give it a shake, and the hot coals will spill out into your grill. Now start cookin'.

To Tenderize the Meat

Use This!   *Not That!*

MEAT MALLET   MEAT TENDERIZER WITH BLADES

> **OUR PICK**
> **KITCHEN CRAFT MEAT MALLET**
> $12.99, Amazon.com

The classic meat tenderizer, a metal mallet with a textured striking surface, is a perfect tool. But in an ill-conceived attempt to innovate, manufacturers have begun producing blade-style tenderizers: meat-mangling weapons that impale your steak with dozens of steel spikes. The result is a mushy hunk that falls somewhere between whole and ground meat. A few thwacks with the mallet (or failing that, a heavy pan) is all the tenderizing your steak needs.

To Flip the Steak

Use This!

Not That!

TONGS

BARBECUE FORK

> OUR PICK
>
> **OXO GOOD GRIPS 18" BBQ TONGS**
> $14.99, OXO.com

You know what a barbecue fork is good for?
Prodding cattle, fixing divots on the putting green,
and mutilating your dinner. Each time you jab the tines of
a fork into a piece of meat, you create tiny ducts
that juices use to travel to the surface and burble out onto
the coals. Tongs are just as easy to operate,
they're better at scraping up clingy bits,
and they're designed to preserve the quality of your pork chop.

To Spread the Sauce

Use This!

Not That!

NATURAL-BRISTLE BRUSH

SILICON BRUSH

> OUR PICK
>
> **GRILLPRO 18" BASTING BRUSH**
> $3.99, GrillPro.com

Silicon brushes rinse easily in the sink,
but that's their only real virtue. What you want is
a brush that sops up the most sauce and spreads it on
evenly, and for that you can do no better
than big, soft, natural bristles. When you're done
just toss it in the dishwasher.
Bonus: Natural-bristle brushes cost about as much as
a pint of beer at your local watering hole.

To Roast the Chicken

Use This!

BEER CAN

OUR PICK

A FIZZY LAGER LIKE PABST BLUE RIBBON

Not That!

VERTICAL CHICKEN ROASTER

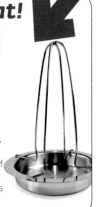

Sure you can buy fancy wire scaffolding to prop a chicken up on your grill, but what's the point? It's just one more bulky piece of equipment taking up space in your cupboard. Besides, a beer can is better since it serves both to prop up the chicken and to provide a moist cooking environment. Simply crack open the can, drink half of the suds, then lodge the can in the open cavity of the chicken. Now use the protruding end of the beer can as a stand. Your bird remains upright and stays moist from beer simmering inside.

To Test the Doneness

Use This!

MEAT THERMOMETER

OUR PICK

THERMOWORKS SUPER-FAST POCKET THERMOMETER
$24, ThermoWorks.com

Not That!

KNIFE

Slicing open a steak to peek inside will give you a good indication of doneness, but it will also decimate an otherwise pristine piece of meat. So do like the pros and use a thermometer. Touch and appearance can serve as rough indicators, but ultimately it's the internal temperature that determines the doneness of meat. For more on how to know when your meat is perfectly cooked, see "Is It Done Yet?" on page 70.

Thermometers run the price and tech spectrum, from $4 basic probes to instant thermometers that would make Steve Jobs proud. Our favorite of the high-end camp is Taylor's Waterproof Dual Temperature Thermacouple and Infrared Thermometer, which measures up to 626°F in one second. ($99; Taylorusa.com)

5 KILLER Grill Gadgets

PACIFIC NORTHWEST FINE WOOD PRODUCTS CEDAR BARBECUE PLANKS

Set of 6, $17.95

PacificNorthwestPlanks.com

Even easier than a wood-chip box? Planks—slices of wood that you set directly on the grill with steaks or fish on top. Pacific Northwest's are thick enough to use a few times, but they'll still cost you more than the wood chips you load into a wood-chip box. Save some cash by asking your local lumberyard if they carry untreated cedar shingles. If they do, stock up. You're essentially getting the same product for a fraction of the cost.

MR. BAR-B-Q PLATINUM PRESTIGE STAINLESS STEEL WOK TOPPER

$19.90, MrBarBQ.com

Asparagus spears and portobello caps can go directly on the grill grates, but unless you want to lose smaller vegetables to the fire, you'll need some protection. This perforated grill basket exposes vegetables directly to the flames without the risk of sacrificing anything to the grill gods. Use it to cook chopped vegetables, roast the skins off small peppers, or add a nice char to green beans. Mr. Bar-B-Q backs this one with a lifetime warranty, but we're guessing you won't need it.

4

CHAR-BROIL CAST-IRON SMOKER BOX

$15.99, CharBroil.com

A wood-chip box is the easiest way to earn big smoky flavor without investing in a dedicated smoker grill. Just load it with soaked wood chips, set it over the flame, and let the smoke permeate your food. This cast-iron version from Char-Broil will handle the heat with ease and cost you less than a steakhouse rib eye.

5

CHARCOAL COMPANION 13" NONSTICK GRILLING KABOB SKEWERS

$6.98, Amazon.com

Skewers are perhaps the most underutilized of all cooking implements. They're the grilling equivalent of the one-pot meal, allowing you to balance a meal's worth of meats and vegetables on a single scrap of metal and requiring very little cleanup effort. Opt for metal over wood and you can skip the soaking step, and with flat skewers like these, you don't have to worry about foods spinning around and cooking unevenly.

ITALIAN VILLA PIZZA PEEL

$14.99, Amazon.com

Several recipes in this book show you how to cook pizza directly on the grate of your grill, but transferring a pie on and off a hot gridiron can be tricky. Forgo the blistered knuckles by purchasing a pizza peel, the pie-shoveling device preferred by pros from New York to Naples. The price tag here is modest, and the stubby handle makes it ideal for grillwork.

5 Gadgets to Avoid

1. BURGER PRESS

Pressing ground beef too firmly gives you tough, rubbery patties. For juicy burgers that melt in your mouth, there's no better compression contraption than two human hands.

2. SMOKING GUN

In order for smoke to permeate food, you need time and heat. Using a "gun" to blast smoke at a cooked brisket won't provide more than a fleeting scent.

3. RIB RACK

Propping your ribs vertically saves a little space on the grill, but you can achieve the same effect by wrapping them in aluminum foil and stacking them directly on the grill.

4. ROTISSERIE SHISH KEBAB WHEEL

A chicken is a large, tricky piece of meat that benefits from the rotation of a rotisserie. A kebab? Drop it on the grill, give it a good high-heat sear, and enjoy. Let's not make this fussy.

5. HOT DOG BASKET

A basket designed to holster your dogs while they cook. The purpose? We don't know either.

Is It DONE Yet?

When it comes to grilling, it's the most important question of all. Here's how to get it right every time.

We've all been there before: You go down to the market, carefully pick out a beautiful piece of beef, shell out $15 a pound for it, and return home to lovingly cook it. But by the time you sit down to eat, it looks like a hockey puck and tastes like leather. You owe it to yourself, your dining mates, the butcher, and the cow to cook that steak as skillfully as possible.

To avoid any major grilling mishaps, it's essential to always have a thermometer on hand—especially for bigger cuts of meat. But with enough practice, you can turn your finger into a divining rod capable of properly judging steaks, burgers, and chops with a single touch. We've broken it down for you both ways, with the empirical data of doneness as well as the keys and clues that will help sharpen your tactile instincts.

Fish

Target Temperatures:
MEDIUM: 130°F
MEDIUM-WELL: 140°F
WELL-DONE: 170°F

The thickest part of any fish fillet should flake with gentle pressure from your fingertip. Or use this great chef trick: Insert a metal skewer (or the tip of a paring knife) into the thickest part of the fillet. After three seconds remove it and touch it to the base of your thumb (where the skin is especially sensitive). If it's warm to the touch, it's perfectly cooked; if it's hot, it's overdone. When cooking salmon, watch out for white spots that form on the surface; those deposits of coagulated protein mean your salmon is overcooked.

Shrimp

Target Temperatures:
SHRIMP ARE TOO SMALL FOR THERMOMETERS.

Shrimp go from raw to perfect to dry all in a matter of 3 minutes, so look alive! Luckily, there are a few visual clues to guide you:

The translucent flesh will turn the lightest shade of pink and the tails will begin to slowly curl inward. You want your shrimp to look more like Js than Cs, so once the tails begin to curl, they're done.

Pork

Target Temperatures:
MEDIUM: 145°F
MEDIUM-WELL: 155°F
WELL: 165°F

Great restaurants cook their pork to medium, with a light pink center, and if you know that your pork comes from a reputable source, you can follow suit. For those squeamish about seeing pink in their pork, aim to cook it to 155ºF; go much above and you'll see why so many people complain about pork being dry.

Chicken

Target Temperatures:
MEDIUM-WELL: 155°F
WELL: 165°F

A perfectly cooked boneless,

skinless chicken breast will feel firm and bouncy to the touch, like a tennis ball. For chicken cooked on the bone, look for the juices that escape to run clear, meaning the last of the pink by the bones has been cooked off. If the meat on the drumstick begins to pull away from the bone, it probably means it's overcooked.

Beef and Lamb

Target Temperatures:
RARE: 125°F
MEDIUM-RARE: 135°F
MEDIUM: 145°F
MEDIUM-WELL: 155°F
WELL: 170°F

People's taste for red-meat temperature runs from nearly mooing to burnt to a crisp, so much of what you're looking for is a personal judgment call.

Some experts swear by the thumb method, which works by touching the tip of your thumb with the tips of your other fingers. As you work your way from index

finger to pinkie, the fleshy base of your thumb firms up, representing the various degrees of doneness. This method works for all meat.
Index Finger: RARE
Soft and squishy, like a pink sponge
Middle Finger: MEDIUM-RARE
Firm but yielding, like a Nerf football
Ring Finger: MEDIUM
Barely yielding, like a racquetball
Pinky Finger: WELL
Hard yet springy, like a tennis ball

Burgers
(Beef, Turkey, Etc)

Target Temperatures:
RARE: 125°F
MEDIUM-RARE: 135°F
MEDIUM: 150°F
MEDIUM-WELL: 155°F
WELL: 160°F

Burgers, especially ones made from lean cuts like sirloin or buffalo, are fickle creatures, going from juicy to arid in a matter of a minute. If it's the former you seek, the center of the burger should feel firm, but easily yield. Once the patty begins to feel springy, you've entered the medium-well stages of doneness.

GRILL
THIS
NOT
THAT!

BURGERS&
SANDWICHES

THE PERFECT
Grilled Burger

There are burgers, and then there are burgers, those juicy, beefy objects of our desire that linger around on our taste buds and our memories long after we've devoured them. What follows is the formula to ensure every burger you grill falls into the second camp. Use these tips and techniques for all the burgers in this chapter, and for all the burgers you make from this day forward.

Use only the freshest ground beef.

Ideally, that means grinding your own at home. If you have a KitchenAid mixer, you can buy a grinding attachment ($65), one of the greatest investments a burger hound can make. Make sure both the attachment and the beef are very cold before grinding on the coarsest setting. The easy alternative to grinding at home is asking the butcher to do it for you at the store. Purchase a whole chunk of brisket (or, failing that, chuck or sirloin) and ask him to grind it and wrap it up.

Don't overwork the meat.

The worst thing you can do to a burger, besides overcook it, is overpack it. No kneading, massaging, punching, or hard-packing necessary. Bring the meat loosely together, just enough to hold its shape, and leave it at that.

Salt at the last moment.

Salt the meat before you form the patties and the sodium chloride will work to break down protein strands, creating a dense texture closer to sausage than the loose, tender ideal you're looking for. Always salt your burgers seconds—not minutes—before grilling.

Cook the patties over a steady heat.

After testing a dozen different cooking methods, we came up with one clear path to juicy, medium-rare results: Form the patties and let them sit at room temperature for 15 minutes before cooking; in our tests, allowing the temperature of the chilled meat to rise made for more even cooking results. After 15 minutes, cook the burgers, with the lid up, over a medium flame—enough heat to give the patties a nice char, but not so much that you cook the outside before the center of the burger reaches a perfect pink.

You'll Need:

- 1 lb freshly ground brisket
- Salt and black pepper to taste
- 4 slices American cheese
- 4 potato buns, lightly toasted
- 1 large, very ripe tomato
- 1 yellow onion, thinly sliced
- Lettuce
- Sliced pickles

- Form the beef into four equal patties, being careful not to overwork the meat. Allow the meat to sit at room temperature for at least 15 minutes before cooking (about as much time as it takes for the grill to heat up).

- Preheat a grill or grill pan over medium heat. Just before cooking, season the burgers all over with salt and pepper. Place on the grill and cook for 4 minutes, until light grill marks have developed. Flip the patties, cover with the cheese, and continue grilling for 3 to 4 minutes, until the center of a burger feels firm but yielding, like a Nerf football, and an instant-read thermometer inserted in the thickest part of a burger registers 135°F.

- Serve the burgers on the buns with tomato, onion, lettuce, pickles, and any other condiments you like. Makes 4 servings.

The Burger Matrix

Beef will always be our first love when it comes to burgers, but anything that can be formed into a patty and inserted in a bun has the potential to be something special. Turkey and salmon are two common alternatives, but ground chicken, tuna, bison, and lamb all can be shaped into outstanding burgers. Avoid the temptation to overdress the burger: A balance among bun, patty, and condiments is at the heart of every great burger recipe.

Four Quick Recipes

Burgers by their very nature are prime canvases for creative cooking. Consider these a mere jumping-off point. Choose your toppings carefully and cook your burger skillfully and you can't go wrong.

CHOOSE A PROTEIN

PORK

CHICKEN

LAMB

BISON

CHOOSE A BUN

SESAME-SEED BUN

DELI FLATS

With the exception of lettuce leaves, these restrained pockets from Pepperidge Farm are the lightest option, packing about 100 calories apiece.

POTATO ROLL

CHOOSE A CHEESE

SWISS

SHARP CHEDDAR

AMERICAN

CHOOSE VEGETATION

ROASTED PEPPERS

AVOCADO

RAW OR GRILLED ONIONS

GRILLED PINEAPPLE

CHOOSE CONDIMENTS

SPECIAL SAUCE

Mix together two parts ketchup, two parts mayo, one part regular mustard, and a scoop of finely chopped pickles.

GUACAMOLE

Much like pesto, this garlicky herb sauce pairs great with any type of patty. See the recipe on page 47.

CHIMICHURRI

THE ALOHA BURGER
Turkey + English muffin + Swiss + grilled onions + pineapple + teriyaki

THE BIG KAHUNA
Chicken + sesame bun + pepper-Jack + salsa + guacamole + jalapeños

TUNA

To form tuna or salmon patties, chop 1 pound of meat very finely and combine with 1 egg, ½ cup bread crumbs, and any seasonings you want to add.

SALMON

Make your own veggie patties by pureeing ½ pound mushrooms, 1 cup black beans, ¾ cup bread crumbs, 1 egg, and a few shakes of Worcestershire food processor.

VEGGIE

LETTUCE

Large, foldable leaves like Bibb and red leaf lettuce are your best options.

ENGLISH MUFFINS

We don't normally love upscale buns like focaccia or ciabatta, but they pair well with tuna and salmon burgers.

"FANCY" ROLL

BLUE

While crumbled cheeses like feta, goat, and blue don't melt as well as the other options here, they pair well with burgers that are dressed with bold condiments.

PEPPER-JACK

When grating cheese for burgers, always use the smallest holes—that way the cheese melts more quickly and covers the burger more thoroughly.

MOZZARELLA

SAUTÉED MUSHROOMS

PICKLES

LETTUCE

TOMATOES

A.1. OR OTHER STEAK SAUCE

TERIYAKI SAUCE

You can use the Pico de Gallo recipe on page 46, or turn to your favorite bottled salsa.

SALSA

BLACK AND BLUE
Bison + potato roll + blackening spices + blue cheese + sautéed mushrooms + A.1.

THE FANCY PANTS
Tuna + focaccia + roasted peppers + arugula + chimichurri

Burger Basics

Rule 1
Lightly pack your patties. Overwork the meat and you'll have a dense, tough burger, rather than a light, juicy one.

Rule 2
Only use produce that tastes great on its own. A tomato flown in from halfway around the world that tastes like wet cardboard isn't doing your burger any favors. Neither is that brown lettuce in the refrigerator.

Rule 3
Match the intensity of the meat with the condiments. A tuna burger with blue cheese isn't going to win anyone's heart, but ground bison dusted with spices and topped with crumbled blue is a winning combination.

Rule 4
Bun-to-burger ratio is key: You don't want a huge bun dominating your burger. Not only does it throw off the balance, it also invites unwanted calories. Lightly toast the inside parts of the bun only: The contrast between soft, warm top and crunchy inside is what a good bun is all about.

Lamb Burgers
with Roasted Red Pepper Spread

Beyond beef, lamb may be our favorite protein for making burgers. Its rich, mildly gamy flavor takes well to smoke and char, just as it takes well to heady spices and boldly flavored condiments like this goat cheese-red pepper spread.

You'll Need:

- ½ cup bottled roasted red peppers
- ¼ cup fresh goat cheese
- ¼ cup plain low-fat Greek yogurt
- 1 clove garlic, smashed and peeled
- 1 lb ground lamb
- ½ tsp fennel seeds
- ¼ tsp ground coriander
- ¼ tsp ground cumin
- Salt and black pepper to taste
- 4 slices yellow onion, skewered with toothpicks
- 4 potato rolls
- Bibb Lettuce or arugula

If your market doesn't sell ground lamb, ask the butcher to grind a pound of lamb leg or shoulder meat.

How to Make It:

- Preheat a grill or grill pan over medium-high heat. In a food processor, combine the peppers, goat cheese, yogurt, and garlic. Pulse until thoroughly pureed and uniform in color.

- Combine the lamb with the fennel seeds, coriander, and cumin. Gently mix with your hands, then form into four equal patties. Just before grilling, season both sides of the patties with salt and pepper.

- Grill the burgers for 4 to 5 minutes per side, until firm but still giving to the touch (like a Nerf football). At the same time, grill the onion slices for 3 to 4 minutes per side, until soft and lightly charred. While the burgers rest, lightly toast the insides of the buns.

- Divide the red pepper spread among the buns. Place lettuce on the bottoms of each, top with a burger, then crown with the grilled onions and bun tops.

Makes 4 servings

Per Serving:	490 calories
$3.03	28 g fat (10 g saturated)
	580 mg sodium

Master **THE** **TECHNIQUE**

Toasting spices

Preground spices like cumin, coriander, and fennel lose much of their punch during the processing. To maximize flavor, buy whole seeds and grind them yourself. First, warm the spices in a dry stainless-steel pan set over medium-low heat until the volatile oils begin to release and fill the kitchen with a deep aroma. Transfer to a clean coffee grinder and pulse. Do this just before cooking to ratchet the flavor of your food up a few notches.

Steak Tortas

The *torta* may be the greatest sandwich you've never heard of. Born in Mexico, a culinary culture blessed with amazing meat preparations and world-class condiments, the pillowy sandwich comes stuffed with an embarrassment of culinary riches: grilled meat and onions, fresh avocado, salsa, chiles, a swipe or two of refried beans. It's everything we love about burritos, but on a roll that packs a fraction of the calories of a large tortilla.

You'll Need:

- 1 lb flank or skirt steak
- ½ tsp cumin
- ⅛ tsp cayenne pepper
- Salt and black pepper to taste
- 1 medium red onion, sliced into ¼"-thick rings and skewered with toothpicks
- 4 crusty rolls, lightly toasted
- ½ cup low-fat refried beans, warmed
- 1 avocado, peeled, pitted, and thinly sliced
- 1 cup shredded Jack cheese
- Pico de Gallo (page 46)
- Hot sauce for serving (optional)

How to Make It:

- Preheat a grill or grill pan over high heat. Season the steak all over with the cumin, cayenne, and salt and black pepper. Grill the steak, turning, for about 10 minutes, until a nice char has developed on the outside, the flesh feels firm but yielding to the touch, and an instant-read thermometer inserted into the thickest part of the steak registers 135°F. While the steak cooks, grill the onions, turning, for about 10 minutes, until caramelized and soft. Allow the steak to rest for at least 5 minutes, then slice into thin pieces against the natural grain of the meat.

- Spread the roll bottoms with a thin layer of refried beans, then pave each with avocado slices and grilled onions. Top with the steak slices, cheese, and pico de gallo, then the roll tops. Serve with hot sauce if you like.

Makes 4 servings

Mexicans will eat their tortas with whole chipotle peppers on top, but a less-incendiary alternative would be a few pickled jalapeños or a hit of hot sauce.

Per Serving:
$4.74

450 calories
22 g fat (7 g saturated)
570 mg sodium

MEAL MULTIPLIER

Tortas can be made with dozens of different fillings playing the lead role. These are some of our favorites:

- Grilled chicken breast marinated in lime juice, cilantro, and chipotle pepper
- Grilled portabella mushroom caps
- Al pastor–style pork (see Tacos al Pastor, page 190)
- Tequila-Jalapeño Shrimp (page 230)

Shrimp Po' Boys

The po' boy is a New Orleans classic, a hearty grab-and-go lunch for the blue collar and white tablecloth sets alike. The blueprint is simple: A long crusty roll is split, layered with a generous amount of traditional sandwich fixings, then piled high with everything from cold cuts to fried oysters. We ratchet up the classic flavors by pairing Old Bay-spiked grilled shrimp with remoulade, a tartar-like sauce that binds the sandwich together. Nothing po' about that.

You'll Need:

- 2 Tbsp Worcestershire sauce
- 2 Tbsp olive oil mayonnaise
- 1 Tbsp grainy mustard
- 1 Tbsp ketchup
- 2 Tbsp chopped pickles
- 1 lb medium shrimp, peeled and deveined
- 1 tsp Old Bay Seasoning
- ⅛ tsp cayenne pepper
- Salt and black pepper to taste
- Metal skewers, or wooden skewers soaked in water for 30 minutes
- 1 large French loaf or baguette
- 1 large tomato, sliced
- 4 cups shredded iceberg lettuce
- ½ yellow onion, thinly sliced

How to Make It:

- Preheat a grill or grill pan over high heat. For the remoulade, combine the Worcestershire, mayonnaise, mustard, ketchup, and pickles in a mixing bowl and stir together. Set aside.

- Season the shrimp with the Old Bay, cayenne, salt, and black pepper and thread onto the skewers. Grill for 1 to 2 minutes per side, until pink and just firm.

- Cut the bread in half horizontally and scoop out a bit of the bread from the top and bottom halves. Slather the bread with the remoulade, then dress with the tomato slices, lettuce, onion, and shrimp. Cut into 4 sandwiches and serve.

Makes 4 servings

Traditional po' boy bread is actually a hybrid of a French loaf and a baguette: crunchy crust with a pillowy interior. A French loaf is probably the best compromise in most American markets.

Per Serving:

$3.17

370 calories
5 g fat (1 g saturated)
860 mg sodium

Spicy Asian Pork Burgers

For the purists who say that a burger must be made from beef and topped with the same predictable toppings, we say lighten up! The burger is an ingenious delivery system for protein and produce and its general awesomeness should not be limited to ground chuck and American cheese. This pork patty, infused with garlic and ginger and dabbed with chili mayo, is delicious testament to the versatility of the burger.

You'll Need:

½ **English cucumber,** thinly sliced

½ **cup rice wine vinegar**

Salt to taste

1 **lb ground pork**

2 **cloves garlic, minced**

1 **Tbsp minced fresh ginger**

2 **scallions, thinly sliced**

2 **Tbsp mayonnaise**

1 **Tbsp Asian-style chili sauce like sriracha**

4 **sesame seed hamburger buns,** lightly toasted

¼ **cup hoisin sauce**

How to Make It:

● Preheat a grill or grill pan over medium heat. Combine the cucumber, vinegar, and a few pinches of salt in a bowl and set aside.

● In a large mixing bowl, combine the pork, garlic, ginger, and scallions. Gently shape the meat into 4 equal patties. Season the burgers on both sides with salt and grill the burgers for about 5 minutes per side, until nicely browned on the outside and firm to the touch.

● Combine the mayonnaise and sriracha and spread on the bottom buns. Top with the burgers and then a small pile of cucumbers. Spread the bun tops with the hoisin and place on top of the burgers.

Makes 4 servings

Per Serving:
$2.39

490 calories
28 g fat (10 g saturated)
770 mg sodium

SECRET WEAPON

Sriracha

If you've read any of our cookbooks before, you'll know that we're addicted to this stuff, but so is anyone who's ever squirted it onto a hot dog or stirred it into a barbecue sauce. It's made primarily from pureed red chilies, but sriracha is more than just firepower: It adds a touch of sweetness, acidity, and garlic bite to raw and cooked dishes alike. Many of the recipes in this book call for sriracha or some form of Asian chili sauce. Our favorite brand has a red rooster on the label; these days, you can find it in nearly every supermarket in America.

Grilled Pork Sandwiches
with Broccoli Rabe

This sandwich is inspired by the roast pork sandwiches of Philadelphia, which live in the long, greasy shadow cast by the city's handheld titan, the cheesesteak—despite being vastly superior (and considerably healthier).

You'll Need:

- 4 cloves garlic, minced
- 1 tsp chopped fresh rosemary
- 1 tsp fennel seeds, roughly chopped
- 3 Tbsp olive oil
- 1 lb pork tenderloin
- Salt and black pepper to taste
- 1 bunch broccoli rabe, bottom half of stems removed
- ½ tsp red pepper flakes
- ½ cup jarred roasted red peppers
- 4 slices sharp provolone
- 4 seeded hoagie rolls

How to Make It:

- Combine half of the garlic, the rosemary, and fennel seeds in a mixing bowl with 2 tablespoons of the olive oil. Season the pork all over with salt and pepper and combine in a sealable plastic bag with the rosemary mixture. Seal and refrigerate for at least 1 hour (or up to 6 hours).

- Bring a pot of salted water to a boil. Add the broccoli rabe and cook for about 7 minutes, until just tender. Drain. Heat the remaining 1 tablespoon olive oil in a large sauté pan. Add the remaining garlic and the red pepper flakes and sauté for 2 minutes. Add the broccoli rabe and cook for 3 minutes, until very tender. Season with salt and pepper.

- Preheat a grill over medium-high heat. Remove the pork from the bag and grill, turning occasionally, for about 12 minutes, until the surface is lightly charred and firm but gently yielding to the touch, and an instant-read thermometer inserted into the thickest part of the meat registers 150°F. Rest the pork for 5 minutes before slicing into thin rounds.

- Divide the pork, broccoli rabe, peppers, and provolone among the hoagie rolls. Place the sandwiches on the grill and cook for about 2 minutes per side, until the bread is lightly toasted.

Makes 4 servings

Per Serving:
$2.88

510 calories
23 g fat (8 g saturated)
660 mg sodium

Grilled Chicken & Pineapple Sandwich

Not even the relatively healthy genre of grilled chicken sandwiches is a safe bet when you seek sustenance away from home. That's because restaurants go long on the oil and the dressing, producing high-fat, high-sodium sandwiches. Our version is a spicy-sweet combination of teriyaki-glazed chicken, juicy grilled pineapple, and fiery jalapeños —a chicken sandwich to end all fatty chicken sandwiches.

You'll Need:

- 4 **boneless, skinless chicken breasts** (4–6 oz each)
- ½ cup **teriyaki sauce**
- 4 slices **Swiss cheese**
- 4 **pineapple slices** (½" thick)
- 4 **whole-wheat buns**
- 1 **red onion**, thinly sliced
- **Fresh sliced or pickled jalapeños** to taste

Whole-wheat buns are often made with a small percentage of whole grains and a surplus of sugar. Settle on a brand with 3 grams of fiber and fewer than 130 calories per bun.

How to Make It:

- Combine the chicken and the teriyaki sauce in a resealable plastic bag and marinate in the refrigerator for at least 30 minutes and up to 12 hours.

- Heat a grill or grill pan over high heat. Remove the chicken from the marinade and place on the grill; discard any remaining marinade. Cook for 4 to 5 minutes on the first side; flip and immediately add the cheese to each breast. Continue cooking until the cheese is melted and the chicken is lightly charred and firm to the touch.

- While the chicken rests, add the pineapple and the buns to the grill. Cook the buns until they're lightly toasted and the pineapple until it's soft and caramelized, about 3 minutes per side. Top each bun with chicken, red onion, jalapeño slices, pineapple, and a bit more teriyaki sauce, if you like.

Makes 4 servings

Per Serving: $2.64	400 calories 11 g fat (6 g saturated) 640 mg sodium

Teriyaki Sauce

There are a few decent teriyaki sauces in the supermarket aisles, but making a superior version at home requires just a few basic pantry items and about 10 minutes of your time. In a small pan, combine ½ cup reduced-sodium soy sauce with ¼ cup brown sugar, a clove of minced garlic, a table-spoon of grated ginger, and a tablespoon of cornstarch dissolved in a bit of water. Simmer for 5 minutes until thickened and you've got homemade teriyaki.

Cowboy Burgers

We're not afraid to admit when a fast-food joint has a good idea. The inspiration for this burger comes from a Carl's Jr. classic, the Western Bacon Cheeseburger, a how-can-it-not-be-delicious comingling of beef, barbecue sauce, and fried onions. Problem is, the small version of Carl's burger packs 740 calories and a full day's worth of saturated fat. This version uses naturally lean bison and replaces the breaded onion rings with sweet grilled ones.

You'll Need:

- 1 lb ground bison or beef sirloin
- 1 medium red onion, sliced into ¼"-thick rings and skewered with toothpicks
- ½ Tbsp finely ground coffee
- 1 tsp chipotle or ancho chile powder
- Salt and black pepper to taste
- 4 slices sharp Cheddar
- 4 sesame seed buns, lightly toasted
- 6 strips bacon, cooked until crisp and halved
- 4 Tbsp Classic Barbecue Sauce (page 45 or store-bought)

How to Make It:

- Gently form the beef into 4 patties, being careful not to overwork the meat. Let the patties rest for 15 minutes.

- Preheat the grill or grill pan over medium heat. Grill the onion slices, turning, for about 10 minutes, until soft and lightly charred. Just before cooking the patties, season them on both sides with the coffee, chile powder, and salt and pepper. Grill the patties alongside the onions for about 4 minutes, until nicely browned. Flip, top with the cheese, and continue grilling for 3 to 4 minutes longer, until the centers of the patties are firm but gently yielding to the touch and an instant-read thermometer inserted into the thickest part of a burger registers 135°F.

- Place the burgers on the bun bottoms, top with onions, bacon, and barbecue sauce.

Makes 4 servings

We have no idea if cowboys actually eat burgers, but if they did, they would taste an awful lot like this one.

Normally we're not huge fans of heavily spiced burgers, but the coffee here adds a roasted depth to the burger that pairs beautifully with the barbecue sauce and bacon.

Per Serving:
$2.62

460 calories
22 g fat (11 g saturated)
850 mg sodium

Italian Sausage Sandwiches

Ground chicken and turkey make for heroic sausage, capable of capturing all of the rich flavors of pork sausage for about half the calories. They've become an indispensable part of our grilling pantry. Sausage and peppers is a classic pairing that can never be wrong, whether eaten alone, slathered with spicy mustard, or covered in tomato sauce and a thin layer of bubbling cheese.

You'll Need:

- **4 Italian-style chicken or turkey sausages**
- **1 large green bell pepper, stemmed, seeded, and quartered**
- **1 yellow onion, sliced into ¼"-thick rings and skewered with toothpicks**
- **4 sesame seed hoagie rolls, split**
- **½ cup Tomato Sauce (page 110) or store-bought marinara sauce, heated**
- **¾ cup shredded Provolone or mozzarella cheese**

Pork sausage can be substituted, but add about 120 calories to the nutrition numbers.

How to Make It:

- Preheat a grill or grill pan over medium heat. When hot, place the sausages, peppers, and onions on the grill. Cook the sausages, turning, for about 12 minutes, until lightly charred and crispy on the outside and cooked all the way through. Cook the onions and peppers for about 5 minutes per side, until soft and caramelized.

- Preheat the broiler. Chop the onion rings in half and slice the peppers. Place each sausage inside a hoagie roll and top with onions and peppers. Spoon on enough marinara to cover and top with the cheese. Place the hoagies under the broiler and cook for about 3 minutes, until the cheese is fully melted and the top of the rolls are lightly toasted.

Makes 4 servings

Per Serving:
$1.89

490 calories
16 g fat (5 g saturated)
890 mg sodium

Upgrade

NUTRITIONAL

As much fun as it is to eat this dish with your hands, the roll is by no means necessary. Like nearly every sandwich in this chapter, the flavors and ingredients are strong enough to stand on their own. By serving the sausage straight off the grill, swaddled in peppers, onions, and tomato sauce (and maybe a grating of Parmesan cheese), you'll save 150 calories and still have something hugely satisfying to sit down to. (It will, however, require a knife and fork.)

Stuffed Meat Loaf Burgers

Much like Thanksgiving turkey, the best part about making meat loaf is the sandwiches the next day. But why not skip right to the good stuff? The good stuff here means a turkey patty infused with the classic flavors of meat loaf (ketchup, Worcestershire, caramelized onion), then stuffed with a molten pocket of smoked Gouda cheese. It's not your mama's meat loaf, but that's the whole point.

You'll Need:

- 1 tsp butter
- 1 large yellow onion, diced
- 1 clove garlic, minced
- ½ cup ketchup
- ¼ cup chicken stock
- 1 Tbsp Worcestershire sauce
- 1 tsp dried thyme
- 1 lb ground turkey
- 1 egg
- ½ cup bread crumbs
- ¾ cup shredded smoked Gouda
- 4 potato buns, toasted

How to Make It:

- Melt the butter in a large sauté pan or cast-iron skillet over medium heat. Add the onion and garlic and cook for about 5 minutes, until the onion is soft and translucent. Add the ketchup, stock, Worcestershire, and thyme. Simmer for about 10 minutes, until the liquid has reduced enough to cling to the onions. Allow the mixture to cool for at least 10 minutes.

- Combine the turkey, egg, bread crumbs, and half of the onion mixture in a mixing bowl. Gently mix together. Form four patties, making a very large indentation in the center of each. Fill each indentation with Gouda, then carefully fold the meat over the top of the cheese and reshape the patties.

- Preheat a grill or grill pan over medium heat. Grill the burgers for about 5 minutes per side, until lightly charred on the outside and cooked all the way through. Place on the buns and top with the remaining onion mixture.

Makes 4 servings

Per Serving:
$1.83

460 calories
20 g fat (8 g saturated)
965 mg sodium

Kimchi Dogs

Once upon a time, on the corner of Ludlow and Stanton on New York's Lower East Side, a young cook named Sam would spend every weekend night cooking a full menu of classic street food. Sam's claim to fame? Every item could be topped with kimchi, spicy pickled cabbage that is the cornerstone of Korean cuisine and serves as a perfect foil to burgers and hot dogs (think sauerkraut). A decade later, North American streets are flooded with food trucks and sidewalk vendors doing the same, but we'll always remember Sam as the guy who pioneered this funky combination.

You'll Need:

- 4 cups thinly sliced Napa cabbage
- Juice of 1 lime
- 1 Tbsp olive oil mayonnaise
- 1 Tbsp toasted sesame seeds
- ½ Tbsp sesame oil
- Salt and black pepper to taste
- 4 all-beef hot dogs (we like Applegate Super Natural Uncured Beef Hot Dog)
- 4 potato hot dog buns, lightly toasted
- ½ small onion, minced
- ½ cup kimchi

How to Make It:

- Preheat a grill or grill pan over medium heat. In a large mixing bowl, combine the cabbage, lime juice, mayonnaise, sesame seeds, sesame oil, and salt and pepper. Toss until the cabbage is evenly coated.

- Grill the hot dogs, turning, for about 10 minutes, until the skin is lightly charred. Place in the buns and top each with minced onion, kimchi, and the cabbage mixture.

Makes 4 servings

Find kimchi in the international section of large supermarkets, in Asian grocery stores, or online at AsianFoodGrocer.com.

Per Serving:
$1.79

260 calories
9 g fat (2.5 g saturated)
830 mg sodium

SECRET WEAPON

Kimchi

"Fermented cabbage" doesn't do much as a description to endear kimchi to first-time eaters, but this Korean staple, with its bold balance of chili spice and vinegar tang, has a profound ability to turn skeptics into life-long devotees. It's most often made by pickling Napa cabbage with red chiles, garlic, ginger, and a host of other rotating ingredients. It's an amazing foil to grilled foods, either as a topping for burgers, a stuffing for cheesy quesadillas, or pureed and served alongside a steak or slices of pork tenderloin.

Teriyaki Dogs
with Grilled Pineapple

A bacon-wrapped dog might seem a little extreme, and perhaps it is, but sometimes we all need to cut loose, and 35 calories' worth of smoked pork is a fine way to do so in our book. As the bacon sizzles and the fat melts away, it forms a tight, crispy skin around the dog, which matches up perfectly with the sweetness of the teriyaki glaze and grilled chunks of pineapple. The jalapeños are there to bring some heat to the equation, but a squeeze of chili sauce or a shake of Tabasco would have the same effect.

You'll Need:

- **4 all-beef hot dogs (we like all dogs from Applegate Farms)**
- **4 slices bacon**
- **2 thick slices peeled fresh pineapple**
- **¼ cup teriyaki sauce**
- **4 potato hot dog buns, lightly toasted**
- **Pickled jalapeño peppers, or thinly sliced fresh jalapeños (optional)**

How to Make It:

- Preheat a grill or grill pan over medium heat. Wrap each hot dog with a slice of bacon, stretching the bacon so that it covers the dog as tautly as possible (you may end up using less than a full slice—simply cut off any unused end).

- Place the hot dogs and the pineapple slices on the grill and cook, turning and basting both occasionally with the teriyaki sauce, for 10 to 12 minutes, until the bacon fat has rendered and the meat is browned and crispy and the pineapple flesh is soft and has nice grill marks.

- Chop the pineapple into bite-size pieces, discarding the tough core. Place the dogs in the toasted buns and top with the pineapple, jalapeños (if using), and another swipe of teriyaki sauce.

Makes 4 servings

Per Serving:
$1.65

270 calories
9 g fat (3 g saturated)
880 mg sodium

Teriyaki Salmon Burgers

Burger patties can be made out of anything that can be ground up and bound together, from bison to black beans to ostrich. It's a fine line between gimmicky and gourmet, but a few proteins are particularly well-suited to stand in for beef in the burger-making business: lamb, turkey, tuna, and salmon. The latter takes well to sweet and spice, the better for cutting through the healthy fats that abound in salmon. Be mindful of the cooking time, though, because overcooked salmon is a drag. Think of salmon like ground beef: It's best when cooked to medium, so that the fish emerges juicy and tender rather than dry and chewy.

You'll Need:

- 1 lb salmon, finely chopped
- 1 egg
- ½ cup bread crumbs (preferably panko), plus more if needed
- 4 scallions, thinly sliced
- 1 Tbsp soy sauce
- Asian-style chili sauce like sriracha to taste
- 2 Tbsp teriyaki sauce, plus more for serving
- 4 whole-wheat sesame seed buns, toasted
- 1 cup Asian Slaw (page 340)

How to Make It:

- Preheat a grill or grill pan over medium heat. Combine the salmon, egg, bread crumbs, scallions, soy sauce, and chili sauce in a bowl and mix thoroughly. Use your hands to gently form 4 patties. The patties will be very moist, but if the mixture is too loose to form patties, stir in more bread crumbs until it firms up enough to shape.

- Brush the tops of the burgers with about half the teriyaki sauce and place on the grill, sauce side down. Grill for about 4 minutes, until the meat firms up and easily pulls away from the grill. Brush the tops with the remaining teriyaki sauce and flip. Continue grilling for 4 minutes longer, until the burgers are cooked all the way through.

- Divide the burgers among the buns, brush with a bit of additional teriyaki sauce, and top with generous piles of the slaw.

Make 4 servings

Per Serving:

$3.13

350 calories
11 g fat (2 g saturated)
910 mg sodium

Cubano Sandwiches

People routinely invest hundreds of dollars in a fancy panini press when they have the world's largest crispy-sandwich maker sitting idly by outside. That's right, a hot grate and a little bit of weight is all you need to transform a cold sandwich into a crispy, melty marvel. We put the grill into action here, first using it to cook the pork tenderloin, then using the hot grate and a few foil-wrapped bricks to press the sandwich—the amazing Miami staple known as a Cubano—into cheesy submission.

You'll Need:

- 1 lb pork tenderloin
- ½ Tbsp chili powder
- Salt and black pepper
- ¼ cup deli-style mustard
- 1 baguette, cut in half lengthwise, or 4 soft hoagie rolls
- 12 pickle slices
- 4 slices Swiss cheese
- 4 slices deli ham

How to Make It:

- Preheat a grill or grill pan over medium heat. Rub the pork tenderloin with the chili powder and a few pinches each of salt and pepper. When the grill is hot, cook the tenderloin, turning, for 10 to 12 minutes, until just cooked through. Allow the tenderloin to rest for at least 5 minutes, then slice into ¼"-thick pieces.
- Spread the mustard on the bottom half of the baguette, top with the pickles, tenderloin slices, Swiss, ham, and the other half of the baguette. Cut into four equal sandwiches.
- Place the sandwiches directly on the grill grate and place something heavy over them (a cast-iron skillet or a brick wrapped in a foil both work great); this will help flatten and crisp them up the same way a panini press does. Cook for 2 minutes per side, until the bread is toasted and the cheese is melted.

Makes 4 servings

Per Serving:
$2.97

380 calories
11 g fat (5 g saturated)
680 mg sodium

Cheesesteak Sandwich

The famous sandwich from Philly is a nutritionist's nightmare: mounds of greasy beef and fried onions; a massive, oil-soaked hoagie roll; and to top it all off, a viscous deluge of Cheez Whiz (that's right, traditional cheesesteaks are made with Whiz). But we want you to have your steak and eat it, too, so we came up with this version, which relies on a lean flank steak, a whole-wheat roll, and a yogurt-based blue cheese sauce. It's a bit fancier than the sandwich from the City of Brotherly Love, but to our tastes, it's also better.

You'll Need:

- 2 Tbsp plain Greek-style yogurt (we like Fage 2%)
- 2 Tbsp olive-oil mayonnaise
- ¼ cup crumbled blue cheese
- 16 oz skirt or flank steak
- Salt and black pepper to taste
- 1 yellow onion, sliced and skewered with toothpicks
- 2 cups arugula
- 2 tomatoes, sliced
- 4 whole-wheat or sesame-seed rolls

How to Make It:

- Combine the yogurt, mayonnaise, and blue cheese. Set aside.

- Heat a grill or grill pan over high heat. Season the steak with salt and pepper and cook for 3 to 4 minutes per side, until the steak is firm but still gives with gentle pressure. While the steak cooks, grill the onions, turning, until soft and caramelized, about 10 minutes. Allow the steak to rest for at least 5 minutes before slicing into thin strips.

- Divide the arugula and tomatoes among the rolls. Top with the steak and grilled onions and drizzle each sandwich with the blue cheese mayo.

Makes 4 servings

Diffuse the caloric heft of mayo-based condiments by cutting the goop with 50 percent Greek yogurt.

Per Serving:
$5.00

400 calories
14 g fat (4 g saturated)
730 mg sodium

PIZZA & PASTA

THE PERFECT
Grilled Pizza

After a decade of cooking pizzas in every device possible—from a toaster oven to a 1,000°F, centuries-old oven in Italy—one immutable truth has emerged: Short of owning a $5,000 hand-built oven imported from Naples, nothing captures the magic—the blistered crust, the smoke-perfumed sauce and cheese—of real wood-fired pizza quite like a grill can. Master this technique and you will be putting out pies that will be the envy of even the finest local pizzerias.

Ease up on the toppings.

Pizza is about the union of bread, sauce, and cheese—a harmony totally disturbed by a thick blanket of melted dairy. There's also a structural-integrity element at play here: Because wood-fired pizzas are thinner than classic American chain pizza, they aren't built to support a barrage of toppings. Use just enough sauce to lightly blanket the dough (about three good spoonfuls), and scatter just enough cheese to cover about half the surface area of the pizza—about 3 ounces per pizza. As the cheese melts, it will spread out and cover the perfect amount of pizza real estate.

Use two kinds of heat.

If using charcoal, bank all of the hot coals onto one side of the grill. If using gas, turn the left burners all the way up and the right burners all the way down. Start the pizza over high heat, effectively searing the raw dough to create a charred, puffy crust and suffuse the whole pie with smoke. When you flip it, move it over to the cooler side of the grill. The lower temperature will give you ample time to top the pizza and close the lid. Keep the lid closed as much as possible: A closed grill functions as both a grill and an oven, charring the bottom of the crust while melting the cheese and crisping the toppings.

Have all your ingredients ready.

In Naples, pizzas cook in under 90 seconds. These pies take a few minutes longer, but they grill up very quickly all the same. Because of the unique cooking process, one that requires quick action and careful monitoring, you'll need to have your sauce, cheese, and other toppings fully ready to go when you start grilling. As soon as you flip the pizza, start in with the toppings: cheese first (so it melts easily from the heat of the crust), then sauce, then basil (or anything else you're adding to personalize your pie).

Pizza

You'll Need:

Pizza Dough

Olive oil for brushing and drizzling

1½ cups fresh mozzarella, chopped

Normal packaged mozzarella is a fine substitute, but it's not as delicious.

1 cup Tomato Sauce

About 10 fresh basil leaves

- Preheat a grill using a two-zone fire (see page 40), one zone over high heat and the other over low. Close the lid so that the heat can effectively build up.

- Divide the dough into two equal balls. Working with one ball at a time on a well-floured work-space, use a rolling pin to stretch the dough into 10" circles.

- Have all of your toppings pre-pared and within arm's reach of your grill. Place one of the dough circles on a lightly floured pizza peel. Brush the top with oil and slide the dough directly onto the hot part of the grill. Cook for about 30 seconds, until the dough begins to brown and firm up, then use a pair of tongs to rotate

45 degrees and grill for another 30 seconds, creating diamond-shaped grill marks on the crust. Flip and place the raw side of the dough down on the cooler side of the grill. Working quickly, top with half of the mozzarella first, then half the sauce and basil leaves, and a drizzle of olive oil. Close the top and let the pizza grill for 2 to 3 minutes, until the cheese begins to melt. Use your tongs to carefully rotate the pizza 45 degrees and continue grilling for another minute or two, until the crust is lightly charred and crisp beneath and the cheese is fully melted. Repeat with the other pizza. Cut the pizzas into 6 slices each before serving.

Makes 4 servings

Pizza Dough

You'll Need:

1 cup hot water

1 Tbsp sugar or honey

½ tsp salt

1 envelope instant yeast

2½ cups flour (we like King Arthur), plus more for kneading and rolling

Any of the pizzas in the coming pages can be made healthier by using half whole-wheat and half all-purpose flour. That will boost both protein and fiber counts in all of your creations.

- Combine the water, sugar, and salt in a large bowl and sprinkle with the yeast. Allow to sit for 10 minutes while the water activates the yeast. Stir in the flour, using a wooden spoon to incorporate. When the dough is no longer sticky, place on a cut-ting board, cover with more flour, and knead for 5 minutes, folding the dough over on itself and using the heel of your hand to push it into the cutting board. Return the dough to the bowl, cover with plastic wrap, and let the dough rise at room tempera-ture for at least 90 minutes. Makes enough dough for two 10" pizzas. The dough will keep, cov-ered, in the refrigerator for up to 2 days.

Tomato Sauce

You'll Need:

1 can (28 oz) whole peeled tomatoes

Whole, peeled tomatoes are best because they are minimally processed and allow you to dictate the texture of your sauce.

1 Tbsp olive oil

½ tsp salt

- Discard the excess tomato juice in the can. Use your hands to thoroughly crush the tomatoes (careful, they're loaded with juice!) into a puree. Stir in the olive oil and salt. Makes about 2 cups sauce; keeps in the refrig-erator for up to 1 week.

America's
WORST Pizza

While it's our goal to teach you how to make the perfect pizza at home, remember there are hundreds of seriously imperfect pies lurking behind every delivery dude and deep-dish dispensary. These five offenders represent just a glimpse of what you're up against when you venture out into the pernicious world of mass-produced pizzas.

Uno Chicago Grill Chicago Classic Deep Dish Pizza (Individual)

2,310 calories,
165 g fat (54 g saturated)
4,650 mg sodium

Think of a deep dish pizza as a bread bowl filled with flab-inducing grease. We've chastised Uno for this "individual" pie before, but the chain refuses to lighten it up. Add one of these to your weekly diet and you'll gain nearly 8 pounds in 3 months.

Domino's Deep Dish ExtravaganZZa Feast (2 slices, 14" pie)

840 calories
44 g fat
(16 g saturated)
2,280 mg sodium

Despite the fun name, this pie is a nutritional downer that derives nearly half its calories from fat. Blame the extra cheese and the fact that Domino's crowns it with four different meats. You know what's not fun? Jogging for an hour and a half to burn off your dinner.

Pizza Hut Stuffed Crust Meat Lover's Pizza (2 slices, 14" pie)

960 calories
52 g fat
(22 g saturated)
2,760 mg sodium

If this book proves anything, it's that we have no qualms about meat. But with this pie, Pizza Hut goes too far. They've piled this crust with pepperoni, ham, beef, bacon, and sausage. And they finish the pie—and your diet—by piping gobs of molten cheese into the crust. Urp. Hope you brought your Rolaids.

California Pizza Kitchen Tostada Pizza with Grilled Steak (½ pie)

840 calories
16 g saturated fat
1,649 mg sodium

This is the melting pot of pizza pies, drawing culinary influence from Italy, Mexico, and the dressing aisle of your local Piggly Wiggly. That's right, CPK has topped an Italian dish with Tex-Mex tortilla chips and fat-heavy ranch dressing. The innovation would be more laudable if it didn't come at such a staggering nutritional price.

DiGiorno Traditional Crust Four Cheese (1 pie)

710 calories
30 g fat
(11 g saturated, 3.5 g trans)
1,190 mg sodium

No, it's not delivery, but it's just as bad. Not only is DiGiorno's pie heavy with sodium and calories, but it also delivers nearly twice the maximum amount of trans fats that you should take in over the entire course of your day. Very few of DiGiorno's pizzas are fit for consumption.

Meatball Pizzas
with Olives & Caramelized Onion

Great cooking is all about balance, and that goes especially for pizza. A pepperoni, sausage, and bacon pie, for example, doesn't quite get you there; it's all fat and salt. This pie, our version of a slimmed-down supreme pizza, is sweet, salty, and savory in equal measure—an addictive equilibrium.

You'll Need:

- 1 Tbsp olive oil, plus more for brushing
- 2 medium onions, thinly sliced

Salt

Pizza Dough (page 110)

- 1½ cups chopped fresh mozzarella
- 1 cup Tomato Sauce (page 110), heated
- 8 leftover Grilled Meatballs (from recipe on page 258), or store-bought meatballs, sliced
- ¼ cup Kalamata olives, chopped

Homemade dough is always best, but for this and all the pizza recipes, fresh, store-bought dough will work just fine.

How to Make It:

- Heat the olive oil in a large saucepan over low heat. Add the onions and a pinch of salt and cover. Cook, stirring occasionally so that the onions don't stick, for about 15 minutes, until very soft and lightly browned.

- Preheat a grill using a two-zone fire (see "Go High and Low," page 40), one zone high and the other low. Close the lid so that the heat can effectively build up. While the grill heats, divide the dough into two equal balls. Using a well-floured work surface and a rolling pin, stretch the dough into 12" circles.

- Place one of the dough circles on a lightly floured pizza peel. Brush the top with oil and slide the dough directly onto the hot part of the grill. Cook for about 30 seconds, until the dough begins to brown, then use a pair of tongs to rotate it 45 degrees. Cook for another 30 seconds, creating diamond-shaped grill marks on the crust. Flip the dough and place, raw side down, on the cooler side of the grill. Working quickly, top first with half the mozzarella, then half the sauce, meatballs, olives, and onions. Close the grill top and let the pizza cook for 2 to 3 minutes, until the cheese begins to melt. Use your tongs to carefully rotate the pizza 45 degrees and continue cooking for another minute or two, until the crust is crisp beneath and the cheese is fully melted. Repeat with the other pizza.

Makes 4 servings

Per Serving:

$3.12

540 calories
18 g fat (6 g saturated)
900 mg sodium

Artichoke Pesto Pizzas

Pizza done properly, with a fine balance of cheese, sauce, and toppings, can make for a surprisingly healthy meal. This is our favorite vegetarian pie of all time, equal parts nutritional powerhouse and deeply delicious comfort food.

You'll Need:

- ½ Tbsp olive oil, plus more for brushing
- 4 oz cremini mushrooms, stemmed and sliced
- 1 clove garlic, minced
- Salt and black pepper to taste
- Pizza Dough (page 110)
- ½ cup soft goat cheese
- ½ cup marinated artichoke hearts
- ¼ cup oil-packed sundried tomatoes
- ¼ cup prepared pesto
- 1 cup Tomato Sauce (page 110)

How to Make It:

- Heat the olive oil in a sauté pan over medium-high heat. Add the mushrooms and garlic and sauté for about 5 minutes, until the mushrooms are caramelized and soft. Season with salt and pepper.

- Preheat a grill using a two-zone fire (see "Go High and Low," page 40), one zone high and the other low. Close the lid so that the heat can effectively build up. While the grill heats up, divide the dough into two equal balls. Using a well-floured work surface and a rolling pin, stretch the dough into 12" circles.

- Place one of the dough circles on a lightly floured pizza peel. Brush the top with oil and slide the dough directly onto the hot part of the grill. Cook for about 30 seconds, until the dough begins to brown, then use a pair of tongs to rotate it 45 degrees. Cook for another 30 seconds, creating diamond-shaped grill marks on the crust. Flip the dough and place, raw side down, on the cooler side of the grill. Working quickly, top first with half of the cheese, then half the artichokes, sundried tomatoes, mushrooms, pesto, and pizza sauce. Close the top and cook for 2 to 3 minutes, until the cheese begins to melt. Use your tongs to carefully rotate the pizza 45 degrees and continue cooking for another minute or two, until the crust is crisp and the cheese is fully melted. Repeat with the other pizza.

Makes 4 servings

Per Serving: $1.94	510 calories 16 g fat (6 g saturated) 910 mg sodium

Sausage & Pepper Pizzas

We've spilled quite a bit of ink over the years warning readers about the hazards of sausage pizza at places like Pizza Hut. At home, though, you can have your sausage and eat it too, just as long as it's chicken or turkey sausage.

You'll Need:

- 2 **links uncooked chicken sausage**
- 2 **medium bell peppers (green, red, or yellow), stemmed, cored, and quartered**
- 1 **large red onion, sliced into ¼"-thick rings and skewered with toothpicks**
- 2 **jalapeño peppers (optional)**

Pizza Dough (page 110)

Olive oil for brushing

1½ **cups diced fresh mozzarella**

1 cup **Tomato Sauce (page 110)**

You can also use cooked chicken sausage from companies like Al Fresco. Just slice and lay them on top of the pizza.

How to Make It:

- Preheat a grill using a two-zone fire (see "Go High and Low," page 40), one zone high and the other low. Place the sausages, peppers, onions, and jalapeños (if using) over the hottest section of the fire. Grill, turning, for about 10 minutes, until the sausage is cooked all the way through, the onions are soft and browned, and the skin on the peppers is blistered. Slice both the sausage and the bell peppers into bite-size pieces and thinly slice the jalapeños.

- Divide the dough into two equal balls. Using a well-floured work surface and a rolling pin, stretch the dough into 12" circles.

- Place one of the dough circles on a lightly floured pizza peel. Brush the top with oil and slide the dough directly onto the hot part of the grill. Cook for about 30 seconds, until the dough begins to brown, then use a pair of tongs to rotate it 45 degrees. Cook for another 30 seconds, creating diamond-shaped grill marks on the crust. Flip the dough and place, raw side down, on the cooler side of the grill. Working quickly, top first with half the mozzarella, then half the sauce, sausages, onions, and peppers. Close the grill top and let the pizza cook for 2 to 3 minutes, until the cheese begins to melt. Use your tongs to rotate the pizza 45 degrees and continue cooking until the crust is lightly charred and the cheese is fully melted. Repeat with the other pizza.

Makes 4 servings

Per Serving:	
$2.87	550 calories 15 g fat (8 g saturated) 950 mg sodium

Kale & Bacon Pizzas

We've seen pizza topped with oysters, quail eggs, hot dogs, and dozens of other previously unthinkable pizza components. If there's anything America has taught the world about pizza, it's that anything goes, as long as it tastes good. Crispy kale, smoky bacon, and piquant provolone definitely qualify.

You'll Need:

Pizza Dough (page 110)

Olive oil for brushing

1½ cups shredded provolone, fontina, or smoked mozzarella

1 cup Tomato Sauce (page 110)

4 strips bacon, cooked until lightly crisp and broken into ½" pieces

Crack Kale (page 335), chopped into bite-size pieces

Feel free to replace grilled kale with sautéed spinach or broccoli rabe.

How to Make It:

- Preheat a grill using a two-zone fire, one zone high and the other low. Close the lid so that the heat can effectively build up.

- Divide the dough into two equal balls. Using a well-floured work surface and a rolling pin, stretch the dough into 12" circles.

- Place one of the dough circles on a lightly floured pizza peel. Brush the top with oil and slide the dough directly onto the hot part of the grill. Cook for about 30 seconds, until the dough begins to brown, then use a pair of tongs to rotate it 45 degrees. Cook for another 30 seconds, creating diamond-shaped grill marks on the crust. Flip the dough and place, raw side down, on the cooler side of the grill. Working quickly, top first with half the cheese, then half the sauce, bacon, and kale. Close the grill top and let the pizza cook for 2 to 3 minutes, until the cheese begins to melt. Use your tongs to rotate the pizza 45 degrees and continue cooking until the crust is lightly charred and crisp beneath and the cheese is fully melted. Repeat with the other pizza.

Makes 4 servings

SAVVY SHORTCUT ↑

Homemade dough is an incomparable component of a first-rate pizza. Rather than turning to the store-bought stuff, double or triple the dough recipe (page 110) and freeze the leftovers. It's simple: After the dough comes together, divide it into tennis ball-size portions, drizzle with a bit of olive oil, and wrap tightly in plastic. Place the balls in the refrigerator to defrost the night before.

Per Serving:
$2.17

470 calories
12 g fat (4.5 g saturated)
800 mg sodium

Pasta Primavera

Pasta primavera is one of the most misunderstood dishes in the restaurant universe. It appears on menus, beckoning health-conscious eaters with the promise of a cornucopia of vegetables. What the menu fails to mention is that the average bowl of restaurant pasta primavera contains nearly 1,000 calories, mostly from quick-burning pasta carbs and the oily cream sauce that traditionally dresses the dish. Our version is the real deal, made with more vegetables than pasta and dressed with a drizzle of olive oil and fresh basil.

You'll Need:

- 2 **medium zucchini,** sliced horizontally into ¼"-thick planks
- 2 **medium yellow squash,** sliced horizontally into ¼"-thick planks
- 12 **asparagus spears,** woody ends removed
- 1 **red bell pepper,** seeded, stemmed, and quartered
- 1 **medium red onion,** sliced into ¼" rings and skewered with toothpicks
- 2 **Tbsp olive oil,** plus more for coating the vegetables

Salt and black pepper to taste

12 **oz whole-wheat penne**

20 **cherry tomatoes,** halved

½ **cup grated Parmesan**

1 **cup chopped fresh basil**

How to Make It:

- Preheat a grill over medium heat. Coat the zucchini, squash, asparagus, bell pepper, and onion with olive oil and season with salt and pepper. Grill the vegetables for 8 to 12 minutes (depending on the thickness of the vegetable), until tender and lightly charred on both sides.

- Bring a large pot of water to boil. Season with salt, add the penne, and cook until just al dente. Drain.

- Chop the grilled vegetables into bite-size pieces. In a large bowl, combine the vegetables and pasta with the 2 tablespoons olive oil, tomatoes, Parmesan, and basil.

Makes 4 servings

Any pasta shape will work just fine here, but the key is that the pasta has some fiber. Ronzoni Smart Taste is our favorite of the fiber-packed brands.

Per Serving:
$3.45

510 calories
13 g fat (3 g saturated)
600 mg sodium

Sausage & Peppers
with Orecchiette

This ain't your grandma's bowl of noodles, that's for sure. No, this dish is a break from the standard stovetop creations, one that relies entirely on the power of the flame to create a robust sauce that dresses little ear-shaped shells. It might not be Italian, technically, but like the best Italian food it's based on a few simple ingredients, carefully prepared and thoughtfully combined. The results speak for themselves. (Note to campers, tailgaters, and people with electricity issues: You can even boil the pasta on the grill.)

You'll Need:

- 1 **bunch broccoli rabe,** bottom 2" of stems removed
- 2 **Tbsp olive oil**
- **Salt and black pepper** to taste
- 2 **bell peppers,** stemmed, seeded, and quartered
- 2 **links hot Italian sausage**
- 10 **oz orecchiette pasta**
- **Grated Parmesan** for serving

How to Make It:

- Preheat a grill over medium heat. Toss the broccoli rabe with 1 tablespoon of the olive oil, plus salt and pepper. Place the broccoli rabe, peppers, and sausages on the grill. Cook the peppers, turning, for about 10 minutes, until the flesh softens and the skin picks up a bit of char. Cook the broccoli rabe, turning once, for 12 to 15 minutes, until the stems are soft and tender and the florets begin to crisp up. Cook the sausages, turning, for about 15 minutes, until the skin is blistered and the meat is cooked through.

- Cook the pasta according to package instructions. Before draining, dip a coffee mug into the cooking water and reserve a few ounces for tossing with the pasta. While the pasta cooks, chop the peppers and broccoli rabe into bite-size pieces. Slice the sausages into thin rounds.

- Toss the vegetables and sausage with the drained pasta, the remaining 1 tablespoon olive oil, plus a splash of the pasta cooking water so that the pasta is moist. Serve with Parmesan over the top.

Makes 4 servings

Per Serving: $2.23	520 calories 22 g fat (6 g saturated) 670 mg sodium

POULTRY

CHAPTER **5**

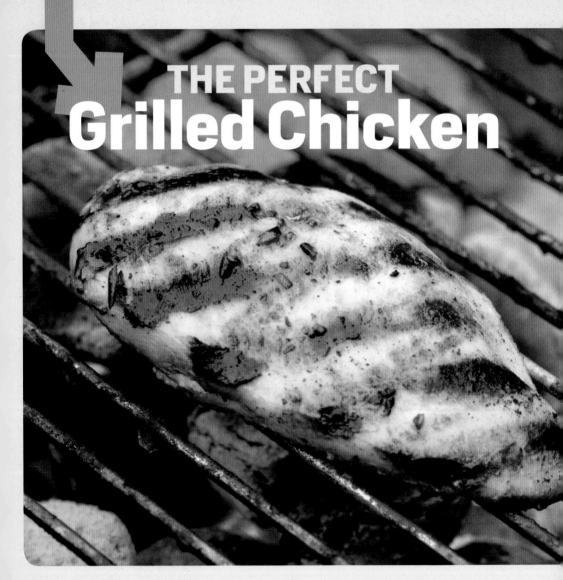

THE PERFECT
Grilled Chicken

The chicken breast is the Mitt Romney of the grill world: It neither excites nor offends anyone with its steady, predictable performance. But with a few minor adjustments, it can become something worthy of loving, even craving. Consider this your master recipe for chicken, whether you're planning to enjoy it in a sandwich, in a salad, or as is, right off the grill.

Buy high-quality chicken.

The reason "it tastes like chicken" became such a popular phrase is because most chicken tastes like nothing at all. Beyond the flavor issue, there's also a health issue at play here (for you and the bird): Most chicken is pumped full of so many drugs it's more science experiment than supermarket staple. Look for antibiotic-free and preferably free-range chickens; you'll pay extra, but you'll taste the difference.

Season in advance.

Every ingredient in the marinade here serves a specific purpose: Garlic, rosemary, and black pepper bring lively, but not over-whelming, flavor. Olive oil and a touch of sugar both help facilitate browning on the surface of the meat— an absolute must for a perfect piece of chicken. The acids in the lemon juice tenderize the meat. But most important, as always, is the salt—salting early will help season the entire chicken, not just the surface.

Cook carefully.

With little to no fat to help insulate it from overcooking, chicken breasts dry out quickly, mercilessly. Cook over a medium-high flame until both sides are nicely charred and the meat feels firm, but still gently yielding, like a tennis ball.

You'll Need:

- 4 boneless, skinless chicken breasts
- ¼ cup olive oil
- Juice of 1 lemon
- 2 cloves garlic, minced
- 1 tsp chopped fresh rosemary, or 1 tsp dried rosemary
- 1 tsp sugar
- 1½ tsp salt
- ½ tsp black pepper

- If the chicken breasts are uneven—thick in some parts, thin in others—cover with plastic and gently pound until they're a uniform ½" thick. Combine the olive oil, lemon juice, garlic, rosemary, sugar, salt, and pepper in a shallow bowl. Add the chicken breasts, turn to coat, and cover. Refrigerate and marinate for 30 minutes.

- Preheat a grill or grill pan over medium-high heat. When hot, remove the chicken from the marinade, pat thoroughly dry, and place on the grill. Cook for 2 minutes, then rotate 45 degrees and continue grilling for another 2 minutes, until the breasts have nice diamond-shaped grill marks. Flip and continue grilling for another 3 to 4 minutes, just until the meat is firm but yielding, like a tennis ball, and an instant-read thermometer inserted in the thickest part of the chicken registers 160°F. Makes 4 servings.

Ways to Cook a
CHICKEN BREAST

Chicken breast is the ultimate canvas, a lean, mild cut of meat that takes well to spice rubs and sauces. With a bit of international inspiration, we've created simple combinations that will turn a weekday staple into something spectacular. With this chart, you can take a spin around the globe without ever leaving your backyard.

	Season with	Sauce with	Serve with
Spanish	Smoked paprika	Romesco (page 50)	Grilled potatoes
Italian	Rosemary, garlic, and lemon	Pesto (page 49) or store bought	Grilled tomatoes
Indian	Curry powder	Mango chutney (page 200) or store bought	Sautéed spinach
Mexican	Chili powder	Grilled Corn Guacamole (page 266)	Black beans
Greek	Oregano, garlic, and olive oil	Tzatziki (page 48)	Warm pita
Argentinean	Cumin	Chimichurri (page 47)	Grilled asparagus
Southwestern	Magic Blackening Rub (page 51)	Mango Salsa (page 47)	Grilled zucchini

Meat Cheat Sheet
Chicken

Sometimes it feels as though the meat case—with its dizzying array of cuts and prices—should come with an instruction manual. To help simplify the process in the next two chapters, we've broken down chicken, beef, and pork by cut, providing you with the nutritional and cost information you need to make the best purchases possible.

Bone-in, skin-on wings (4 oz)
252 calories
21 g protein
18 g fat (5 g saturated)
Grill it right: Direct heat, medium
Average cost per lb: $2.22

Bone-in, skin-on breast (4 oz)
195 calories
24 g protein
10.5 g fat (3 g saturated)
Grill it right: Direct heat, medium
Average cost per lb: $2.56

Boneless, skinless thigh (4 oz)
135 calories
22 g protein
5 g fat (1 g saturated)
Grill it right: Indirect heat, medium
Average cost per lb: $2.92

Boneless, skinless breast (4 oz)
129 calories
24 g protein
3 g fat (0.5 g saturated)
Grill it right: Direct heat, medium-high
Average cost per lb: $3.29

Bone-in, skin-on thigh (4 oz)
248 calories
18.5 g protein
19 g fat (5 g saturated)
Grill it right: Indirect heat, medium
Average cost per lb: $1.66

Bone-in, skin-on drumsticks (4 oz)
180 calories
20 g protein
10.5 g fat (3 g saturated)
Grill it right: Indirect heat, medium
Average cost per lb: $2.16

* Prices for this and the other two Meat Cheat Sheets reflect the average cost obtained from a survey of butcher shops around the country. They may be higher or lower in your local market, depending on where you live.

The SPICE Route

These six exotic spice blends do wonders for food served around the world. They can do the same in your backyard.

ZA'ATAR

This all-purpose blend is used throughout the Middle East, usually as a condiment for sprinkling on breads and meats at the table. Sesame seeds add crunch and nuttiness, while sumac, a purple-hued Syrian spice, brings a pleasant acidic tang.

 Grill This! Lamb chops and chicken drumsticks are prime candidates for a pre- or post-grilling sprinkle of za'atar. Or mix a spoonful with olive oil and use as a dip for toasted pita or a dressing for grilled eggplant, tomatoes, or zucchini.

HERBES DE PROVENCE

Long before spice companies started overcharging for their mediocre blends, cooks in southern France were using this floral mix of fennel, thyme, lavender, tarragon, and bay to season everything from a steak to homemade tomato sauce. This will end up being one of the most useful members of your entire spice rack.

Grill This! Rub all over a whole chicken before cooking it beer-can style, or toss with a mix of vegetables like squash, zucchini, and asparagus prior to grilling.

OLD BAY

This classic Chesapeake Bay spice blend was created by a German immigrant in 1939 as a crab companion, but these days its reach extends well beyond crustaceans. It packs a cabinet worth of seasonings, from ground mustard to cinnamon to mace.

Grill This! Toss medium unpeeled shrimp with a generous amount of Old Bay, then grill for an amazing peel-and-eat snack, or use it to convert wedges of grilled potatoes into Old Bay steak fries.

CHINESE FIVE-SPICE POWDER

This Eastern blend is made predominantly from warm cookie spices like cloves and cinnamon, which makes for a perfect yin-yang combination when rubbed on savory grilled meats. Look for a version with lip-tingling Szechuan peppercorns, which gives the blend some extra firepower.

Grill This! Rub it onto a steak, lamb chop, or duck breast, then serve with a dipping sauce of soy sauce, sesame oil, and a squirt of chili sauce.

SHICHIMI TOGARASHI

You don't have to be able to pronounce it to reap the rewards. This potent blend varies from one batch to the next, but expect sesame seeds, orange peel, dried seaweed, and a few different kinds of chiles.

Grill This! Japanese cooks use it to sprinkle on top of grilled chicken skewers, vegetables, and sliced steaks. You'd be wise to do the same.

GARAM MASALA

Nearly every constituent in this Indian spice blend falls well beyond the realm of the average American spice cabinet, but this heady mixture of star anise, cardamom, kalonji, and other exotic ingredients will feel right at home in your kitchen.

Grill This! Marinate chicken breasts or pork chops for an hour before cooking, or season shrimp, scallops, or vegetables just before grilling.

Power up your pantry:
Your local supermarket may not carry most of these spice blends, but online spice merchants Penzeys.com and Kalustyans.com do— along with hundreds of other exotic seasonings.

131

Classic Barbecue Chicken

There are just two factors that separate good barbecue chicken from bad barbecue chicken: technique and sauce. Barbecue chicken needs to be seasoned early (giving the chicken time to absorb the spices) and cooked over a low flame for even browning. As for sauces, we tested dozens of different recipes until finally settling on this homemade version, a perfect balance of sweet, salty, spicy flavors that will make your chicken sing.

You'll Need:

- 4 chicken legs, thighs and drumsticks separated

- 1 tablespoon All-Purpose Barbecue Rub (page 50)

Classic Barbecue Sauce (page 45)

How to Make It:

- Season the chicken all over with the rub. Do this at least 1 hour before cooking or up to 8 hours ahead, keeping the chicken refrigerated the whole time.

- Preheat a grill over medium-low heat. Pour ½ cup of the barbecue sauce into a small bowl for basting the chicken, reserving the rest to serve at the table. Place the chicken on the grill, skin side down. Grill for about 5 minutes, until the skin begins to lightly brown and the fat begins to render (which may create flare-ups on your grill; if need be, move the chicken to the cooler parts on the grill's perimeter).

- Turn the chicken and baste with the sauce, cooking for another 5 minutes. Continue turning and basting for 15 to 20 minutes total, until the chicken skin is deeply browned, the meat is firm to the touch and beginning to pull away from the bone, and an instant-read thermometer inserted into the thickest part of the meat registers 160°F. Pass the reserved sauce at the table.

Makes 4 servings

Per Serving:
$1.12

480 calories
26 g fat (9 g saturated)
580 mg sodium

Chicken Yakitori

It's a sight beautiful enough to make a grown man weep: Long, narrow streets jam-packed with tiny restaurants serving nothing but grilled chicken parts and ice-cold beer. You'll find more than a few yakitori alleys throughout Tokyo, and you'll know them by the thick cloud of charcoal smoke that hangs over the street. This is the closest you'll get to Japan without a plane ticket.

You'll Need:

- ½ cup soy sauce
- ½ cup sake
- ½ cup mirin
- 2 cloves garlic, crushed and peeled
- 1" piece fresh ginger
- 1 bunch scallions
- 1 lb boneless, skinless chicken thighs, cut into ½" pieces
- Metal skewers, or wooden skewers soaked in water for 30 minutes
- Salt and black pepper to taste

How to Make It:

- Combine the soy sauce, sake, mirin, garlic, and ginger in a small saucepan over medium-low heat. Simmer until the sauce is reduced by three-fourths, about 15 minutes. Discard the garlic and ginger. Pour half the sauce into a small bowl and reserve for brushing on the chicken after it's cooked.

- Preheat a grill or grill pan over high heat. Remove the greens from the scallions and save for another use (or for garnish, if you like). Cut off and discard the bottoms, then chop the white parts into ½" pieces. Alternately thread the chicken and scallion pieces onto the skewers. Season with pepper and a light sprinkle of salt (the yakitori sauce packs plenty of sodium).

- Brush the chicken skewers all over with the sauce from the saucepan. Grill for 8 minutes, turning occasionally, until the chicken and scallions are lightly charred and the meat is firm to the touch and cooked through. Brush the skewers with the reserved sauce before serving. Serve with a scoop of steamed rice, if you like.

Makes 4 servings

Mirin is a sweetened rice wine that plays a huge role in Japanese sauces and marinades. You can find it in the Asian section of larger supermarkets, or you can substitute ½ cup sake plus 1 tablespoon honey.

Per Serving:	
$1.45	260 calories 4.5 g fat (1 g saturated) 780 mg sodium

Prosciutto Pesto Chicken

Wrapping meats in other meats may seem like an overly indulgent way of tackling the issue of a weeknight dinner, but consider this: A slice of prosciutto has just 50 calories, many of which melt away under the intensity of an open flame. What you're left with is a crisp, intensely savory sheath that holds in place soft, melting goat cheese laced with the bright herbal notes of pesto. Try these tasty chicken thighs with a side of sautéed spinach and roasted potatoes, or stack them on toasted wheat buns for a heroic handheld meal.

You'll Need:

4 boneless, skinless chicken thighs (4 oz each)

Salt and black pepper to taste

½ cup fresh goat cheese, softened at room temperature for 30 minutes

2 Tbsp pesto (page 49 or store-bought)

4 thin slices prosciutto

How to Make It:

● Preheat a grill or grill pan over medium heat. Season the chicken all over with salt and pepper. Mix together the goat cheese and pesto until thoroughly incorporated. Slather the mixture down the center of each chicken thigh, then wrap with the prosciutto. The prosciutto should fit fairly tightly around the chicken, but as it cooks and the fat renders, it will tighten up even more.

● Grill the thighs for about 4 minutes per side, until the chicken is firm and cooked through and the prosciutto is browned and crisp around the edges.

Makes 4 servings

Master
THE
TECHNIQUE

Prosciutto wrapping

Chicken is just one of many grilled edibles made more delicious by the addition of a thin layer of prosciutto stretched across its surface. Other favorites include fillets of firm white fish like halibut or cod, scallops, shrimp, asparagus spears, and fresh figs. All follow the same technique: Wrap the meat, fish, fruit, or vegetable in just enough prosciutto to form a single secure layer and grill over medium heat until the prosciutto is crisp.

Per Serving:

$1.83

230 calories
14 g fat (6 g saturated)
600 mg sodium

Hoisin-Lime Duck Breasts

For most people, duck is restaurant food, only to be enjoyed at white-linen fine-dining palaces or out-of-the-way Chinese spots. That's unfortunate, since it's not only intensely enjoyable, but also surprisingly lean and prime for the open flame. Its rich flavor is best when tempered with sweetness and acidity, both of which you'll find in our Asian-inspired glaze. Be sure to score the duck, as it will allow the fat underneath the skin to render out, leaving you with a crispy crust and soft, supple meat.

You'll Need:

¼ cup hoisin sauce

Juice of 2 limes

1 Tbsp reduced-sodium soy sauce

1 tsp toasted sesame oil

4 duck breasts (about 5 oz each)

Black pepper to taste

1 tsp Chinese five-spice powder

How to Make It:

● Preheat a grill or grill pan over medium heat. Combine the hoisin, lime juice, soy sauce, and sesame oil in a mixing bowl. Set aside half the sauce for serving.

● Score the duck: Make 3 diagonal cuts through the skin, then rotate 90 degrees and make 3 more cuts, creating diamonds in the skin. Season with pepper.

● Grill the breasts, skin side down, for 5 minutes, until the fat begins to render and a crust forms. Flip and baste with the hoisin mixture. Continue cooking and basting for 3 to 5 minutes, until the duck is firm but gently yielding to the touch and an instant-read thermometer inserted into the thickest part of the duck registers 135°F. Let the duck rest for 5 minutes before slicing. Serve with the reserved sauce.

Makes 4 servings

Per Serving:
$2.65

230 calories
8 g fat (2 g saturated)
470 mg sodium

SECRET WEAPON

Hoisin

Made from sweet potatoes, vinegar, garlic, and red chiles, among other ingredients, hoisin has become an indispensible part of our grill pantry; try it once and it's likely to get as much use in your kitchen as that bottle of Heinz. Brush this sweet-salty condiment on salmon or beef before grilling, combine with soy sauce and sriracha and use as a marinade for chicken drumsticks or wings, or swipe on burgers and chicken sandwiches for a low-calorie mayo replacement.

Beer-Can Chicken
Peruvian Style

El Pollo Rico, an unassuming Peruvian chicken spot on a tiny Arlington, VA, side street, serves America's greatest chicken, hauntingly delicious birds licked by the open flame of the restaurant's massive rotisserie setup. With a can of beer standing in for the spit and a fiery dipping sauce served on the side, we pay tribute to El Pollo Rico and their indecently juicy birds.

You'll Need:

1 **whole chicken (3½–4 pounds)**

½ **Tbsp ground cumin**

1 **tsp chili powder**

Juice of 2 limes

3 **cloves garlic, chopped**

1 **can (12 oz) beer**

Green Sauce (page 48)

Short of a rotisserie spit, there is no better way to grill a chicken than over a half-full can of beer. The steam from the beer produces an incredibly moist, tender bird.

How to Make It:

- Place the chicken in a large, sealable plastic bag. Add the cumin, chili powder, lime juice, and garlic. Seal, shake, and place in the refrigerator to marinate for at least 1 hour (but no more than 4 hours).

- Preheat a grill over medium-low heat. Open the beer and take a few spirited sips (or pour half of it down the drain, but why waste?). With the drumsticks facing down, carefully slide the chicken cavity over the beer can until it fits snugly. The chicken and beer should be able to stand freely on their own.

- Place the chicken on the grill grate and carefully close the lid. Cook for 35 to 45 minutes, depending on the size of the chicken. The chicken is done when the juices from the legs run clear (or until a thermometer inserted into the deepest part of a thigh reads 160°F). Check on the chicken occasionally; if the chicken fat is causing flare-ups, move the chicken to the coolest part of the grill. Allow the chicken to rest for 10 minutes before carving. Serve with the green sauce.

Make 4 servings

Per Serving:	460 calories
$2.68	26 g fat (7 g saturated)
	680 mg sodium

Balsamic Chicken Breasts

The best thing that can be said about a chicken breast—apart from the fact that it's a lean, powerful source of protein—is that it takes well to outside flavors. This balsamic barbecue sauce is pretty amazing stuff: Six ingredients that everyone has in their pantry come together to make a complex, deeply satisfying sauce that elevates the prosaic chicken breast to delicious new heights. It tastes every bit as good when painted onto pork chops, duck breasts, or flank steak.

You'll Need:

- 1 cup ketchup
- 1 cup balsamic vinegar
- 1 Tbsp brown sugar
- 1 Tbsp Dijon mustard
- 1 Tbsp Worcestershire sauce
- 1 clove garlic, minced
- 4 small chicken breasts (about 6 oz each)
- Salt and black pepper to taste

How to Make It:

- Bring the ketchup, balsamic, brown sugar, mustard, Worcestershire, and garlic to a simmer in a saucepan set over medium heat. Simmer for about 5 minutes, until the liquid has reduced by half and the sauce is thick like a bottled barbecue sauce. Allow the sauce to cool, then set aside half of the sauce to serve with the chicken.

- Preheat a grill over medium heat. Season the chicken with salt and pepper. Paint the chicken all over with a thin layer of sauce from the saucepan and place on the grill. Cook for 2 minutes, turn the breasts 45 degrees, and cook for another 2 minutes, until nice diamond-shaped grill marks have developed. Flip, brush one more time with the sauce, and grill for another 3 minutes, until the chicken is firm to the touch and an instant-read thermometer inserted into the thickest part of the chicken registers 160°F. Brush the chicken with the reserved barbecue sauce before serving.

Makes 4 servings

Per Serving:
$1.97

270 calories
4.5 g fat (1 g saturated)
610 mg sodium

Chimi Skewers

Argentina lays claim to one of the world's greatest grill cultures, thanks in large part to the cattle-wrangling gauchos of Patagonia. Massive *asados,* epic feats of grilling often involving whole animals, are a common catalyst for social gatherings in this magical part of the world. While these spreads usually involve a staggering variety of smoked and grilled meats and fish, the one common thread tying them all together is chimichurri, the garlicky herb sauce that is paired with everything from thick-cut steaks to piles of crispy french fries. Here, we use it to top skewers of grilled chorizo and chicken, but it works just as well with fish, pork, and beef.

You'll Need:

- 1 lb boneless, skinless chicken breasts, cut into ¾" chunks
- 2 links chorizo, cut into ¾" chunks
- 1 medium onion, coarsely chopped
- 1 red or green bell pepper, cored and coarsely chopped
- ½ Tbsp olive oil
- Salt and black pepper to taste
- 8 metal skewers, or wooden skewers soaked in water for 30 minutes
- Chimichurri (page 47)

How to Make It:

- Preheat a grill or grill pan over medium heat. Combine the chicken, chorizo, onion, red pepper, and olive oil in a large mixing bowl. Season with salt and black pepper and toss. Alternating among chicken, chorizo, and vegetables, thread the ingredients onto the skewers.

- Grill the skewers, turning occasionally, for 3 to 4 minutes per side, until the meat and vegetables are nicely colored and the chicken and chorizo are firm to the touch and cooked through. Serve with the chimichurri drizzled over the skewers.

Makes 4 servings

Al Fresco makes an excellent lean chicken chorizo that would be perfect for these skewers.

Per Serving:

$2.24

300 calories
15 g fat (5 g saturated)
500 mg sodium

Smoked Turkey Breast

This recipe is a strong argument for eating fresh-cooked turkey more than once a year. Hot off the grill, it's excellent with all the traditional Thanksgiving fixings, but even better as leftovers. Cook this on Sunday and you'll be eating the best turkey sandwiches of your life all week long.

You'll Need:

- ¼ cup salt
- ¼ cup sugar
- 16 cups water
- 1 boneless turkey breast (3–4 lb)

Black pepper to taste

- 2 cups wood chips (mesquite, oak, or apple), soaked in warm water for 30 minutes
- ¼ cup Dijon mustard
- ¼ cup maple syrup
- 2 Tbsp apple cider vinegar
- 2 Tbsp canola oil, plus more for coating the turkey

Turkey breasts are often sold in mesh netting, ready for cooking. If not, roll the breast and secure it with twine on both ends and in the middle.

How to Make It:

- Heat the salt, sugar, and water in a large pot set over medium heat until the sugar and salt dissolve. Allow to fully cool, then place the turkey in the brine. Refrigerate for at least 4 hours (or up to 12 hours). If the pot doesn't fit in the fridge, add a few big scoops of ice to the brine every few hours.

- Preheat a grill over low heat. Remove the turkey from the brine, pat dry, and lightly coat with oil. Season with pepper. Place the chips in a wood-chip box and place the basket directly over the flame. Place the turkey on the grill and close the lid. Grill, turning occasionally, for about 30 minutes, until the turkey is lightly browned on all sides.

- Combine the mustard, maple syrup, vinegar, and the 2 tablespoons canola oil. Grill the turkey for another 15 minutes, using a brush to continuously glaze the turkey with the sauce. The turkey is done when an instant-read thermometer inserted into the thickest part registers 155°F. Wait 15 minutes before slicing.

Makes 8 servings

LEFTOVER LOVE

As great as this turkey is on its own, it's even better dressed up and stacked between two pieces of bread. Here are three different ways to do it well:

- On a toasted English muffin with tomatoes, pepper-Jack cheese, and guacamole
- On sourdough with avocado and cranberry-spiked cream cheese
- On toasted rye with melted Swiss, sauerkraut, and Thousand Island dressing

Per Serving:

$1.63

270 calories
5 g fat (0.5 g saturated)
620 mg sodium

Korean-Style Drumsticks

Koreans are chicken geniuses, able to perform dazzling acts of alchemy with the humble bird. Unfortunately, most of those acts involve the use of a deep fryer, which is both inconvenient and ultimately deleterious for the home cook. Instead, we've taken some of their classic flavors and adapted them for the grill, using drumsticks to ensure the same type of juicy, succulent chicken you'd get from a deep fryer. This sweet, spicy glaze would work just as well on grilled chicken breasts or pork chops.

You'll Need:

- 3 cloves garlic, minced
- 1 Tbsp minced fresh ginger
- ¼ cup honey
- 2 Tbsp sesame oil
- 2 Tbsp chili garlic sauce (sambal oelek is best, but sriracha will do)
- 2 Tbsp rice wine vinegar
- 8 chicken drumsticks
- Salt and black pepper to taste

How to Make It:

- In a mixing bowl, whisk together the garlic, ginger, honey, sesame oil, chili sauce, and vinegar. Season the chicken all over with salt and pepper. Place the chicken in a sealable plastic bag and pour in half of the marinade, reserving the other half. Seal the bag and refrigerate for at least 1 hour (but not more than 8 hours).

- Preheat a grill over medium heat. Remove the chicken from the marinade and grill, turning occasionally, for about 15 minutes, until the skin is nicely caramelized and the meat feels firm to the touch and is cooked through. If the rendered chicken fat causes flare ups, turn down the heat or move the chicken to a cooler side. Toss the cooked chicken with the reserved marinade and serve.

Makes 4 servings

Per Serving: $1.07	300 calories 16 g fat (4 g saturated) 490 mg sodium

Tandoori Chicken

The Indians know better than anyone the potential for yogurt beyond the breakfast table. It acts as a sauce, a binder, and, perhaps most effectively, an excellent marinade base, where its natural acids help break down tough muscle tissue. Yogurt is at the heart of one of India's most famous dishes, tandoori chicken, where it's combined with a host of aromatic spices to transform an otherwise boring cut of meat. These skewers are killer on their own, but perhaps even better with a bit of Mango Chutney (page 200) drizzled over the top.

You'll Need:

- ¾ cup plain Greek yogurt
- 2 cloves garlic, minced
- 1 Tbsp minced fresh ginger
- ½ tsp cumin
- ½ tsp ground coriander
- ¼ tsp turmeric
- ⅛ tsp cayenne pepper
- 1 lb boneless, skinless chicken breasts, cut into ¾" cubes
- 4 metal skewers, or wooden skewers soaked in water for 30 minutes

How to Make It:

- In a large mixing bowl, combine the yogurt, garlic, ginger, cumin, coriander, turmeric, and cayenne and mix thoroughly. Submerge the chicken in the marinade, cover with plastic, and refrigerate for at least 2 hours (but no more than 8 hours).

- Preheat a grill or grill pan over high heat. Thread the chicken onto the skewers. Cook the skewers, rotating 90 degrees every few minutes, for about 8 to 10 minutes, until the chicken is firm to the touch and nicely browned all over.

Makes 4 servings

Per Serving:

$1.45

160 calories
4 g fat (1 g saturated)
370 mg sodium

Fried Chicken
with Honey and Hot Sauce

We're using the term "fried" very liberally here, as this chicken contains not a single drop of oil. But the spirit of the dish is the same: chicken soaked in buttermilk, dredged in bread crumbs, and grilled until crisp and juicy. It might not replace Grandma's fried chicken in your world of comfort foods, but dipped into a mix of honey and hot sauce, it will wiggle its way into your heart nonetheless.

You'll Need:

- 1 **lb boneless, skinless chicken thighs**
- 1 **cup buttermilk**
- 6 **tablespoons hot sauce (we like Frank's RedHot)**
- 2 **cups panko bread crumbs**
- 1 **Tbsp butter, melted**
- **Salt and black pepper to taste**
- 4 **Tbsp honey**

Panko is a light, flat Japanese bread crumb that produces crispier crusts than standard bread crumbs.

Chicken breasts work fine here, too, but they should first be pounded until they're uniformly ½" thick

How to Make It:

- Combine the chicken, buttermilk, and 2 tablespoons of the hot sauce in a sealable plastic bag. Seal and marinate in the refrigerator for up to 4 hours.

- Preheat a grill or grill pan over medium-low heat. Combine the bread crumbs and butter, plus a few pinches of salt and pepper, in a shallow baking dish. Working with a few pieces at a time, remove the chicken from the buttermilk and roll it in the bread crumbs, using your hands to gently press the crumbs into the flesh.

- Grill the chicken (if using a regular grill, keep the lid closed for about 4 minutes, until the bread crumbs begin to color and turn crisp). Flip and continue cooking for another 3 to 4 minutes, until golden and cooked through and an instant-read thermometer inserted into the thickest part of the chicken registers 160°F.

- Place 1 tablespoon of honey in each of four ramekins. Top with 1 tablespoon of hot sauce and serve alongside the chicken thighs.

Makes 4 servings

Per Serving:

$1.73

360 calories
8 g fat (3 g saturated)
630 mg sodium

Asian Chicken Meatballs

Most of the world has its own spin on the meatball, and you'd be wise to embrace a few in your kitchen. These meatballs are inspired by street-corner grills in Vietnam and Thailand, where ginger, garlic, and chiles reign supreme. Wrap them in lettuce leaves for a lean, boldly-flavored Asian-style burrito.

You'll Need:

- 1 lb ground chicken or pork
- 1 small red onion, minced
- 2 cloves garlic, minced
- 1 Tbsp minced fresh ginger
- 1 Tbsp minced lemongrass (optional)
- 1 jalapeño pepper, minced
- 2 tsp sugar
- 1 tsp salt
- 4–8 wooden skewers, soaked in water for 20 minutes

Boston lettuce, steamed rice, pickled cucumbers and onions (see Master the Technique to the right), hoisin, and/or sriracha for serving

How to Make It:

- Preheat a clean, lightly oiled grill or grill pan over medium heat. In a large mixing bowl, combine the ground meat with the onion, garlic, ginger, lemongrass if desired, jalapeño, sugar, and salt, stirring gently to evenly distribute all the ingredients. Roll the mixture into golf ball–size orbs, then carefully thread 3 or 4 onto each skewer.

- When your grill is hot, add the meatball skewers and grill for 4 to 5 minutes per side, until a light char has developed on the outside and the meatballs are cooked through. When done, they should feel firm, but springy to the touch.

- Use the lettuce and rice to make little Asian-style wraps with the meatballs, topping with cucumbers and your choice of sauces.

Makes 4 servings

Master **THE** **TECHNIQUE**

Quick Pickling

A quick soak in seasoned vinegar can turn a raw vegetable into something special, perfect for topping grilled creations or eaten on its own as a snack. Combine ½ cup rice wine vinegar or white vinegar with ½ cup water and ½ tablespoon each salt and sugar. This basic solution can be used for onions, cucumbers, jalapeños, and pretty much any cooked vegetable you can imagine. Let them soak for at least 15 minutes before eating.

Per Serving:
$2.11

230 calories
12 g fat (3.5 g saturated)
670 mg sodium

Moroccan Turkey Legs

These days it's easy to spot turkey legs at state fairs, carnivals, and ballparks across the country: They're those massive hunks of flesh that look more like caveman clubs than a grab-and-go snack. But the carnies and ballpark vendors are definitely on to something: The hearty cut of turkey makes for good eats hot off the grill—a far cry from the dry turkey most people are used to.

You'll Need:

¼ cup salt

¼ cup sugar

16 cups water

4 turkey drumsticks (about 1 lb each)

1 Tbsp Moroccan Spice Rub (page 51)

¼ cup honey

¼ cup red wine vinegar

2 Tbsp olive oil, plus more for coating the turkey legs

2 cloves garlic, minced

Buy the smallest turkey legs you can find. If your market only sells large legs, count on one leg for two people.

How to Make It:

- Heat the salt, sugar, and water in a large pot over medium heat just long enough to dissolve the salt and sugar. Allow to fully cool, then place the turkey legs in the brine. Refrigerate for 4 to 6 hours (or up to 12 hours). (If the pot doesn't fit in the fridge, add a few big scoops of ice to the brine every few hours.)

- Preheat a grill over low heat. Remove the turkey legs from the brine and pat dry with paper towels. Drizzle the legs with enough oil to lightly coat, then season them all over with the Moroccan Spice Rub.

- Grill the legs with the lid closed, turning occasionally, for about 45 minutes, until the skin is lightly browned all over and the meat begins to pull away from the bone. Stir together the honey, vinegar, the 2 tablespoons olive oil, and garlic. Use a brush to glaze the legs with the mixture, and grill for another 15 to 20 minutes, until the turkey has developed a dark crust all over (if using a gas grill, you can turn the fire up a notch to facilitate the browning) and an instant-read thermometer inserted into the thickest part of the turkey registers 155°F.

Makes 4 servings

Per Serving:
$3.39

380 calories
18 g fat (4.5 g saturated)
900 mg sodium

Chicken Under a Brick

Brick chicken, or *pollo al mattone* as the Tuscans call it, has been a favorite in central Italy for many years; taste it once and you'll see why. The concept is simple: By exposing as much of the chicken as possible to the hot grate, and by weighing it down with something heavy like a foil-wrapped brick, you encourage even cooking and deep crisping of the skin.

You'll Need:

- ¼ cup white or red wine vinegar
- ¼ cup olive oil
- 2 Tbsp Dijon mustard
- 1 Tbsp honey
- 1 tsp black pepper
- 1 tsp chili powder
- 1 tsp smoked paprika
- ½ tsp garlic powder
- ½ tsp cumin
- ½ tsp allspice
- 1 tsp red pepper flakes
- ¾ tsp salt
- 1 whole chicken (about 3 lb), backbone removed
- 2 lemons (optional)

How to Make It:

- Whisk together the vinegar, olive oil, mustard, honey, and ¾ tsp of the black pepper in a bowl. Reserve.

- One hour before cooking, combine the chili powder, paprika, garlic powder, cumin, allspice, red pepper flakes, salt, and remaining ¼ teaspoon black pepper in a bowl, and season the chicken all over with the mixture.

- Preheat a grill over medium-low heat. Grill the chicken, back side down, with the lid closed for 15 minutes, until the bones have begun to brown. Flip, top with a heavy object (preferably a brick wrapped in foil) and close the top. Grill for about 20 minutes longer, until the skin is lightly charred and crispy and an instant-read thermometer inserted into the thickest part of the breast registers 160°F. If the fire flares up, move the chicken to a cooler part of the grill and continue cooking. Serve the chicken with the sauce and grilled lemon halves, if you like.

Makes 4 servings

Per Serving: **$2.83**

470 calories
28 g fat (8 g saturated)
780 mg sodium

Master **THE** TECHNIQUE

Breaking down a chicken

Any butcher worth his salt will remove the chicken backbone with a few cleaver whacks, but doing it yourself at home is easy: Take a pair of kitchen scissors (or, failing that, a sharp, heavy knife) and cut your way through the chicken back immediately to the right of the spine. Repeat on the left side until the entire spine can be separated from the back. Toss the spine (or save for chicken stock), open the bird and flatten it out, and proceed with the recipe.

Paella

When it comes to making authentic paella at home, there's no better place to start than with the grill. That's because the traditional paella of central Spain has always been cooked over an open fire, which perfumes the rice with smoke and assures that the large paella pan cooks the dish evenly.

You'll Need:

- 1 Tbsp olive oil
- 1 small yellow onion, minced
- 1 large tomato, diced
- 2 cloves garlic, minced
- 1 link Spanish-style chorizo, diced
- 4 bone-in chicken thighs
- Salt and black pepper to taste
- 1 cup bomba, Arborio, or other short-grain rice
- 3 cups low-sodium chicken broth
- Pinch of saffron
- 8 medium shell-on shrimp
- 8 mussels, scrubbed under water and debearded

How to Make It:

- Preheat a grill over high heat. Place a large stainless steel sauté pan directly on the grate and close the lid to allow the heat to build up. When the pan is hot, add the olive oil, onion, tomato, garlic, and chorizo and sauté for about 10 minutes, until the vegetables are very soft and caramelized and the chorizo is lightly browned. Remove to a plate and reserve.

- Season the chicken thighs with salt and pepper and place in the pan, skin side down. Cook for about 5 minutes, until the skin is deeply browned, then flip. Return the vegetables and chorizo to the pan, along with the rice, chicken broth, and saffron. Simmer the paella, undisturbed, for 15 minutes, until most of the liquid has been absorbed by the rice (if the liquid isn't simmering, close the lid to speed the process). Arrange the shrimp and mussels around the paella, close the lid, and cook for about 5 minutes, until the shrimp are pink and firm, and the mussels have opened. If you like an extra crispy crust on the bottom of the paella (called *socarrat* in Spain, it's the most important part of paella), leave the pan on the hottest part of the grill for an extra minute or two before serving.

Makes 4 servings

Per Serving:
$2.91

510 calories
21 g fat (5 g saturated)
980 mg sodium

SECRET WEAPON

Paellera

To make a great paella, you can't crowd the rice. Doing so will result in a wet, unevenly cooked paella rather than the dry, almost crunchy rice dish that paella is supposed to be. That's why Spaniards have always used paelleras, flat pans with ample surface area, to give the rice a chance to absorb every last drop of flavorful liquid. Pick one up (along with the chorizo and other great Spanish products) at Tienda.com. If you don't feel like investing in a paella pan, use the largest, shallowest oven-safe sauté pan you have.

RED MEAT

CHAPTER **6**

Beef

We've all been there before: You stand at the meat case and a sprawling diversity of cuts spreads out before you. Unless you grew up in a butcher shop, it's tough to know where to start. There's a time and a place for nearly every cut of cow, but when it comes to everyday grilling, look for lean, affordable beef that can be cooked over direct heat. Take a close look at the chart breakdown and a few favorites stand out: flank steak, skirt steak, and oft-overlooked round provide a great balance of price, protein, and calories, while sirloin emerges as the best of the common steak cuts.

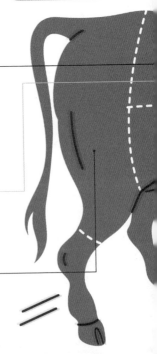

Tenderloin (4 oz)*
280 calories

22 g protein

20.5 g fat
(8 g saturated)

Grill it right: Direct heat, medium

Average cost per lb: $15.16

Sirloin (4 oz)
228 calories

23 g protein

14.5 g fat
(6 g saturated)

Grill it right:
Direct heat, high

Average cost per lb: $7.05

Porterhouse/ T-bone (4 oz)
280 calories

21 g protein

21 g fat (8 g saturated)

Grill it right: Direct heat, medium-high

Average cost per lb: $10.49

Round (4 oz)
188 calories

25 g protein

9 g fat
(3.5 g saturated)

Grill it right: Direct heat, medium-high

Average cost per lb: $5.49

* Fillet (aka filet mignon) comes from the tapered end of the tenderloin. As such, its cost and its nutritional numbers are essentially the same.

Rib-eye/ prime rib (4 oz)
277 calories
21.5 g protein
21 g fat (9 g saturated)
Grill it right: Indirect heat, medium
Average cost per lb: $10.66

Short ribs (4 oz)
266.5 calories
20 g protein
21 g fat (9 g saturated)
Grill it right: Marinate first; indirect heat, low
Average cost per lb: $3.92

Shoulder roast (4 oz)
140 calories
24 g protein
5 g fat (2 g saturated)
Grill it right: Direct heat, medium-high
Average cost per lb: $5.06

Hanger steak (4 oz)
174 calories
24 g protein
8 g fat (3 g saturated)
Grill it right: Direct heat, medium-high
Average cost per lb: $13.32

Brisket (4 oz)
285 calories
21 g protein
22 g fat (8.5 g saturated)
Grill it right: Indirect heat, medium-low
Average cost per lb: $4.66

Flank steak (4 oz)
176 calories
24 g protein
8 g fat (3.5 g saturated)
Grill it right: Direct heat, medium-high
Average cost per lb: $7.66

Skirt steak (4 oz)
212 calories
23 g protein
13 g fat (5 g saturated)
Grill it right: Direct heat, medium-high
Average cost per lb: $6.32

Meat Cheat Sheet
Pork

No animal produces meat with a wider range of nutritional numbers than the humble hog. A serving of pork tenderloin has just 7 more calories than a serving of boneless, skinless chicken breast, while a piece of pork belly the size of a deck of cards packs more than a day's worth of saturated fat. As a general rule, the cuts from the perimeter of the pig are lightest on your wallet, while the center cuts are lightest on your waistline. Your best strategy? Grab any loin cut you can get your hands on.

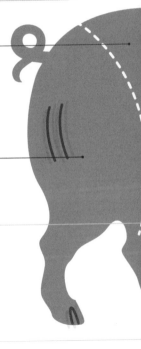

Chops (4 oz)
239 calories
22.5 g protein
16 g fat
(5.5 g saturated)
Grill it right: Direct heat, medium-high
Average cost per lb: $4.83

Tenderloin (4 oz)
136 calories
23.5 g protein
4 g fat
(1 g saturated)
Grill it right: Direct heat, medium-high
Average cost per lb: $3.89

Ham, fresh, uncured (4 oz)
278 calories
20 g protein
21.5 g fat
(7.5 g saturated)
Grill it right: Indirect heat, medium
Average cost per lb: $2.49

Pork belly/fresh bacon (4 oz)
587 calories
10.5 g protein
60 g fat
(22 g saturated)
Grill it right: Indirect heat, medium
Average cost per lb: $3.82

Spareribs/Kansas City ribs (4 oz)
314 calories
17.5 g protein
26.5 g fat
(8.5 g saturated)
Grill it right: Indirect heat, low
Average cost per lb: $2.65

Loin roast (4 oz)
188 calories

24 g protein

9.5 g fat
(2 g saturated)

Grill it right: Direct heat,
medium-high

Average cost per lb: $5.16

Rib roast (4 oz)
211 calories

23 g protein

12.5 g fat
(3 g saturated)

Grill it right: Indirect heat,
medium

Average cost per lb: $5.09

Shoulder roast/
Boston butt (4 oz)
211 calories

20 g protein

14 g fat
(5 g saturated)

Grill it right: Indirect heat, low

Average cost per lb: $2.79

Baby back ribs
(4 oz)
254 calories

22 g protein

18.5 g fat
(6.5 g saturated)

Grill it right:
Indirect heat, low

Average cost per lb: $5.16

Sirloin/roast
(4 oz)
191 calories

23 g protein

10 g fat
(2 g saturated)

Grill it right: Indirect heat,
medium

Average cost per lb: $2.89

THE PERFECT
Grilled Steak

There's a big difference between good steak and great steak. A good steak requires a decent cut of meat and a general idea of what you're doing on the grill; a great steak needs careful provisioning, true finesse, and a bit of patience—but all are within your grasp. Follow these steps to ensure that you never eat a merely good steak again.

Take the chill off the meat.

Allowing the steak to rest at room temperature before grilling helps erase the discrepancy between the warm surface of the meat and the cold center, making for more even cooking. A thick steak needs at least 40 minutes at room temperature; a thinner steak needs about 20 minutes to warm up.

Create a crust.

A steak without a well-developed crust can never be a truly great steak. Meat browns through a process called the Maillard reaction (a process similar to caramelization in vegetables) that is largely responsible for beef tasting, well, beefy. To ensure your steak has a deep, almost-crunchy crust, you need a steak with no excess water on its surface (which will cause it to steam rather than brown) and a very hot grill.

Flip the steak three times.

A hot grill facilitates browning, but you also want even cooking, minimizing that unappetizing gray area between the crust and the pink center of your steak. To do this, ignore the advice of the TV chefs who implore you to flip your meat only once. By flipping your steak more often, the heat of the grill is better distributed throughout the meat, which not only ensures more even cooking, but also encourages faster cooking. Aim for at least three flips in total, one every 2 minutes or so, depending on the thickness of your steak.

Be patient.

We can't say this strongly enough: Cut into your steak hot off the grill and you're compromising your dinner. The juices inside a hot steak are looking for an exit plan and an overeager knife and fork will provide the perfect escape route. By waiting 5 to 10 minutes for the internal temp of the steak to cool, you ensure yourself a juicier steak, from the first bite to the last.

You'll Need:

4 sirloin or strip steaks (about 6 oz each)

Olive oil for coating the steaks

Kosher salt and fresh cracked black pepper

- Preheat a grill or grill pan over high heat. Just before cooking, coat the steaks with a light layer of olive oil and season both sides aggressively with salt and black pepper.

- Place the steaks on the grill and cook for 2 minutes, until light grill marks have developed, then flip. Grill for another 2 minutes and flip again. Flip one more time, grilling for 8 to 10 minutes in total, until the steak is firm but very yielding to the touch. (For medium-rare, an instant-read thermometer inserted into the center of the steak should register between 130 and 135°F). Allow the steak to rest for at least 5 minutes before eating. Makes 4 servings.

These rules apply to any kind of steak you like to cook. Some of our favorites come from Nimanranch. com and Snakeriverfarms.com.

169

THE PERFECT
Grilled Pork Chop

In 1987, the National Pork Board created the slogan "The Other White Meat," meant to tout pork's healthfulness and versatility, but mostly what it achieved was to remind people that pork can be dry and boring. But with our simple steps, you can restore pork to its rightful place as both a lean protein and incredibly delicious hunk of red meat.

Choose wisely.

Major domestic hog producers have steadily bred the flavor out of pork over the years, hence the comparisons to chicken and turkey. Fortunately, excellent small-scale pig farmers are selling high-quality meat that actually tastes like pork at local farmers' markets and grocers like Whole Foods. If you can't find someone locally, order a few chops online from nimanranch.com—they're life changing.

Stick to the bone.

Bones impart both moisture and flavor to meat, which is why buying bone-in chops, steaks, and chicken is always a good idea when looking for full-on meat flavor.

Soak your chops.

Remember osmosis and diffusion from high school science? Well, these are some of the same concepts at work when you brine meat. By submerging a chop in a liquid seasoned with lots of salt and sugar, the end result is a more tender and moist piece of pork. If you don't have time to do a full brine, then salt each chop a few hours before cooking. The meat will absorb the salt, which helps break down tough proteins, leaving you with a more flavorful, tender chop.

Ease off the gas.

It's been beaten into our heads over the years that pork must be incinerated for it to be safe to eat, but according to the Centers for Disease Control and Prevention, trichinosis has been all but eliminated in domestic swine. Just to be safe, harmful bacteria is killed off at 145°F, while the meat begins to dry out around 160°F degrees, so aim for 150°F and you'll be amazed at how juicy a chop can be.

You'll Need:

- ½ **cup salt**
- ½ **cup sugar**
- 8 **cups water**
- 4 **thick bone-in pork chops (about 8 oz each)**

Olive oil for coating the chops

- 1 **tsp fennel seeds, roughly chopped**

Consider the fennel seeds optional, but if Italian sausage has taught us anything, it's that fennel brings out the best in pork.

Black pepper to taste

- Combine the salt, sugar, and water in a large pot and heat just enough for the sugar and salt to dissolve. Cool thoroughly, then place the chops in the brine and refrigerate for at least 2 hours (but no more than 4 hours).

- Preheat a grill or grill pan over medium-high heat. Remove the chops from the brine and pat thoroughly dry. Coat the chops with a thin layer of olive oil, then season on both sides with the fennel and black pepper.

- When the grill is very hot, place the chops on the grate and grill for 2 to 3 minutes, until grill marks have formed. Rotate 45 degrees and continue grilling for another 2 minutes, until you have nice diamond-shaped grill marks. Flip and continue grilling for 4 to 5 minutes, until the chops feel firm but gently yielding to the touch and an instant-read thermometer inserted in the thickest part of a chop registers 150°F. Let the chops rest 5 minutes before serving. Makes 4 servings.

Grill This!
Marinade Matrix

Marinades serve many purposes: First, they infuse cuts of meat and fish with flavor and moisture. The acids in marinades also help break down tough muscle tissue, turning chewy cuts as tender as their more expensive counterparts. But marinades also have a serious health function: Research from the Food Science Institute of Kansas State University found that the polyphenols in marinades cut carcinogen levels in grilled foods by up to 88 percent. Time for a soak!

CHOOSE AN ACID

RED WINE

Balsamic is the sweetest of the vinegars and will cause your food to brown faster. The wine vinegars (red, white, rice) have less sugar and a more intense acidity.

VINEGAR

CHOOSE A LIQUID

SOY SAUCE

WORCESTERSHIRE SAUCE

CHOOSE AROMATICS

GARLIC

FRESH GINGER

Four Quick Recipes

Build the base of your marinade with an acid, fill it out with another source of liquid, then punch up the flavor with aromatics and a secret weapon or two. It's a recipe for grilling greatness every time.

CHOOSE A SECRET WEAPON ▶

Even better than the chipotle peppers themselves is the piquant, smoky sauce they come in. A few spoonfuls add a ton of flavor.

CHIPOTLE PEPPERS

Mirin is a sweet Japanese wine available in the international section of large supermarkets.

MIRIN

RED WINE ROSEMARY
BEST FOR: BEEF, LAMB
Red wine + olive oil + garlic + rosemary

CHIPOTLE ORANGE
BEST FOR: BEEF, PORK
Orange juice + lime juice + cilantro + chipotle

ORANGE JUICE

Plain Greek yogurt is your best bet for marinades

YOGURT

LEMON OR LIME JUICE

Combine with olive oil, lime juice, and honey for a bold beef, pork, and vegetable marinade.

Olive oil is great for Mediterranean-style marinades, sesame oil adds a touch of Asian flavor, and a neutral oil like canola or vegetable helps moisten proteins and keep them from getting dry without altering their inherent flavor.

FISH SAUCE

OIL

SLICED ONIONS

Stronger herbs like rosemary, thyme, oregano, and bay leaf work best.

FRESH HERBS

White miso paste is sweeter and goes best with chicken and seafood, while red miso's intensity pairs nicely with beef and pork.

MISO PASTE

SPICY MUSTARD

SPICY YOGURT
BEST FOR: LAMB, CHICKEN, PORK
Yogurt + lemon juice + garlic + sriracha

SWEET MISO
BEST FOR: FISH, SCALLOPS, CHICKEN
Rice wine vinegar + canola oil + mirin + miso paste

Marinade Basics

Rule 1
As a general rule, the less you spend on a cut of meat, the more likely it is that it will benefit from a marinade. That $20 fillet mignon? Don't bother. The $5 piece of flank steak? Time for a soak.

Rule 2
Marinades by definition contain some type of acid, which is the critical ingredient that helps break down muscle tissue and make proteins more tender. If you're looking for flavor but not tenderness, you can skip the acid, but then it's not really a marinade.

Rule 3
Marinade times should correspond to the size and intensity of the cut. A brisket or a pork shoulder can withstand an overnight marinade, but fish and shrimp should be marinated for no more than 30 minutes, otherwise the acid will begin to "cook" your food, turning your seafood into ceviche. Mid-range cuts like chicken breasts and pork chops are best if marinated between 1 and 4 hours.

173

Porterhouse
with Soy-Dijon Dipping Sauce

There is something magical about meat cooked on the bone, and it's not just the sheer primal joy of having a Flinstonian cut of meat before you. No, bones impart both flavor and moisture to meat, which is why T-bones and porterhouses are the undisputed kings in America's greatest steakhouses. Go for the thickest steak you can get your hands on, even if it means begging the butcher to saw one especially for you. This is caveman eating, with just a hint of sophistication.

You'll Need:

- 1 small shallot, minced
- 2 Tbsp minced fresh ginger
- 2 Tbsp soy sauce
- 2 Tbsp Dijon mustard
- 1 Tbsp honey
- Juice of 1 lime
- ¼ cup canola oil
- 1 very large (18–20 oz) or 2 smaller (10–12 oz) T-bone or porterhouse steaks
- Salt and black pepper to taste

How to Make It:

- Preheat a grill or grill pan over high heat. In a food processor, combine the shallot, ginger, soy sauce, mustard, honey, and lime juice. Pulse, slowly adding the oil to obtain a smooth, nicely emulsified sauce.

- Season the steak(s) all over with salt and pepper. Grill for 3 to 4 minutes, then rotate 45 degrees and continue grilling on the same side for another 2 to 3 minutes. Flip and repeat on the other side. Depending on how thick your steak is, it will take between 12 and 18 minutes total to hit medium-rare, when a thermometer inserted into the center of the steak (close to the bone) reads 135°F. Allow the steak to rest for 10 minutes before slicing into thick pieces. Serve with the soy-Dijon sauce.

Makes 4 servings

Per Serving:
$4.15

460 calories
35 g fat (10 g saturated)
910 mg sodium

Lamb Kofta

Nobody on the planet has been grilling as long and consistently as the rich cultures of the Middle East, so when a popular dish emerges from these parts, savvy cooks should pay attention. Kofta, a mixture of ground meat and spices, is a ubiquitous staple found all across the region, albeit in many different guises. According to a study from 2005, Turkey alone lays claim to 291 different types of kofta. This one here, made from lamb spiced with cayenne pepper and cinnamon, is as good a place to start as any.

You'll Need:

- 1 lb ground lamb
- ¼ cup chopped fresh parsley
- ¼ cup minced onion
- 2 cloves garlic, minced
- ½ tsp cumin
- ⅛ tsp cinnamon
- ⅛ tsp cayenne pepper
- 1 tsp salt
- ½ tsp black pepper
- 4 metal skewers, or wooden skewers soaked in water for 30 minutes

Tzatziki (page 48)

How to Make It:

- Preheat a grill or grill pan over medium-high heat. In a large mixing bowl, combine the lamb, parsley, onion, garlic, cumin, cinnamon, cayenne, salt, and pepper. Gently mix to distribute the spices, then pack around the skewers to form two 3"-long oblong kebabs on each. (The colder the meat is, the more easily it will hold its shape on the skewers. To that end, it may be helpful to refrigerate the formed skewers for 15 or 20 minutes before grilling.)

- Grill the kebabs, turning them so that all sides pick up a nice char from the fire, for about 10 minutes, until the meat is cooked all the way through. Serve each skewer with a generous scoop of tzatziki on the side.

Makes 4 servings

If your market doesn't sell ground lamb, ask the butcher to grind a pound of lamb stew meat, usually cut from the lamb leg or shoulder. Or use ground chuck as a substitute.

Per Serving:

$2.30

290 calories
22 g fat (8 g saturated)
650 mg sodium

Stuffed Pork Chops

A pocket in a pork chop presents the cook with a world of opportunities. Savory, salty, sweet, spicy: All effects can be obtained with just a few carefully considered ingredients stuffed inside the chop. Do it right and there's no sauce or other bells and whistles required. It's restaurant-quality food (and by restaurant, we don't mean Applebee's or Outback, we mean the good ones), achieved for a few bucks a plate in the amount of time it takes you to load up the car and drive to the nearest lackluster chain. Who can argue with that?

You'll Need:

4 **boneless pork chops**
(about 6 oz each)

Salt and black pepper
to taste

½ cup **dried cranberries**

½ cup **fresh goat, feta,**
or blue cheese

¼ cup **walnuts, chopped**

1 tsp **fennel seeds,**
roughly chopped

Look for chops that are at least ¾" thick to make the stuffing easier.

How to Make It:

• Preheat a grill over medium heat. Use a paring knife to cut a pocket in the side of each chop, making it as deep and as long as you can without actually puncturing any other part of the meat. Use your fingers to carefully stretch out the pocket to create a bit of extra space. Season the chops all over with salt and pepper.

• Combine the cranberries, goat cheese, walnuts, and fennel seeds in a mixing bowl. Stuff the chops with the mixture until they're very full and secure with toothpicks. Place the chops on the grill, close the lid, and grill, turning once, for about 15 minutes, until browned and cooked all the way through.

Makes 4 servings

$(\mathbf{Y}+\mathbf{I})^2$

MEAL MULTIPLIER

Three more ways to successfully stuff a chop or a chicken breast:

• Apples, onions, chicken sausage, bread crumbs, fresh sage—all sautéed for 5 minutes in olive oil

• Wild rice, caramelized onions, crumbled bacon

• Sautéed broccoli florets, caramelized onions, and sharp Cheddar cheese

Per Serving:
$2.28

410 calories
19 g fat (8 g saturated)
460 mg sodium

Grilled Steak Fajitas

On paper, fajitas look to be among the healthiest options at any Tex-Mex restaurant. The reality isn't so rosy; excess oil, cheese, and sour cream invariably saddle restaurant fajitas with more than 1,000 calories. Our version, done entirely on the grill, packs half the calories and twice the flavor.

You'll Need:

¼ cup vegetable or canola oil

Juice of 2 limes

1 Tbsp sugar

1 chipotle pepper in adobo

2 cloves garlic, crushed and peeled

1 tsp chili powder

¼ tsp cumin

1 lb skirt or flank steak

Salt and black pepper to taste

1 large sweet onion, sliced into ¼"-thick rings and skewered with toothpicks

2 large bell peppers (a mix of green and red is best), stemmed, seeded, and quartered

FOR SERVING

Guacamole (page 49)

Pico de Gallo (page 46)

Shredded Jack cheese

8 small flour or corn tortillas, warmed on the grill

There are few ingredients we love more than chipotle pepper. Its mixture of spice and smoke is a perfect addition to marinades and sauces.

How to Make It:

● Combine the oil, lime juice, sugar, chipotle, garlic, chili powder, and cumin in a food processor or blender. Puree until you have a smooth, uniform sauce. Combine with the skirt steak in a sealable plastic bag, seal, and marinate in the refrigerator for at least 1 hour (or up to 4 hours).

● Preheat a grill over high heat. Remove the steak from the marinade and pat dry with a paper towel. Season all over with salt and pepper and grill for 4 to 5 minutes per side, until a crust has formed, the meat is firm but yielding to the touch, and an instant-read thermometer inserted into the thickest part of the steak registers 135°F. While the steak cooks, grill the onions and peppers, turning, for 8 to 10 minutes, until soft and caramelized.

● After the steak has rested for at least 5 minutes, slice into thin pieces against the natural grain of the meat. Roughly chop the onions and peppers. Serve the steak and vegetables with the guacamole, pico de gallo, cheese, and warm tortillas.

Makes 4 servings

Per Serving: **$3.86**

430 calories
16 g fat (7 g saturated)
810 mg sodium

Classic Baby Back Ribs

In 2004, *Advertising Age* placed the "Baby Back Ribs" jingle from Chili's restaurant at the top of the list of the "10 songs most likely to get stuck in your head." The rib business exploded, and thousands of American waistlines followed suit, taking in 2,170 calories per rack (not to mention 6,510 milligrams of sodium). Ribs by their very nature are fatty, which is why we crave them, but there are two effective ways to tame the caloric intake: Cut back on the gloppy, candy-sweet sauce and dish out the final product in reasonable portions. We've done both here and still put out ribs with more appeal than those that have been stuck in all of our heads this past decade.

You'll Need:

- 2 small racks baby back ribs
- ¼ cup All-Purpose BBQ Rub (page 50)
- 2 cups mesquite or hickory wood chips, soaked in warm water for 30 minutes

Classic Barbecue Sauce (page 45)

Serve the ribs with a few healthy sides (Barbecued Carrots and Cowboy Beans are perfect), which allow you to dish out smaller serving sizes and save everyone serious calories.

How to Make It:

- Preheat the oven to 250°F. Remove the thin membrane from the back of each rack of ribs (if not already removed by the butcher). Rub the ribs all over with the spice rub. Place in a large baking dish, cover tightly with aluminum foil, and bake for about 90 minutes, until the meat is tender and just beginning to pull away from the bone.

- Preheat a grill over medium heat. Place the mesquite or hickory chips in a wood-chip box and place the box directly over the flame. (If using charcoal, you can add the chips directly to the hot coals.) Brush the ribs with barbecue sauce and place on the grill. Cook, basting continuously with the sauce, for 15 to 20 minutes, until a deep, dark crust forms on the surface of the ribs.

Makes 6 servings

Per Serving:
$2.93

370 calories
15 g fat (4.5 g saturated)
870 mg sodium

Balsamic Lamb Chops

Lamb chops can be pricey, but as a special occasion or an impressive appetizer for a group, they're pretty tough to top. They cook quickly on the grill, emerging juicy even if you go a minute or two too long. And because they're lean and tender, they carry less of the gamy taste many people associate with lamb. Lamb loves rosemary and garlic, which by itself would make this a perfectly good dish, but the sweetness of the balsamic drizzle really takes it over the top.

You'll Need:

- 2 Tbsp olive oil
- 2 cloves garlic, minced
- 1 Tbsp finely chopped fresh rosemary
- 1 lb lamb rib chops
- ½ cup balsamic vinegar
- **Salt and black pepper to taste**

Cut the cost in half by going with shoulder chops. They're not quite as pretty as the petite loin chops, but they're every bit as tasty.

How to Make It:

- Whisk together the olive oil, garlic, and three-fourths of the chopped rosemary. Place the lamb chops in a sealable plastic bag and pour the marinade over them. Seal the bag and refrigerate for up to 4 hours.

- Combine the remaining rosemary and the balsamic vinegar in a small saucepan set over medium heat. Cook until the vinegar reduces by about three-fourths (it should easily coat the back of a spoon), about 10 minutes.

- Preheat a grill over high heat. When very hot, season the lamb chops all over with salt and pepper and cook for 2 to 3 minutes per side, until firm but still yielding. Serve with the balsamic syrup drizzled over the chops.

Makes 4 servings

Per Serving:

$3.66

280 calories
21 g fat (8 g saturated)
435 mg sodium

Carolina Pulled Pork (2 Ways)

The best barbecue in the world comes from the Carolinas, where whole hogs are smoked over hickory until the meat falls off the bone, then dressed in a vinegar-, ketchup-, or mustard-based sauce, depending on where you're eating. Which one is best? We'll let you decide for yourself.

You'll Need:

- 1 8–10-lb piece pork shoulder (preferably one with a generous crown of fat on top)

Salt and black pepper to taste

- 4 cups hickory wood chips, soaked in warm water for 30 minutes

NC Vinegar Sauce (page 46), SC Mustard Sauce (page 46), or Classic Barbecue Sauce (page 45)

Cole Slaw (page 337)

Potato rolls, warmed

How to Make It:

- A few hours before cooking, season the pork shoulder all over with salt and pepper and return to the refrigerator.

- Preheat a grill over low heat. You want to maintain a temperature between 200 and 300°F, which on a large gas grill means lighting just one or two burners on the lowest setting. Place a cup of the hickory chips in a wood-chip box and place the box beneath the grate, over the flame. (If using charcoal, you can add the chips directly to the hot coals.) Place the pork on the grill and close the lid. Grill for 3 to 4 hours, refreshing the wood chips occasionally and basting the meat with half of the NC Vinegar Sauce every 30 minutes or so. The exterior of the pork should be a deep amber color and the meat should pull away easily with a set of tongs.

- Let the pork rest for 15 to 20 minutes, then use tongs or forks to shred it into long strands. Alternatively, you can use two knives to chop it into fine pieces (the traditional way Eastern-style Carolina barbecue is served).

- Serve the barbecue with any or all of the sauces, along with slaw and buns on the side for making sandwiches.

Makes 12 to 16 servings (depending on the size of the shoulder)

The fat cap renders slowly while it cooks, basting your pork naturally without dramatically affecting the calorie count.

Per Serving:
$1.31

350 calories
16 g fat (5 g saturated)
650 mg sodium

Grilled 'Carpaccio' with Arugula

Raw slices of beef have been a staple on fancy restaurant menus for decades now, allowing diners the privilege of paying $15 for what amounts to a couple ounces of meat and some token greenery. We propose you could do a better job at home for a third of the cost, especially with the help of a screaming-hot grill. A quick sear on all sides gives the carpaccio texture and depth of flavor while making it easier to eat for those squeamish about eating rare meat.

You'll Need:

- ¼ cup pine nuts
- 1 lb beef tenderloin (about 2 medium steaks)
- Salt and black pepper to taste
- 4 cups baby arugula
- 2 Tbsp olive oil (the best you have)
- Juice of 1 lemon
- Shaved Parmesan

How to Make It:

- Preheat a grill or grill pan over high heat. While the grill warms up, toast the pine nuts in a lightly oiled sauté pan set over medium heat until lightly browned, about 3 minutes.

- Season the tenderloins all over with salt and pepper and grill on the hottest part of the grill for no more than 2 to 3 minutes per side, until the outside of the meat is nicely browned but the inside is still rare. Rest the meat for 5 minutes before slicing into thin pieces.

- Toss the arugula with the toasted pine nuts, olive oil, and lemon juice and season with salt and pepper. Arrange the slices of beef in a wide circle on each of 4 plates and season with a pinch of salt. Place a pile of the arugula mixture in the center of each circle and garnish with the shaved Parmesan.

Makes 4 servings

Per Serving:	320 calories
$4.96	21 g fat (5 g saturated)
	440 mg sodium

SAVE-MONEY STRATEGY

It's true that tenderloin makes for fine eating, especially in a dish as straightforward as this, but at $15 a pound or more, it's just not in the budget for most people. Truth is, many restaurants make their expensive carpaccio plates with cheaper cuts of beef, so there's no reason you can't do the same. Your best bets are eye of round or sirloin, both of which will cost you less than half of what you pay for tenderloin.

Tacos al Pastor

In Mexico, the *al pastor* taco is king. All throughout Mexico City you'll find late-night *taquerias* outfitted with giant spits of chile-rubbed pork turning over an open flame. Most wear a pineapple crown, the warm juices dripping down to commingle with the rendered pork fat. It's a glorious union of smoke and spice and sweet, one that we've done our best to recreate here.

You'll Need:

- 2 Tbsp white vinegar
- ½ Tbsp orange juice
- 1 onion, chopped
- 2 cloves garlic, chopped
- 2 Tbsp chipotle pepper in abodo
- ½ Tbsp guajillo chile powder
- Pinch cinnamon
- 1 lb pork loin, sliced into ½" rounds
- Salt and black pepper
- 1 avocado, peeled and pitted
- 1 cup Tomatillo Salsa (page 204) or store-bought salsa verde
- 2 thick slices pineapple
- 8 corn tortillas
- 1 handful cilantro, chopped
- Lime wedges

How to Make It:

- In a food processor or blender, combine the vinegar, orange juice, onion, garlic, chipotle pepper, guajillo, and cinnamon and pulse to a uniform puree. Season the slices of pork all over with salt and pepper, then combine with the marinade in a sealable plastic bag. Seal and refrigerate for at least 1 hour (or up to 4 hours).

- In a small mixing bowl, mash the avocado into a smoothish puree, then stir in the salsa to form a thick sauce. Reserve.

- Preheat a grill or grill pan over high heat. Remove the pork pieces from the marinade and grill for 2 to 3 minutes per side, until browned on the outside, firm to the touch, and cooked through. While the pork cooks, grill the slices of pineapple for 2 to 3 minutes per side, until light grill marks develop on the flesh.

- Warm the tortillas (on the grill or in a clean, damp towel in the microwave), then fill each with pork and pineapple and top with the avocado mixture and cilantro. Serve with lime wedges on the side.

Makes 4 servings

If you can't find guajillo chile powder, a standard chili powder can be substituted.

Per Serving:	370 calories
$3.12	11 g fat (2 g saturated)
	380 mg sodium

Santa Maria Tri-Tip
with Pico de Gallo

Tri-tip is a cut of meat taken from the bottom sirloin. It's an inexpensive and intensely beefy cut, and if cooked correctly and sliced across the natural grain of the meat, it can be perfectly tender and juicy too. Originally available primarily on the West Coast, supermarkets and independent butchers around the country are finally recognizing tri-tip's inherent awesomeness. This recipe is based on the specialty of Santa Maria, a farming town in central California with a long history of putting out soulful hunks of garlicky tri-tips.

You'll Need:

- 1 tri-tip steak (about 1½ lb)
- 1 Tbsp garlic powder
- Salt and black pepper to taste
- Mesquite or oak chips soaked in warm water for 30 minutes (optional)
- Pico de Gallo (page 46)
- Cowboy Beans (page 341)

How to Make It:

- Rub the tri-tip with the garlic, plus plenty of salt and pepper, using your fingers to gently press the spices into the meat. Let stand for 30 minutes at room temperature.

- Preheat a grill over medium-low heat. If using the wood chips, place them in a wood-chip box and place the box directly on the fire just before you start grilling. (If using charcoal, you can add the chips directly to the hot coals.) Grill the tri-tip, turning occasionally, for 20 to 25 minutes, until firm but yielding and a thermometer inserted into the thickest part of the meat registers 135°F. Rest for at least 10 minutes before slicing against the natural grain of the meat. Serve with the Pico de Gallo and Cowboy Beans.

Makes 4 servings

Santa Maria tri-tip is traditionally cooked over big hunks of red oak. Even a touch of smoke from a handful of chips will add to its authenticity.

Per Serving:
$2.36

280 calories
15 g fat (6 g saturated)
675 mg sodium

Chinese Spareribs

As much as we love baby back ribs for being obscenely tender, spareribs pack more protein and generally cost about half as much as the more popular baby backs. The trick to making them every bit as rib-stickingly delicious is a low, slow cook in the oven, which helps to break down the tough muscle tissue that holds the ribs together. Then a high-heat blast on the grill imparts that smoky outdoor flavor we crave from ribs and turns the sweet, sticky hoisin glaze into a lovely crust that contrasts nicely with the moist, tender meat inside.

You'll Need:

- 1 rack St. Louis–style spareribs, cut into individual ribs
- 1 Tbsp Chinese five-spice powder
- 1 cup hoisin sauce
- ½ cup soy sauce
- ¼ cup honey
- 2 Tbsp rice wine vinegar
- 2 cloves garlic, minced
- 1 Tbsp minced fresh ginger

Because spareribs are naturally such a fatty cut, this is the most caloric recipe in the book. Our suggestion? Serve just a few ribs per person and round out dinner with plenty of grilled vegetables.

How to Make It:

- Rub the ribs with the five-spice powder and place inside a sealable plastic bag. Combine the hoisin, soy sauce, honey, vinegar, garlic, and ginger in a bowl and whisk thoroughly. Pour half of the sauce over the ribs, seal the bag, and refrigerate the ribs overnight. Reserve the sauce remaining in the bowl.

- Preheat the oven to 300°F. Remove the ribs from the marinade and spread across a wire rack set in a baking dish. (If you don't have a rack, oil the baking dish and place the ribs directly in it.) Cover with aluminum foil. Bake for 1 hour, until the meat begins to pull away from the bone.

- Preheat a grill over high heat. Baste the ribs with some of the reserved marinade and grill for about 15 minutes, until the sauce caramelizes and the ribs pick up a nice char. Serve with the leftover sauce for slathering.

Makes 4 servings

Per Serving:	600 calories
$1.97	35 g fat (11 g saturated)
	1,010 mg sodium

Strip Steaks
with Blue Cheese Butter

Beef and blue cheese are common menu partners for a reason: The subtle funk of blue cheese echoes and elevates the beefiness of a good steak, creating something much more than the sum of the two parts. If you don't have the time to form the butter and refrigerate, simply mix the ingredients in a bowl and serve each plate with a scoop slowly melting on top of the beef.

You'll Need:

- ¼ cup (½ stick) butter, softened at room temperature for 30 minutes
- 2 Tbsp crumbled blue cheese
- 1 Tbsp chopped fresh chives
- 1 shallot, minced
- 1 clove garlic, minced
- Black pepper and salt to taste
- 1 lb New York strip steak (about 2 medium steaks)
- 1 tsp smoked paprika

Normal paprika has almost no flavor at all, but Spanish-style smoked paprika is an explosive spice, perfect for steaks, chops, and chicken breasts.

How to Make It:

- Mix the butter, blue cheese, chives, shallot, garlic, and pepper together in a bowl. Spoon the butter into the center of a long piece of plastic wrap, fold the plastic around the butter, and twist the ends to create a log about an inch in diameter. Place in the refrigerator to firm up. Before cooking, remove the butter and slice into 4 thick coins.

- Preheat a grill or grill pan over high heat. Season the steaks with the paprika, salt, and pepper. Grill the steaks, flipping every two minutes, until nice grill marks have developed, the steaks are firm but still yielding to the touch (like a Nerf football), and an instant-read thermometer inserted into the thickest part of the steaks registers 135°F. Allow the steaks to rest for at least 5 minutes before slicing into thick pieces. Arrange on 4 plates and top with the butter.

Makes 4 servings

Per Serving:

$2.92

300 calories
20 g fat (10 g saturated)
510 mg sodium

Master THE TECHNIQUE

Flavored butters

Spiking softened butter with assertive flavors is a great way to add an instant "sauce" to your dinner. And adding coins of compound butters (which keep for weeks in your fridge) to high-carb foods like baked potatoes actually works to mitigate blood-sugar spikes. Try any of these combinations on meat, fish, or vegetables.

- Reduced red wine, garlic, and rosemary
- Maple syrup and a slug of bourbon
- Minced sundried tomatoes and olives with goat cheese

Steak-and-Potato Skewers
with Horseradish Steak Sauce

The classic steak-and-potato dinner can pack up to 1,200 calories on its own. This interpretation retains all the best parts of the steak dinner but puts it all on one skewer, shedding more than 700 calories in the process.

You'll Need:

16 golf-ball size yellow or red potatoes

Salt

2 Tbsp prepared horseradish

2 Tbsp ketchup

2 Tbsp Dijon mustard

2 Tbsp brown sugar

2 Tbsp Worcestershire sauce

1 Tbsp honey

1 lb sirloin, cut into ¾" cubes

Freshly cracked black pepper to taste

4 metal skewers, or wooden skewers soaked in water for 30 minutes

How to Make It:

- Place the potatoes in a pot, cover with water, season with salt, and set over high heat. Cook for about 15 minutes, until just tender. Drain.

- Preheat a grill over high heat. To make the sauce: Combine the horseradish, ketchup, mustard, brown sugar, Worcestershire, and honey in a mixing bowl. Set aside a few tablespoons of the sauce to serve with the grilled steak and potatoes.

- Season the sirloin with salt and lots of black pepper. Thread the skewers with chunks of sirloin and the potatoes. Grill the skewers, turning once and basting with the sauce, for about 5 minutes per side, until the steak is browned, slightly firm to the touch, and an instant-read thermometer inserted into the thickest part of the steak registers 135°F. Brush the reserved sauce on the steak and potatoes just before serving.

Makes 4 servings

If you can't find small potatoes, buy normal Yukon gold potatoes and cut them into ¾" pieces.

Per Serving:
$2.74

440 calories
15 g fat (6 g saturated)
710 mg sodium

Curried Lamb Chops
with Mango Chutney

The average American consumes more than 60 pounds of beef a year. By comparison, that same average American consumes less than 1 pound of lamb a year. It's an astounding discrepancy, especially when you consider that lamb is widely available, easy to cook, and relatively lean. Here's a recipe we hope takes a bit of the pressure off the cows of this country.

You'll Need:

MANGO CHUTNEY

2 fresh mangos, peeled and diced

1 small red onion, diced

½ Tbsp minced fresh ginger

1 jalapeño pepper, minced

1 cup orange juice

2 Tbsp apple cider vinegar

2 Tbsp brown sugar

½ Tbsp curry powder

Salt and black pepper to taste

LAMB CHOPS

1½ lb lamb shoulder or loin chops

½ Tbsp curry powder

Salt and black pepper to taste

How to Make It:

● To make the mango chutney: Combine the mangos, onion, ginger, jalapeño, orange juice, vinegar, brown sugar, and curry powder in a saucepan set over medium heat. Simmer, stirring occasionally, for about 20 minutes, until the liquid has reduced into a thick syrup and the fruit and vegetables are very soft. Season with salt and pepper.

● To grill the lamb chops: Preheat a grill or grill pan over high heat. Season the lamb chops on both sides with the curry powder and salt and pepper. Grill for about 5 minutes per side, until nicely charred on the outside, firm but yielding to the touch, and an instant-read thermometer inserted into the thickest part of the lamb registers 135°F. Serve with the mango chutney.

Makes 4 servings

Shoulder lamb chops are cheaper, but also contain more fat than loin chops. The choice is yours.

Frozen mango also works great here. Defrost 2 cups, then chop into small pieces before cooking.

Per Serving:

$3.84

380 calories
10 g fat (3.5 g sat)
510 mg sodium

LEFTOVER LOVE

Mango chutney is one of those heroic condiments that seems to make most everything better—duck breast, bone-in pork chops, salmon steaks, even turkey sandwiches. Make up a double batch and keep it on hand for any time you're looking for a quick cure for the common dinner. Here's a favorite: Rub a chicken breast with chili powder and grill until cooked through. Serve over basmati rice with a side of sautéed spinach and a huge scoop of mango chutney.

Stuffed Flank Steak

Stuffing meat is one of those great kitchen tricks that takes very little time or effort, but makes you look like a culinary genius. This is a simple three-step process: Pound the meat until flat, spread with the spinach-raisin mixture, then roll up and tie with a few pieces of butcher twine. To turn this into an Italian-style braciole, all you need is a few ladles of simmered tomato sauce.

You'll Need:

- 1 flank steak (1–1½ lb)
- 1 tsp olive oil
- 2 cloves garlic, thinly sliced
- ¼ cup pine nuts
- 1 bunch spinach, washed, bottom half of the stems removed
- ¼ cup raisins (preferably golden raisins)
- Pinch of nutmeg
- Salt and black pepper to taste
- 1 cup shredded provolone (or 3 thin deli slices)
- Butcher twine

How to Make It:

- Preheat a grill over medium heat. Place the steak on a cutting board, cover with a sheet of plastic wrap, and using a meat mallet or a heavy-bottomed pan, pound the meat until it's uniformly about ¼" thick.

- Heat the oil in a large sauté pan over medium heat. Sauté the garlic and pine nuts for a minute, until the garlic softens, then stir in the spinach and cook until it's fully wilted, about 5 minutes. Pour off any water in the bottom of the pan, then add the raisins, nutmeg, and salt and pepper.

- Season the steak on both sides with salt and pepper. Distribute the spinach mixture and provolone evenly over the meat. Roll the meat up tight, as if making a jelly roll (or rolling a sleeping bag). Use butcher twine to secure the meat on both ends and in the middle.

- Place the flank steak on the grill and close the lid. Grill until the bottom is nicely browned, about 5 minutes, then roll 90 degrees and continue grilling. Repeat the process until the steak is browned on all sides and cooked all the way through (an instant-read thermometer inserted into the thickest part should read 135°F). Wait 10 minutes before slicing.

Makes 4 servings

Per Serving:	430 calories
$3.35	23 g fat (9 g saturated) 610 mg sodium

Pork Tenderloin
with Grilled Tomatillo Salsa

Pork tenderloin offers everything you should be looking for in a cut of meat: It's inexpensive (about $5 a pound), lean (with about the same amount of fat found in a chicken breast), and packs more flavor than any other protein in its calorie range. It also takes well to bold flavors and a huge variety of treatments, from spice rubs to sauces, both of which are in use here.

You'll Need:

- 1 **pork tenderloin (1–1½ lb)**
- 1 **Tbsp Southwestern Rub (page 51)**

Salt to taste

TOMATILLO SALSA

- 1 **lb tomatillos, husks removed**
- 1 **small yellow onion, halved**
- 1 **jalapeño pepper**
- ½ **cup cilantro leaves**

Juice of 1 lime

- 2 **cloves garlic, chopped**
- 8 **corn tortillas, heated on the grill**

How to Make It:

- Season the pork with the spice rub and salt, cover, and refrigerate for at least 1 hour (or up to 8 hours).

- Preheat a grill over medium heat. When hot, grill the pork, turning occasionally, for 12 to 15 minutes, until nicely browned on all sides, firm but gently yielding to the touch, and an instant-read thermometer inserted into the thickest part of the pork registers 150°F. While the pork cooks, grill the tomatillos, onion, and jalapeño, turning, for about 10 minutes, until soft and lightly blistered from the heat.

- While the pork rests, combine the tomatillos, onion, jalapeño, cilantro, lime juice, and garlic in a blender. Pulse until smooth. Season with salt.

- Slice the pork and serve with the tomatillo salsa and tortillas.

Makes 4 servings

MEAL MULTIPLIER

Pork tenderloin is a perfect canvas for a grill master to paint with spices and sauces. Here are a few ideas to get the creative juices flowing:

- Rub with curry powder and serve with Mango Chutney (page 200)
- Brush with a mixture of Dijon, bourbon, and maple syrup during and after grilling and serve with grilled peaches
- Marinate in fish sauce, garlic, and honey and serve with a generous scoop of Peanut Sauce (page 48)

Per Serving: $2.37	320 calories 6 g fat (1.5 g saturated) 550 mg sodium

Smoked Brisket
with Chimichurri

Brisket offers tough love for the home cook, but when it's done right, few things are better. Great brisket demands slow, steady cooking in a moist environment, which is achieved easily enough with a bit of help from Mr. Beer. By placing a pan of beer next to the huge hunk of beef, you create a constant source of moisture that bastes the brisket as it cooks. Save this recipe for a down weekend. Though it cooks for a long time, it requires absolutely nothing from you, so just take it easy and let the grill do the work.

You'll Need:

- 2 **cups wood chips (preferably oak), soaked in warm water for 30 minutes**
- 1 **center-cut beef brisket (3–4 lb)**
- 2 **Tbsp Southwestern Rub (page 51)**
- 1 **can beer**

Chimichurri (page 47)

How to Make It:

- Preheat a grill over low heat. You want to maintain a temperature between 200 and 300°F, which on a large gas grill means lighting just one or two burners on the lowest setting. On a charcoal grill, this means banking all of the charcoal to one side, leaving a generous space for indirect cooking. (For more on two-zone fires, see "Go High and Low," page 40). Place the 2 cups of hickory chips (or as many as will fit) in a wood-chip box and place the box beneath the grate, directly over the flame. (If using charcoal, you can add the chips directly to the hot coals.)

- Season the brisket all over with the rub and place on the coolest part of the grill. Pour the beer into a flame-proof baking dish and place beside the brisket. Close the lid and grill, turning, over low heat for 3 to 4 hours, until the brisket is very tender and an instant-read thermometer inserted into the thickest part of the meat registers 180°F. Let rest for at least 15 minutes before slicing. Serve with the chimichurri.

Makes about 8 servings (depending on the size of the brisket)

Per Serving: **$2.38**

360 calories
20 g fat (6 g saturated)
790 mg sodium

Eat This!

Grilled Pork & Peaches

Restaurant pork chops are usually Flintstonian in size and skirted with enough fat to keep a bear warm in the winter. To wit: Cheesecake Factory's Grilled Pork Chops contain 347 percent of your day's saturated fat, plus more sodium than you'd find in nearly 2 pounds of salted peanuts. Our dish takes its cue from classic pork chops and applesauce, using grilled fruit and blue cheese to boost the flavor without skyrocketing the calorie count.

You'll Need:

4 **thick-cut (1"), bone-in pork chops (8 oz each)**

Olive oil

Salt and black pepper to taste

2 **firm peaches or nectarines, halved and pitted**

2 **Tbsp pine nuts, toasted**

1 **small red onion, thinly sliced**

½ **cup crumbled blue cheese**

1 **Tbsp balsamic vinegar**

How to Make It:

● Heat a grill or grill pan over high heat. Brush the pork with olive oil and season with salt and pepper. Grill for 4 to 5 minutes on each side, until the outside is lightly charred and an instant-read thermometer inserted into the thickest part of the pork registers 150°F.

● While the chops cook, brush the peach halves with oil and add them to the grill, cut side down. Grill for 5 minutes, until soft, then flip and grill for another 2 minutes. Remove, slice, and toss with the pine nuts, onion, blue cheese, and vinegar; season with salt and pepper. Top each chop with a quarter of the peach mixture and serve.

Makes 4 servings

Prepackaged pork chops are cut too thin, so they dry out easily. Have the butcher cut them thick and leave them on the bone.

SAVE-MONEY STRATEGY

Savvy swaps

As much as we love the combination of funky blue cheese and sweet caramelized peaches, the ingredients aren't set in stone. Blue cheese pricey at your market? Try feta or goat cheese. Apricots or nectarines on sale today? Ditch the peaches for either. Price of pine nuts too high for your budget? Almonds, pecans, or walnuts all work beautifully. The point is, there's always room to adapt.

Per Serving:	
$3.86	430 calories 24 g fat (8 g saturated) 530 mg sodium

Leg of Lamb
with Gremolata

Few cuts of meat are better suited for the grill than a leg of lamb. The mix of lean meat studded with small, soft deposits of fat means you get juicy results off the grill without a glut of calories. Gremolata, the classic Mediterranean-style mix of garlic, parsley, and lemon, can be sprinkled on pretty much anything—chicken legs, flank steak, pork tenderloin— to great effect, but it works especially well when bringing lamb to life.

You'll Need:

¼ cup olive oil

4 cloves garlic, peeled

2 Tbsp chopped fresh rosemary

1 boneless leg of lamb (2–3 lb)

Salt and black pepper to taste

Butcher twine

GREMOLATA

Zest of 2 lemons

4 cloves garlic, finely minced

1 cup finely minced parsley

To make the gremolata, simply mix together the three ingredients in a bowl.

How to Make It:

- Combine the olive oil, garlic, and rosemary in a food processor and pulse. Place the lamb in a shallow dish, season with salt and pepper, and spread the garlic mixture all over. Cover and marinate in the refrigerator for at least 1 hour (or up to 4 hours).

- Preheat a grill over medium-low heat. Remove the lamb from the marinade, roll tight like a jelly roll, and tie at both ends and in the middle with the twine.

- Place the lamb on the grill and close the lid. Grill, turning occasionally, for about 25 minutes, until the outside is deeply browned and an instant-read thermometer inserted into the thickest part of the meat registers 130°F.

- Allow the lamb to rest for 10 minutes before slicing. Serve with a bit of gremolata sprinkled on top.

Makes about 6 servings (depending on the size of the lamb)

Per Serving:	340 calories
$3.34	19 g fat (5 g saturated) 660 mg sodium

LEFTOVER LOVE

These are precious leftovers to have on hand. Make the most of them with one of these next-day treatments:

- Stuff into a toasted pita with tomato and onion, then top with Greek yogurt spiked with garlic and lemon

- Cradle in warm tortillas with salsa and guacamole

- Stack on focaccia (or a crusty roll), then top with caramelized onions, olives, roasted red peppers, and a few crumbles of feta

GRILL
THIS
NOT
THAT!

FISH & SEAFOOD

CHAPTER **7**

THE PERFECT
Grilled Fish

Even the most confident spatula-wielders tend to seize up in terror at the prospect of grilling fish. It's too expensive, they say, too delicate, too easy to mess up. Our response? Fish is at its finest hot off the grill, which means it's time to conquer any fears and hesitations and learn how to do it right every time. This is your blueprint.

Shop at a market with a real fish counter.

Too many American supermarkets have traded in a dedicated fishmonger for a section of shrink-wrapped plastic trays of fish. More than any other purchase you make in the market, fish is one that demands some basic inquiries, which requires human contact. You'll find it at places like Whole Foods, though it can be pricey. An even better source? Asian markets, where high turnover, low prices, and expert fishmongers make buying fresh fish simple and inexpensive.

Choose freshness over fish type.

The first question you ask your fish guy should always be: "What's fresh today?" No fish dish can be rescued if it starts with lousy fish, so make sure you source the fillet carefully. More important than getting the exact fish in the recipe is getting a piece of fish that's as fresh as possible, so substitute freely with any of the recipes in this chapter.

Scrape the grate.

You want clean grill grates for everything you cook, but nowhere is it more essential than when you cook fish. Use a grill brush, or failing that, a large piece of crumpled aluminum foil, to scrape away any lingering adherents from the grate, then thoroughly oil the grill (and the fish) before you cook.

Leave it alone.

Fish will stick to the grate every time if you try to flip it too early. Place the more attractive side of the fillet down on the grill (always start with the side you want to see when you sit down to eat) and leave it untouched for 3 to 4 minutes. Once grill marks develop, the flesh will release naturally from the grate. Flip and continue cooking for another minute or two.

- Preheat a grill or grill pan over medium heat. As the grill is warming up, drizzle a bit of oil onto a paper towel and use it to wipe down the grate.

- Coat the fish with a light layer of oil and season on both sides with salt and pepper. When the grill is hot, place the fish on the grate with the pretty side facing down (this is the side you want to see when you serve the fish). Grill without touching for 3 to 4 minutes, until nice grill marks have developed and the flesh releases easily from the grate. Flip and continue grilling for another 2 to 3 minutes, until the thickest part of the fillet flakes with gentle pressure from your finger and an instant-read thermometer inserted in the thicket part of the fish registers 140°F. Makes 4 servings.

Grill This!
The Packet Matrix

The French call it *en papillote;* for the Italians it's en *cartoccio;* but for us, it's simply a meal in a bag. It might not sound as fancy in English, but it makes for an extraordinary way to eat dinner. And regardless of how refined your grill skills are, the method is almost impossible to screw up because the food steams inside the enclosed packet, making for moist, flavorful results. It's the grilling equivalent of the one-pot meal, with even less cleanup.

CHOOSE A PROTEIN

This technique works best with fish and other types of seafood because they're naturally so tender. When it comes to meat, chicken is best.

CHICKEN BREAST

SCALLOPS

CHOOSE A LIQUID

When cooking with wine, no need to break out the big expensive guns, but if you wouldn't drink it, you shouldn't cook with it.

WHITE WINE

REDUCED-FAT COCONUT MILK

CHOOSE VEGETABLES

CHERRY TOMATOES

SLICED POTATOES

Potatoes work best when sliced and parboiled for 10 minutes.

SLICED ONION OR FENNEL

Four Quick Recipes

Place a piece of fish or chicken on a sheet of foil, drizzle with a bit of flavorful liquid, top with a few vegetables, and seal the deal. The ratio of effort to deliciousness is unmatched anywhere in the culinary galaxy.

CHOOSE AROMATICS

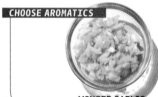

MINCED GARLIC

Parsley, basil, tarragon, thyme, and oregano are all excellent herb choices.

FRESH HERBS

CATFISH CURRY
Catfish + coconut milk + broccoli + red curry paste + ginger

DIJON CHICKEN
Chicken breast + white wine + cherry tomatoes + potatoes + Dijon + garlic

216

Peeled shrimp cook very fast inside the packet. Be ready to pull them off the grill in about 5 minutes.

SALMON

SHRIMP

MUSSELS

To avoid a salt overload, opt for reduced-sodium soy sauce.

BEER

SOY SAUCE

OLIVE OIL

Want a vegetarian meal? Skip the protein entirely and load up on the vegetables. The combo of mushrooms, broccoli, and butternut squash is an excellent way to start.

Sliced white or cremini mushrooms or shiitake caps work best.

BROCCOLI FLORETS OR ASPARAGUS

MUSHROOMS

Squeeze in the juice, grate in the rind, or top the protein with thin slices of the citrus.

MINCED FRESH GINGER

CHILES

LEMON OR LIME

DRUNKEN MUSSELS
Mussels + dark beer + fennel + fresh parsley + Dijon + garlic + butter

SOY-GINGER SALMON
Salmon + soy sauce + asparagus + mushrooms + ginger + garlic

Packet Basics

Rule 1
Everything you place in the packet needs to cook in the same amount of time. A big hunk of carrot or potato will still be raw by the time a catfish fillet is cooked through. When using denser vegetables, slice them thin so they cook fast.

Rule 2
Create a sturdy, fully enclosed packet. Fold a two-foot piece of heavy-duty foil in half. Place all of the ingredients on the bottom third of the foil, then fold the opposite end of the sheet over to completely cover the food. Roll up the edges of the foil tightly.

Rule 3
Cooking time is essential. A medium chicken breast cooked over medium heat takes about 12 minutes; a thin fish like catfish cooks in about half that time. It's better to err on the side of overcooking. Because of the abundance of moisture trapped inside the packet, you can afford to cook the protein an extra minute without losing much in terms of flavor or texture.

Grill This!
The Sauce Matrix

Why work so hard to grill something correctly only to cover it in a tide of sugary, salty goop? That's what you get more often than not when you invite a bottled sauce into your backyard. As long as you have a decently stocked pantry, an incredible homemade sauce is never more than a few minutes away. Balance the flavors by choosing one product from each category and you'll have something that will improve your next meal without tarnishing the health benefits of grilling.

Four Quick Recipes

A properly made sauce is the kind of game-changing flourish that makes culinary geniuses out of every-day cooks. Use these creations before, during, and after cooking for amazing results.

CHOOSE SOMETHING SWEET

KETCHUP

HONEY

BROWN SUGAR

CHOOSE SOMETHING SALTY

SOY SAUCE

Fish sauce is at the heart of Southeast Asian cuisine. It adds an addictive salty-sweet punch to sauces for everything from catfish to steak.

FISH SAUCE

CHOOSE SOMETHING SOUR

BALSAMIC VINEGAR

RED OR WHITE WINE VINEGAR

APPLE CIDER VINEGAR

CHOOSE SOMETHING SPICY

ASIAN CHILI SAUCE

Sriracha is king of the chili sauces, but chili-garlic and sweet chili sauces are also great.

HOT SAUCE

Tabasco and Frank's Red Hot are our favorite sources of heat and vinegar tang.

GRATED HORSERADISH

HOISIN LIME
BEST FOR: SALMON, DUCK, BEEF
Hoisin + soy sauce + lime juice + sriracha

MAPLE DIJON
BEST FOR: PORK CHOPS, CHICKEN
Maple syrup + Worcestershire + white wine vinegar + Dijon

MOLASSES

MAPLE SYRUP

HOISIN

WORCESTERSHIRE

MISO PASTE

PEANUT BUTTER

LEMON OR LIME JUICE

ORANGE JUICE

DIJON MUSTARD

You're not after the peppers themselves, but rather a spoonful or two of the spicy sauce they come packed in.

CHIPOTLE PEPPERS

CAYENNE PEPPER

TANGY HORSERADISH
BEST FOR: STEAK, CHICKEN
Ketchup + Worcestershire + apple cider vinegar + horseradish

SPICY PEANUT
BEST FOR: CHICKEN AND PORK SKEWERS, AS A DIPPING SAUCE FOR GRILLED SHRIMP
Honey + peanut butter + fish sauce + lime juice + sriracha

Sauce Basics

Rule 1
Balance is everything. Make a sauce with ketchup, honey, brown sugar, and maple syrup and you'll bury your taste buds in a tide of sweetness. As a general principle, try to make your sauces with nearly equal amounts (by volume) of sweet, salty, and sour ingredients, then adjust the heat level to your liking.

Rule 2
Thickness counts. Make your sauce too thin and it will slide off the food rather than cling to it; make it too thick and it will dominate whatever dish it touches. The consistency of bottled barbecue sauce is ultimately what you're aiming for.

Rule 3
Know when to sauce. Thinner cuts of meat can be spread with sauce before cooking, but if you sauce items like thick steaks or whole chickens too early, the sugars will burn long before the meat is fully cooked. A good rule of thumb: If it takes more than 10 minutes to cook, don't sauce the food before it goes on the grill.

Grilled Whole Fish

We tend to like our meat and fish to resemble anything but the animals they come from. We're accustomed to packaged chicken breasts, neatly trimmed steaks, and ivory fillets of fish. Fair enough, but when it comes to seafood, that means missing out on one of the best ways to eat fish—and easily the most common form of fish consumption beyond the borders of the United States. Since the bones help impart moisture and the skin protects the flesh from the intensity of direct heat, fish cooked whole emerges effortlessly moist and tender. All it needs is a squeeze of lemon and a drizzle of olive oil.

You'll Need:

4 whole sea bass
(1–1½ lb each)

Olive oil, for coating
and drizzling

Salt and black pepper
to taste

Fresh thyme sprigs
(optional)

2 lemons, halved

Asian markets are the best places to buy whole fish. If you can't find fish this small, buy larger fish, about 2 pounds each, and divide between two people.

How to Make It:

- Preheat a grill over medium heat. Coat the fish with olive oil and season all over with salt and pepper. Place the thyme, if using, inside the fish cavities.

- Place the fish on the grill, close the lid, and grill for 6 to 7 minutes, until the skin is browned and easily pulls away from the grill. Flip and repeat, grilling for 5 to 7 minutes longer, until the flesh at the thickest part flakes with gentle pressure from your finger and an instant-read thermometer inserted into the thickest part of the fish registers 140°F. While the fish cooks, place the lemons on the grill, cut side down, and grill for about 5 minutes, until deeply caramelized and juicy.

- Serve the fish with the grilled lemons and an extra drizzle of olive oil.

Makes 4 servings

Per Serving:
$7.35

210 calories
10 g fat (1.5 g saturated)
295 mg sodium

Master THE TECHNIQUE

Filleting fish

You can serve these lovely whole fish as is, or you can quickly fillet these after cooking. Run a long, thin knife along the spine of the fish, from head to tail, to loosen the meat from the bones. Gently slide a spatula underneath the fillet, starting at the tail and moving it up toward the head. The fillet should slide effortlessly off the spine and onto the spatula. It's so easy that servers at fancy restaurants often do it with a spoon.

Cedar Plank Salmon

The tradition of cooking salmon over cedar comes from the Pacific Northwest, where Native Americans have been using large planks over fire pits for hundreds of years. For the home cook equipped with a few store-bought slats of cedar, it's an easy way to suffuse salmon with toasty, smoky flavor without calories and without the fear of the fish drying out. Whatever you do, don't throw the plank out. You paid serious cash for that little piece of wood and you should be sure to reuse it.

You'll Need:

- 2 Tbsp grainy mustard
- 2 Tbsp light brown sugar
- ½ Tbsp fresh thyme leaves (or 1 tsp dried thyme)
- 1 large salmon fillet (1–1½ lb)
- 1 large cedar plank, soaked in water for 30 minutes

Salt and black pepper to taste

No planks? No problem. This is a simple, satisfying way to prepare salmon directly on the grill or in a 300°F oven.

How to Make It:

- Preheat a grill over medium-low heat. Combine the mustard, brown sugar, and thyme in a bowl. Place the salmon, skin side down, on top of the cedar plank, season with salt and pepper, and spread the mustard mixture on the top.

- Place the plank directly on the grill grate and close the lid. Grill for about 20 minutes, until the center of the fillet flakes with gentle pressure from the finger and an instant-read thermometer inserted into the thickest part of the salmon registers 135°F.

Makes 4 servings

MEAL MULTIPLIER

Salmon is the most famous of the planked proteins, but the plank is no one-trick pony. Save the slats of cedar and use them to add a dimension of smoke to any of the following dishes:

- Burgers topped with sautéed mushrooms, Swiss, and steak sauce
- Chicken breasts brushed with Classic Barbecue Sauce (page 45)
- Pork chops glazed with a mixture of honey, bourbon, and spicy mustard

Per Serving:
$2.91

240 calories
9 g fat (1.5 g saturated)
470 mg sodium

Scallops
with Orange-Soy Glaze

Scallops rarely make an appearance in the average American kitchen. Perhaps that stems from the days when supermarket seafood sections were awash in shrimp, mussels, and lobsters, but finding a scallop required a scuba mask and an oxygen tank. But now that scallops are a steady staple of the American food supply, they should be regular guests in your backyard. They are lean, meaty, take well to big flavors, and, best of all, impossible to screw up.

You'll Need:

- 1 cup orange juice
- 1 Tbsp soy sauce
- 2 Tbsp butter
- 1 lb large sea scallops, tough muscles removed

Salt and black pepper

- 1 Tbsp minced fresh chives or scallions

Make sure there is no milky liquid accumulated beneath the scallops in the fish case, a sign that the scallops have likely been dyed or pumped full of additives.

How to Make It:

- Combine the orange juice and soy sauce in a small saucepan over medium heat. Simmer until the liquid is reduced by three-fourths (it should easily cling to the back of a spoon). Remove from the heat and stir in the butter.

- Preheat a grill or grill pan over high heat. Season the scallops with a bit of salt and pepper. Pour about 1 tablespoon glaze into a small bowl and use to brush both sides of the scallops with a light film. Grill the scallops on one side for 2 to 3 minutes, until a nice char has developed. Flip and grill for 1 more minute, until just firm to the touch. Brush with the glaze in the saucepan and top with the chives.

Makes 4 servings

SAUCE
selector

Scallops' creamy texture and neutral flavor make them a perfect canvas for improvised sauces and toppings. Feel free to swap out the orange-soy glaze for one of these tasty stand-ins:

- Equal parts Dijon mustard, white wine vinegar, honey, and crumbled bacon
- Tomatillo Salsa (page 204)
- Smoky Aioli (page 242)
- Chimichurri (page 47)

Per Serving:
$3.60

180 calories
7 g fat (3.5 g saturated)
550 mg sodium

Snapper à la Veracruz

Veracruz is a coastal city in southern Mexico with a rich culinary history, one largely revolving around heaps of insanely fresh seafood. The most famous dish involves roasting a whole snapper, then topping it with a tomato sauce spiked with salty notes from capers and olives. This streamlined approach puts all the same great flavors inside a single package, quickening the cooking time (and the cleanup), but still giving you a dish elegant enough to serve on a serious occasion.

You'll Need:

1 **pint cherry tomatoes**

1 **handful fresh parsley or cilantro, roughly chopped**

¼ **cup chopped green olives**

2 **Tbsp capers, rinsed**

Juice of 1 lime

¼ **cup olive oil**

Chopped fresh or pickled jalapeño peppers (optional)

4 **snapper (or other firm white fish like cod or halibut) fillets (4–6 oz each)**

Salt to taste

How to Make It:

● Preheat a grill over medium-low heat. Combine the cherry tomatoes, parsley, olives, capers, lime juice, olive oil, and jalapeños (if using) in a mixing bowl.

● Lay out one 2' sheet of aluminum foil on the kitchen counter and fold in half lengthwise. Season one snapper fillet with salt and place toward the right edge of the folded sheet. Top with one-fourth of the olive-tomato mixture. Fold the foil over so that it covers the fish completely, then carefully roll the corners tightly to create a fully sealed package. Repeat to make 4 packets.

● Place the packets directly on the grill grate and close the top (with the top closed, the grill temperature should max out around 450°F). Cook for 8 to 10 minutes, depending on the thickness of the fillets and the heat of the grill. Slash open the packets just before eating. The fish is done when it flakes with gentle pressure from your fingertip.

Makes 4 servings

Per Serving:
$4.28

290 calories
12 g fat (2 g saturated)
370 mg sodium

Grilled Halibut Skewers with Charmoula

Charmoula is one of those magical herb sauces, like pesto and chimichurri, that works wonders on almost any food that touches the grill: chicken legs, pork tenderloin, zucchini, asparagus. More than anything, though, charmoula is fit for fish. The cilantro- and spice-charged sauce is uniquely capable of elevating tender chunks of firm white fish (like halibut, cod, and swordfish) into near-sacred territory.

You'll Need:

- 1 cup fresh parsley leaves
- 1 cup fresh cilantro leaves
- 2 cloves garlic, peeled
- Juice of ½ lemon
- ½ cup olive oil
- 1 tsp paprika (preferably smoked paprika)
- ½ tsp ground cumin
- ½ tsp cayenne pepper
- Salt and black pepper to taste
- 1 lb halibut, cut into 1" pieces
- Metal skewers, or wooden skewers soaked in water for 30 minutes

How to Make It:

- Combine the parsley, cilantro, garlic, lemon juice, olive oil, paprika, cumin, and cayenne, plus a few pinches of salt and pepper, in a food processor or blender. Puree until you have a smooth, uniform sauce.

- Preheat a grill or grill pan over medium heat. Thread the halibut chunks onto the skewers and season with salt and pepper. Spoon enough of the charmoula over the skewers to cover the fish; let sit for 10 minutes.

- Grill the halibut, turning once, for 3 to 4 minutes per side, until the fish is lightly charred and flakes with gentle pressure from your finger. Serve with more charmoula spooned over the top.

Makes 4 servings

Per Serving:
$4.47

280 calories
22 g fat (2 g saturated)
510 mg sodium

Tequila-Jalapeño Shrimp

Shrimp need help. With nary a speck of fat to insulate them from the heat of the flame, they go from perfectly cooked to dry and lifeless in a matter of seconds. That's where our boozy, jalapeño-laced marinade comes into play: Not only does it impart huge amounts of spicy flavor to a normally neutral protein, it also helps keep the shrimp as juicy as possible while they cook. Still, the shrimp require careful monitoring on the grill: When they've turned pink and their tails begin to curl, they're done. These spicy shellfish are best served alongside a scoop of black beans and a few warm tortillas.

You'll Need:

Juice of 1 lime

2 Tbsp tequila

1 Tbsp vegetable oil

½ medium onion, chopped

Handful of cilantro

2 jalapeño peppers, chopped

1 clove garlic

Salt and black pepper

1 lb medium shrimp, peeled and deveined

Metal skewers, or wooden skewers soaked in water for 30 minutes

How to Make It:

- Preheat a grill or grill pan over high heat. Combine the lime juice, tequila, oil, onion, cilantro, jalapeños, garlic, and a few pinches of salt and pepper in a food processor. Pulse until the mix has the consistency of a pesto.

- Thread the shrimp onto the skewers. Slather the shrimp with enough marinade to fully cover; let marinate for 15 minutes.

- Grill the shrimp for 1 to 2 minutes per side, until pink and firm.

Makes 4 servings

Per Serving:
$2.98

170 calories
5 g fat (0.5 g saturated)
410 mg sodium

Grilled Mussels
with Garlic Butter

Compared with other shellfish stars like shrimp, clams, and oysters, mussels get little love from cooks. It's tough to imagine why: Not only are mussels considerably cheaper than their more popular counterparts, they also cook in a matter of minutes and are nearly impossible to mess up. And, surprisingly enough, they're perfect grill food. Contained within a foil packet with white wine, garlic, and butter, they're steamed into a state of sauce-absorbing submission. Use the side of grilled bread to soak up all that luscious liquid.

You'll Need:

- 4 (2'-long) pieces aluminum foil
- 1 lb mussels, scrubbed under water and debearded
- 4 cloves garlic, minced
- 2 Tbsp butter, cut into small pieces
- ½ cup chopped fresh parsley
- ½ cup white wine
- 4 thick slices sourdough or country-style bread, grilled for a few minutes

How to Make It:

- Preheat a grill over medium-low heat. Fold the sheets of foil in half crosswise. Place an equal amount of mussels in the center of each sheet, then divide the garlic, butter, and parsley among the four piles. For each packet, bring the ends of the foil up over the mussels to create a tent, then fold the foil together to create a tightly sealed package. Just before making the final seal, pour a few tablespoons of white wine into each packet.

- Place the packets directly on the grill grate, fold side facing up, and grill for 10 minutes, until the mussels have all opened. Serve with wedges of grilled bread for dipping.

Makes 4 servings

Debearding just means removing any of the long "hairs" that sometimes come attached to mussel shells.

Per Serving:
$2.83

260 calories
10 g fat (4 g saturated)
530 mg sodium

Upgrade

NUTRITIONAL

Mussel power

When it comes to nutrition, mussels are no wimps. Three ounces of cooked mussels packs in more than a day's worth of selenium and three days' worth of manganese, a mineral best known for strengthening bones and stabilizing blood sugar levels. Mussels also really flex in the B12 department, boasting three full days' worth of the vitamin, which is essential in keeping your cells (i.e., your body and everything that it does) functioning properly.

Mahi-Mahi
with Fennel-Orange Salsa

Mahi is perhaps the most grill-friendly fish of all: Not only does its meaty flesh stand up beautifully to the heat, but its skin is perfect for crisping over the open flame. Most people are accustomed to peeling off the skin, either before cooking or after, but with the right fish (sea bass, salmon, snapper), the skin is not only the healthiest part of the fillet, but also the most delicious, contrasting a deep, almost nutty flavor and a satisfying crunch with the flaky meat of the fish. To do it right, you want to grill the fish 75 percent of the way on the skin, then flip and finish it off quickly on the flesh side.

You'll Need:

2 **medium oranges (preferably blood oranges, if available), peeled**

1 **bulb fennel, cored and thinly sliced**

½ **small red onion, very thinly sliced**

½ **Tbsp minced fresh ginger**

2 **Tbsp olive oil, plus more coating the fish**

1 **Tbsp reduced-sodium soy sauce**

Salt and black pepper to taste

4 **mahi-mahi fillets (4–6 oz each)**

How to Make It:

- Preheat a grill over high heat. To make the salsa, use a paring knife to cut out the individual segments of the oranges, leaving the tough membranes behind. Combine the orange segments with the fennel, onion, ginger, olive oil, and soy sauce in a mixing bowl. Stir in a handful of chopped fennel fronds (the leafy tops of the fennel bulb) and season with pepper.

- Coat the fish with olive oil and season on all sides with salt and pepper. Place skin side down on the grill and cook for 5 to 6 minutes, until the skin is crispy and easily pulls away from the grill. Flip and cook for about 2 minutes longer, until the flesh is nicely browned and flakes with gentle pressure from your finger and an instant-read thermometer inserted into the thickest part of the fish registers 140°F. Serve the fish with the crispy skin facing up and the salsa on the side.

Makes 4 servings

Per Serving:
$4.11

230 calories
8 g fat (1 g saturated)
290 mg sodium

Grilled Lobster Tails with Chipotle-Lime Butter

It's not an exaggeration to say that 95 percent of all lobsters consumed are boiled. Both for convenience and for tradition, boiling has always been the preferred cooking method, but that doesn't make it the only way, or even the best way. The clean, sweet flavor of lobster is especially excellent when grilled over a hot flame and braced with a bit of fat (olive oil or butter) and a few drops of acidity (lemon, lime, vinegar). While grilling isn't the most convenient way to cook whole lobsters, it works perfectly for the individual lobster tails that are sold frozen in larger supermarkets everywhere.

You'll Need:

¼ cup (½ stick) butter, softened at room temperature

½ cup chopped cilantro

Zest of 1 lime

1 Tbsp chipotle pepper puree

1 clove garlic, minced

4 lobster tails (about 7 oz each; if frozen, thawed)

Olive oil for drizzling

Salt and black pepper to taste

How to Make It:

● Preheat a grill over medium heat. Combine the butter, cilantro, lime zest, chipotle, and garlic in a small mixing bowl. Squeeze in a few drops of lime juice and stir to combine.

● Drizzle the lobster tails with olive oil and season with salt and pepper. Place flesh side down on the grill and cook for 5 minutes, until the meat is lightly browned. Flip and continue grilling for about 5 minutes, until the meat pulls away from the shell. Immediately serve each tail with a generous scoop of the compound butter over the top.

Makes 4 servings

Per Serving:
$9.23

220 calories
15 g fat (8 g saturated)
420 mg sodium

SAUCE selector

Grilled lobster tails are perfectly delicious with nothing more than a bit of butter, but it never hurts to dress them up a bit. Here are a few suggestions:

● Juice of 1 lemon, ¼ cup olive oil, 2 cloves minced garlic, and 1 cup fresh herbs like parsley and basil

● 1 cup chopped scallions, 2 tablespoons minced ginger, ¼ cup canola oil, and the juice on 1 lime

● Chimichurri (page 47)

Eat This!

Grilled Fish Tacos

The famous fish tacos of Baja California are born of a simple formula: warm tortilla, fried fish fillet, mayonnaise-based sauce. Delicious for a bite or two, but by the time the fried crust is reduced to a mushy paste under the cover of the mayo, you have to wonder what you're wasting all of those calories on. That's why we prefer the fish in our tacos grilled: Smoky, tender, and the perfect vessel for bold condiments, it won't ever cross your mind how healthy this meal really is.

You'll Need:

Juice of 4 limes

¼ cup canola oil

1 tsp chili powder

1 lb fresh white fish (tilapia, catfish, snapper, halibut, etc.)

Salt and black pepper to taste

½ cup reduced-fat sour cream

½ cup chopped cilantro

8 corn tortillas

Pico de Gallo (page 46)

Hot sauce to taste

Any hot sauce will do, but the smokiness of Tabasco Chipotle really ties this dish together beautifully.

How to Make It:

● Preheat a grill or grill pan over medium-high heat. Combine half of the lime juice, the oil, and chili powder in a sealable plastic bag. Season the fish with salt and pepper and place in the marinade for no more than 20 minutes (any longer and the citric acid from the lime juice will begin to "cook" the fish). In a small mixing bowl, combine the remaining lime juice with the sour cream and cilantro.

● Grill the fish for 3 to 4 minutes, until the flesh begins to brown and easily pulls away from the grill. Flip and continue grilling for 3 to 4 minutes longer, until the fish flakes with gentle pressure from your finger and an instant-read thermometer inserted into the thickest part of the fish registers 140°F. Grill the tortillas until lightly toasted.

● Divide the fish among the tortillas and top with the lime sour cream, pico de gallo, and hot sauce.

Makes 4 servings

Per Serving:
$2.89

320 calories
13 g fat (2 g saturated)
490 mg sodium

SAUCE selector

When it comes to dressing up a fish taco, there are many paths to success. Our tacos here combine lime-spiked sour cream with pico de gallo, but any of these other condiments would make a delicious alternative:

● Mango Salsa (page 47)
● Tomatillo Salsa (page 204)
● Grilled-Corn Guacamole (page 266)
● Asian Slaw (page 340)

Salmon
with Ginger Soy Butter

It's well known that salmon is one of the world's healthiest foods, dense with protein and flush with a tide of heart-protecting, cancer-fighting omega-3 fatty acids. And yet, it's not uncommon to find restaurant salmon dishes packing 800 calories or more. Even with a generous mound of this incredible compound butter, our salmon doesn't break the 400-calorie barrier.

You'll Need:

- 2 Tbsp unsalted butter, softened
- ½ Tbsp minced chives
- ½ Tbsp grated fresh ginger
- Juice of 1 lemon
- ½ Tbsp low-sodium soy sauce
- 4 salmon fillets (4–6 oz each)
- Salt and black pepper to taste
- 1 Tbsp olive oil

The best way to peel ginger? With a spoon. That's right; the edge of a spoon easily scrapes away ginger's thin skin without wasting any of the fragrant flesh inside.

How to Make It:

- Mix the butter, chives, ginger, lemon juice, and soy sauce. Set aside.

- Preheat a grill or grill pan over medium heat. Season the salmon with salt and pepper and rub with the oil. Wipe the grill grates clean and rub with a paper towel dipped in oil. Add the salmon skin side down and cook for 4 to 5 minutes, until the skin is lightly charred and crisp.

- Flip the fish and cook for another 2 to 3 minutes on the flesh side, until the flesh flakes with gentle pressure from your finger but is still slightly translucent in the middle. (We believe salmon is best served medium, but if you want yours completely cooked, leave it on for another 2 minutes.)

- Serve the salmon with a generous spoonful of the flavored butter, which should begin to melt on contact.

Makes 4 servings

Per Serving:
$2.46

390 calories
26 g fat (7 g saturated)
710 mg sodium

MEAL MULTIPLIER

Salmon's rich flavor stands up to more aggressive spices and sauces than white fish. Try one of these potent spice rubs to bring out the best in this versatile superfood:

- Pastrami Salmon: Rubbed with equal parts ground ginger, allspice, onion powder, garlic powder, paprika, and ground mustard

- Moroccan Salmon: Rubbed with the Moroccan Spice Blend (page 51)

- Thai Salmon: Rubbed with red curry paste and served with Peanut Sauce (page 48)

Grilled Swordfish
with Smoky Aioli

Sometimes the only thing dividing good food from great food is a simple embellishment: a quick spice rub, a light dressing, an improvised sauce. The only rule we stick to is that the embellishment, whatever it may be, doesn't overpower the dish. A red wine sauce on a fish fillet? Too much. But a smoky, garlic-spiked mayonnaise on a meaty swordfish steak? Just right.

You'll Need:

- 3 Tbsp olive oil mayonnaise
- 1 Tbsp olive oil, plus more for coating the fish

Zest and juice of 1 lemon

- 2 cloves garlic, finely minced
- 1 tsp smoked paprika
- 4 swordfish steaks (about 6 oz each)
- 1 tsp fennel seeds, roughly chopped

Salt and black pepper to taste

How to Make It:

- Preheat a grill or grill pan over high heat. To make the aioli, combine the mayonnaise, olive oil, lemon zest and juice, garlic, and paprika in a small mixing bowl. Stir until thoroughly blended.

- Coat the swordfish with a light film of olive oil, then season on both sides with the fennel, salt, and pepper. Grill for 4 to 5 minutes, until the first side has developed some nice grill marks and the flesh pulls away easily from the grate. Flip and continue grilling for another 4 minutes, until the fish flakes with gentle pressure from your finger and an instant-read thermometer inserted into the thickest part of the steaks registers 140°F. Serve each steak with a spoonful of the aioli.

Makes 4 servings

SAVE-MONEY STRATEGY

Swordfish is an excellent fish for grilling, its meatiness standing up nicely to the intense heat. But like so many great fish out there, it can be pricey, running up to $15 or more per pound. Mahi-mahi and tuna both make excellent alternatives and are usually gentler on the wallet. Even better are bluefish and mackerel, both of which are excellent for grilling and cost around $7 per pound. Plus, these two neglected fish are loaded with huge deposits of heart-healthy omega-3 fatty acids.

Per Serving:
$4.04

280 calories
14 g fat (2.5 g saturated)
490 mg sodium

CHAPTER **8**

APPETIZERS, SNACKS & SMALL BITES

Artichoke-Lemon Crostini

Crostini means "toast" in Italian, but let's be clear now that there is a gaping chasm between toast and flame-grilled bread. The former is merely crunchy, while the latter soaks up the smoke and the char of the open flame, making it the perfect vessel for a variety of toppings—meat, vegetables, cheeses, anything really. Below and the recipes that follow are our favorite crostini, but by all means, grill the bread and top however you see fit.

You'll Need:

- 1 jar (5 oz) marinated artichoke hearts
- ¼ cup grated Parmesan
- Juice of 1 lemon
- 1 Tbsp olive oil, plus more for brushing on the bread
- 2 cloves garlic, minced
- Salt and black pepper to taste
- 4 (½"-thick) slices ciabatta or country bread

How to Make It:

- Preheat a grill or grill pan over high heat. While the grill is heating up, combine the artichoke hearts, Parmesan, lemon juice, olive oil, garlic, and a good pinch of salt and pepper in a food processor. Pulse until pureed but still slightly chunky.

- Lightly brush the bread on both sides with olive oil and grill over high heat for about 2 minutes per side, until lightly charred on the outside but still a bit soft in the center. Slather the toasts with the artichoke puree and serve.

Makes 4 servings

MEAL MULTIPLIER

When it comes to crostini, you are only limited by your imagination. Consider these just a few among the hundreds of possibilities for amazing crostini toppings.

- Grilled rounds of eggplant tossed with vinegar, red pepper flakes, and mint
- Chopped tomatoes, garlic, basil, and olive oil
- Canned white beans pureed with olive oil, garlic, and rosemary
- Fresh ricotta and grilled bell peppers

Per Serving:
$1.19

130 calories
8 g fat (1.5 g saturated)
290 mg sodium

Fig & Prosciutto Crostini

We're helpless junkies for the combination of pork and fruit, and this crostini takes that enduring combination to its most delicious extreme. Strips of salty, porky, glorious prosciutto are offset by the full-throttle sweetness of ripe, juicy figs. The surrounding cast—peppery arugula, goat cheese, honey—are only there to further strengthen this sacred union.

You'll Need:

- ½ cup fresh goat cheese
- 8 fresh figs, quartered
- 2 cups arugula
- 4 slices prosciutto, cut into strips
- 1 Tbsp balsamic vinegar
- 1 Tbsp olive oil, plus more for brushing on the bread
- Salt and black pepper to taste
- 4 (½"-thick) slices ciabatta or country bread
- 1 Tbsp honey

How to Make It:

- Preheat a grill or grill pan over high heat. While the grill is heating up, combine the goat cheese, figs, arugula, prosciutto, balsamic, and olive oil. Mix until the ingredients are evenly coated and season with salt and pepper.

- Lightly brush the bread on both sides with olive oil and grill over high heat for about 2 minutes per side, until lightly charred on the outside, but still somewhat soft in the center. Divide the fig mixture among the toasts and drizzle each with a bit of honey before serving.

Makes 4 servings

Per Serving:
$2.56

260 calories
11 g fat (4 g saturated)
450 mg sodium

Chickpea Crostini

Every meal at Babbo, Mario Batali's flagship restaurant in New York, begins with a simple chickpea crostini that hits all the right notes to rouse the appetite—sweet, sour, salty, hot. It takes divine intervention to score a reservation at Babbo, but thankfully, one of the best parts of the meal is easy enough to re-create at home. This is our take on the first bite.

You'll Need:

- **1 can (14 oz) garbanzo beans (aka chickpeas), drained and rinsed**
- **2 Tbsp olive oil, plus more for brushing on the bread**
- **2 Tbsp tapenade**
- **1 Tbsp balsamic vinegar**
- **¼ tsp fresh rosemary**
- **1 pinch red pepper flakes**
- **Salt and black pepper to taste**
- **4 (½"-thick) slices ciabatta or country bread**

How to Make It:

- Preheat a grill or grill pan over high heat. While the grill is heating up, combine the chickpeas, olive oil, tapenade, balsamic, rosemary, and pepper flakes. Mix until the chickpeas are evenly coated. Season with salt and pepper.

- Lightly brush the bread on both sides with olive oil and grill over high heat for about 2 minutes per side, until lightly charred on the outside but still a bit soft in the center. Top each piece of bread with enough chickpea mixture to cover. You'll likely have leftover chickpeas, which can be served as a side dish or with more toasted bread. Covered, they keep in the refrigerator for up to 1 week.

Makes 4 servings

These garbanzos are amazing on their own or served alongside grilled chicken, steak, or lamb.

Per Serving:	
$0.88	200 calories 8 g fat (1 g saturated) 340 mg sodium

Chipotle Honey Wings

The deep fryer has one prevailing virtue: It makes food crisp. But in exchange for the crunch, you get saddled with hundreds of worthless calories every time you tussle with fried food. We think you can do better—and here's a perfect example how. Wings are never better than when they're hot off the grill, skin beautifully browned and meat suffused with smoke, which is why it's so surprising to see the same boring oil-soaked wings on every restaurant menu in America. We hope these will be all the proof you need to make the switch from the fryer to the grill.

Master THE TECHNIQUE

You'll Need:

1–2 chipotle peppers in adobo

2 Tbsp honey

2 cloves garlic, chopped

Juice of 1 lime

2 lb chicken wings

Salt to taste

Chopped cilantro

These wings will be pretty fiery with two full chipotles. If you want to tone down the heat, stick to a single pepper.

How to Make It:

- In a blender or food processor, puree the chipotle peppers, honey, garlic, and lime juice. Reserve.

- Preheat a grill over medium-low heat. Season the wings all over with salt. Grill the wings for 5 to 7 minutes per side, until the skin is nicely browned and crispy and the meat is cooked through. Combine the wings and the sauce in a large mixing bowl and toss until the wings are thoroughly coated. Top with the cilantro.

Makes 6 servings

Crispy low-cal wings

Want the crisp without the calories? Try this simple trick: Toss the whole batch of wings in ½ tablespoon each baking powder and salt, then lay them out on a baking rack set on a sheet pan and place in the fridge overnight, being careful the wings don't come into contact with other foods. The air will help remove moisture from the skin while baking powder helps weaken protein strands. Both are key to producing crispier wings.

Per Serving:
$1.62

360 calories
24 g fat (7 g saturated)
390 mg sodium

Tuna Satay Skewers

Appetizer sections are home to the densest caloric concentrations on America's menus. It's hard to find anything in the starters section that hasn't touched the deep fryer or isn't built entirely out of refined carbs and cheap fat. What you really want to start your meal with is a big dose of protein: Not only does it get your metabolism firing, protein also keeps your belly full, which helps ward off overeating later in the meal. Luckily, these grilled tuna skewers are nearly pure protein.

You'll Need:

- 1 lb ahi tuna, cut into 8 long pieces

- 8 metal skewers, or wooden skewers soaked in water 30 minutes before cooking

Salt and black pepper to taste

Peanut Sauce (page 48)

How to Make It:

- Heat a grill or stovetop grill pan until hot. Thread the tuna onto the skewers, season all over with salt and black pepper, and paint with the peanut sauce. Cook for 2 minutes per side, until charred on the outside but still pink in the center. Serve the skewers with the remaining sauce.

Makes 4 servings

LEFTOVER
LOVE

Find yourself with more peanut sauce than you need for the tuna? Perfect. It will keep in the fridge for up to 3 days and is perfect for quick stir-fries on busy weeknights. Heat a wok or sauté pan over high heat; sauté chicken, beef, or pork with broccoli, asparagus, bell peppers, and onions. When the produce and protein are almost fully cooked, dump in the peanut sauce, along with a splash of water or chicken broth to thin it out. Cook for 2 to 3 minutes more. Serve sprinkled with crushed peanuts and accompanied by lime wedges.

Per Serving:
$3.32

300 calories
8 g fat (2 g saturated)
270 mg sodium

Grilled Baba Ghanoush

Think of baba ghanoush as hummus, but with eggplant standing in for chickpeas. Most recipes for this Middle Eastern specialty call for the eggplant to be baked in the oven, which misses the point entirely: This dip is all about the sweet-smoky combination that comes from grilled eggplant. This is the perfect appetizer to put out to tame raging appetites while you move on to the meatier matters of grilling.

You'll Need:

1 large eggplant

Olive oil for rubbing on the eggplant

2 Tbsp tahini

Juice of 1 lemon

2 cloves garlic, chopped

¼ tsp cumin

Salt and black pepper

Chopped fresh parsley (optional)

4 whole-wheat pitas

Tahini is a paste made from ground sesame seeds. Can't find it? Peanut butter will work in a pinch.

How to Make It:

● Preheat a grill over medium heat. Prick the eggplant all over with a fork and rub with a thin coating of olive oil. Grill, turning occasionally, for about 15 minutes, until the skin is charred and the inside is very soft. Allow the eggplant to cool for at least 5 minutes before handling. (This step can be done up to a day ahead.)

● Peel back the charred skin and scoop out the soft innards of the eggplant, using a spoon to scrape off every last bit of flesh from the skin (it's quite alright if a bit of charred skin makes it into the mix). Pulse the eggplant in a food processor with the tahini, lemon juice, garlic, and cumin until smooth. Season with salt and pepper. Transfer to a serving bowl and top with chopped parsley, if you like.

● Heat the pitas on the grill, in a toaster, or in the oven until very warm and soft. Cut into wedges and serve with the baba ghanoush.

Makes 4 servings

Per Serving:
$0.93

200 calories
5 g fat (1 g saturated)
250 mg sodium

Grilled Meatballs
with Smoky Tomato Sauce

We wanted to keep the essential awesomeness of meatballs and red sauce intact but ditch about 80 percent of the calories, so we nixed the mountain of spaghetti and turned to our friend Old Smoky for the solution.

You'll Need:

MEATBALLS

- ½ lb ground sirloin
- ½ lb ground pork
- ¼ cup bread crumbs
- ¼ onion, minced
- ¼ cup grated Parmesan
- 1 egg, beaten
- 1 clove garlic, minced
- ½ tsp fennel seeds
- ½ tsp salt

SMOKY TOMATO SAUCE

- 1 lb Roma tomatoes, tops removed, halved
- 1 small onion, sliced

Olive oil

- 1 clove garlic, minced (or 2 cloves Grilled Garlic, page 50)

Salt and black pepper to taste

How to Make It:

- Preheat a grill over medium heat. While the grill heats up, make the meatballs: Combine the sirloin, pork, bread crumbs, onion, Parmesan, egg, garlic, fennel seeds, and salt in a large mixing bowl. Gently roll the mixture into golf ball–sized orbs, being careful not to overwork the meat (which will give you tough, chewy meatballs).

- To make the tomato sauce, drizzle the tomatoes and onion with enough olive oil to lightly coat. Place on one side of the grill and cook for about 10 minutes, until the onions are very soft and the tomato skins begin to blister. Peel off the tomato skins and puree the rest in a blender with the onion, garlic, 1 tablespoon olive oil, and salt and pepper.

- While the tomatoes and onions are grilling, place the meatballs on the other side of the grill and cook on all sides for 8 to 10 minutes, until they are charred and firm to the touch.

- Serve the meatballs with the tomato sauce and slices of grilled bread, if you like.

Makes 4 servings

Per Serving:
$2.04

350 calories
21 g fat (7 g saturated)
540 mg sodium

MEAL MULTIPLIER

Pork and beef are traditional meatball fodder for a reason, but limit yourself to them and you're missing out on a world of exciting possibilities. Combine any of the following with bread crumbs and eggs for a tasty departure from the standard meatball:

- Finely minced tuna with toasted pine nuts and raisins
- Ground chicken with minced ginger and scallion, served with Mango Chutney (page 200)
- Ground lamb with garlic, red pepper flakes, and chopped fresh mint, served with the same tomato sauce used on this page

Ham & Pineapple Quesadillas

Most quesadillas in America are made either in a skillet or, worse, the microwave, while the best cooking implement goes entirely overlooked. The grill not only adds a smoky char and a lasting crisp to a quesadilla, it also allows you to cook two or three at a time, making this one of the quickest, easiest recipes in the entire book. The inspiration here comes from that uniquely American take on pizza, the Hawaiian pie. Try dipping wedges into warm marinara to complete the effect.

You'll Need:

- 4 (8" diameter) tortillas
- 1 cup shredded Jack cheese
- 1 cup shredded Swiss cheese
- 4 slices deli ham, cut into thin strips
- 1 cup chopped pineapple
- Pickled jalapeño peppers (optional)
- Canola oil for brushing
- Pico de Gallo (page 46), Smoky Tomato Sauce (page 258), or your favorite store-bought salsa for serving

How to Make It:

- Preheat a grill or grill pan over medium heat. Place two tortillas on a large cutting board or clean kitchen surface. Evenly divide the cheeses, ham, pineapple, and jalapeños (if using) between them. Top each with another tortilla.

- Brush the top tortillas lightly with oil, then place directly on the grill, oiled side down. (If you're using a grill pan, you'll need to cook one quesadilla at a time.) Lightly brush the tortillas now facing up with oil. Grill, turning 45 degrees midway through, for 4 to 5 minutes. Flip the quesadillas and grill on the other side, turning 45 degrees midway through, for another 4 to 5 minutes, until the tortillas are lightly toasted and the cheese is fully melted. (The cheese will melt better if you close the lid while cooking.) Cut into wedges and serve with pico de gallo or salsa.

Makes 4 servings

Per Serving: **$1.77**

370 calories
18 g fat (10 g saturated)
620 mg sodium

Tomato Bread (2 Ways)

It seems so basic, but when the tomatoes are ripe and the bread is good, few combinations are as satisfying. In Spain, they smash ripe tomatoes directly on the bread to create one of the country's iconic dishes. The other take is a nod to the South, where thick-cut tomatoes team up with mayo for a summer treat.

Spanish Style

You'll Need:

- 2 **very ripe large tomatoes, halved**

- 2 **Tbsp olive oil, plus more for brushing on the bread**

Coarse sea salt to taste

- 4 **(½"-thick) slices ciabatta or country bread**

- 1 **clove garlic, peeled and halved**

It's helpful to have two types of olive oil on hand: one normal bottle for cooking, one nice bottle for drizzling on raw or cooked foods. Both of these recipes are best with high-quality oil.

How to Make It:

- Using a large box grater, grate the flesh side of the tomatoes through the largest holes until everything but the skin has passed through. Stir the olive oil into the tomato pulp and season with salt.

- Preheat a grill or grill pan over high heat. Brush the bread on both sides with olive oil and grill over high heat for about 2 minutes per side, until lightly charred on the outside, but still a bit soft in the center. While the bread is still hot, rub one side with a cut garlic clove. Spoon the tomatoes over the toasts and top with a few flakes of coarse salt.

Makes 4 servings

Per Serving: $1.56

130 calories
8 g fat (1 g saturated)
120 mg sodium

American Style

You'll Need:

- 4 **(½"-thick) slices ciabatta or country bread**

- 2 **Tbsp olive oil, plus more for brushing**

- 1 **clove garlic, peeled and halved**

- 3 **very ripe medium heirloom tomatoes (preferably different colors), sliced**

- 2 **Tbsp chopped fresh chives**

Coarse sea salt and black pepper to taste

How to Make It:

- Preheat a grill or grill pan over high heat. Lightly brush the bread on both sides with olive oil and grill over high heat for about 2 minutes per side, until lightly charred on the outside, but still a bit soft in the center. While the bread is still hot, rub one side with a cut garlic clove.

- Layer the tomatoes across the bread, varying colors if you're lucky enough to find a variety of heirlooms. Top with the chives and 2 tablespoons olive oil and season with salt and pepper.

Makes 4 servings

Per Serving: $1.82

130 calories
8 g fat (1 g saturated)
120 mg sodium

Oysters
with Garlic Butter and Tabasco

If there is one unconventional grilled food that everybody should try once, it's the grilled oyster. As the shell heats up from the bottom, the oyster begins to cook gently in the bath of garlic, butter, and brine. It ends up somewhere between the soft, slippery texture of a raw oyster and the creamy, slightly chewy effect of a cooked one. A bit of bubbling garlic butter and a shake of Tabasco take the experience over the top. Be sure to have a cold beer, or a glass of sparkling wine, close at hand.

You'll Need:

- 12 oysters, shucked
- 2 Tbsp salted butter, cut into small pieces
- 2 cloves garlic, very finely minced
- Tabasco to taste
- Lemon wedges

How to Make It:

- Preheat a grill or grill pan over medium heat. Divide the butter and garlic among the oysters. When the grill is hot, place the oysters directly on the grate, shell side down. Grill for about 5 minutes, until the butter has fully melted and the oysters have begun to firm up. Serve with hot sauce and lemon wedges.

Makes 4 servings

Master THE TECHNIQUE

Shucking oysters

Place the oysters in the freezer for 15 minutes; the cold helps to loosen the muscle that holds the shell closed. Using a towel to hold the oyster, insert an oyster knife (or any thin blade—like a paring knife) in the oyster's back hinge. Rotate the knife 90 degrees, rocking it back and forth to pop the top open. Slide the knife across the oyster to sever the connective tissue, being careful not to lose the precious oyster liquor in the shell.

Per Serving:
$3.12

80 calories
7 g fat (3 g saturated)
130 mg sodium

Grilled-Corn Guacamole

Normally our guacamole ethos boils down to this: Less is more. It's tough to watch people pollute the enduring union of avocado, salt, and citrus with high-calorie intruders like mayonnaise and sour cream. But this recipe, like so many great ones out there, was born out of serendipity, the result of having some leftover grilled corn and a handful of cherry tomatoes. It's not better than classic guac, it's just different—in the best possible way. Serve with tortillas warmed on the grill, tucked into tacos, or spooned over the top of grilled chicken or fish. Or with tortilla chips, of course.

You'll Need:

- 1 ear corn
- 2 medium Hass avocados, pitted and peeled
- 1 clove garlic, minced

Salt to taste

- 1 cup cherry tomatoes, halved
- 1 handful cilantro, chopped

Juice of 1 lime

How to Make It:

- Preheat a grill over medium heat. Peel the corn husk back, being careful so it remains attached to the base of the cob, and remove the silk inside. Re-cover the ear with the husk and soak in cold water for 5 minutes.

- Grill the corn for 10 minutes, turning a quarter-turn every few minutes. Peel back the husk and place the corn back on the grill. Grill, turning occasionally, for 5 minutes more, until the kernels are nicely browned. When the corn is cool enough to handle, use a knife to cut the kernels from the cob.

- Combine the avocado, garlic, and a few good pinches of salt in a mixing bowl. Use a fork to mash the avocado until you have a consistency somewhere between smooth and chunky. Fold in the corn kernels, tomatoes, cilantro, and lime juice.

Makes 4 servings

Per Serving:
$1.69

200 calories
15 g fat (2.5 g saturated)
325 mg sodium

Grilled Raisin-Walnut Bread
with Ricotta and Grapes

By themselves, grilled grapes are the world's healthiest dessert. Paired with ricotta, fresh rosemary, and cracked black pepper, they create something that straddles the sweet-savory world in a deeply delicious way. It's the kind of dish that people will question at first, but as they bite down, their eyes will open wide and eventually sink into the backs of their heads—a powerful reminder that experimentation in the kitchen is always a good thing.

You'll Need:

- 1 **medium bunch (about ½ lb) red grapes**
- 4 **(½"-thick) slices raisin-walnut bread**
- 1 **cup part-skim ricotta**
- 1 **tsp chopped fresh rosemary**

Black pepper to taste

Want to turn this into dessert? Omit the black pepper and drizzle on a light stream of honey instead.

How to Make It:

- Preheat a grill over high heat. Place the grapes directly on the grate and grill for about 10 minutes, until the skins are blistered and the insides are hot and juicy. While the grapes grill, grill the bread, turning, until lightly browned and crisp.

- Spread the ricotta in a thick layer on the slices of bread. Remove the grapes from the stems and arrange on top of the ricotta, along with the rosemary and a generous amount of freshly cracked black pepper.

Makes 4 servings

A more traditional bread like ciabatta will work fine. So will cinnamon-swirl bread sold by makers like Sun-Maid.

Per Serving:
$1.71

200 calories
6 g fat (3.5 g saturated)
180 mg sodium

Chorizo Tostadas

Buy a box of tostada shells in the supermarket and you'll get a few flat, dry pieces of additive-addled corn that look more like flying saucers than dinner. But put a fresh corn tortilla on the grill until it perfectly straddles the tender-crispy spectrum and you have the base for something spectacular. You can vary this recipe dozens of different ways, but the mix of spicy chorizo, fresh avocado, and crumbled cheese is as good a place to start as any.

You'll Need:

- **6 oz fresh Mexican-style chorizo**
- **1 avocado, peeled and pitted**
- **1 cup Tomatilla Salsa (page 204 or store-bought)**
- **4 corn tortillas**
- **½ Tbsp canola oil for brushing**
- **½ cup Cotija cheese**

Cotija is a dry, crumbly Mexican cheese available in Latin markets. If you can't find it, feta or even fresh goat cheese works nearly as well.

This recipe makes more salsa than you'll need. Use the leftovers to slather on sandwiches or for topping fried eggs in the morning.

How to Make It:

- Remove the chorizo from its casing and cook in a medium-sized sauté pan set over medium heat for 7 to 8 minutes, until just cooked through. Remove to a plate lined with paper towels to absorb the excess fat.

- Place the avocado in a mixing bowl and mash with a fork until smooth. Stir in the tomatillo salsa.

- Preheat a grill over low heat. Brush the tortillas on both sides with oil and grill for 3 to 4 minutes, until the bottoms are crispy and browned. Flip, top with the chorizo, and continue grilling for another 3 to 4 minutes, until the bottoms begin to crisp. Top the tostadas with the avocado salsa and the crumbled cheese.

Makes 4 servings

MEAL MULTIPLIER

Crunchy grilled tostadas are the perfect vehicles for dozens of Latin-inspired toppings. Here are three other combinations worth trying:

- Refried beans, pepper Jack cheese, and grilled chicken
- Grilled strips of zucchini, mushrooms, and jalapeños, topped wtih Tomatillo Salsa
- Mashed avocado, finely chopped raw ahi tuna, lime juice, and arugula
- Grilled Scallop Ceviche (page 276)

Per Serving:
$1.87

310 calories
18 g fat (8 g saturated)
740 mg sodium

Sweet & Spicy Ahi

Ahi tuna is one of the greatest grill ingredients of all—lean, meaty, and incredibly simple to cook. The key to great ahi is a screaming hot flame, which allows you to sear the outside while leaving the center raw—a nod to its role as a star of the sushi bar. As such, it takes well to Asian flavors like ginger, soy, and rice wine vinegar. Serve this as is for an impressive appetizer, or with a bit of steamed brown rice for an ultra-lean dinner.

You'll Need:

- ¼ cup rice wine vinegar
- ¼ cup soy sauce
- 1 Tbsp honey
- 1 Tbsp minced ginger
- 1 jalapeño pepper, minced
- ¼ cup chopped cilantro
- ¼ cup peanut oil
- 1 English cucumber, sliced into thin rounds
- 1 lb ahi tuna (2–3 fillets)

Salt and black pepper to taste

How to Make It:

- Combine the rice wine vinegar, soy sauce, honey, ginger, jalapeño, and cilantro in a medium mixing bowl. Slowly drizzle in the oil, whisking to fully incorporate. Add the cucumber and let soak at least 10 minutes before you cook the tuna.

- Preheat a grill or grill pan over high heat. Season the tuna all over with salt and pepper. Place on the hottest part of the grill and grill for 2 minutes per side, until grill marks have developed but the center is still raw. (If you like your tuna cooked through, cook for 4 minutes per side.)

- Slice the tuna into thin pieces and divide among four plates. With a slotted spoon, place a pile of cucumbers on each plate. Drizzle the remaining sauce over the tuna.

Makes 4 servings

Per Serving:
$3.83

280 calories
15 g fat (2 g saturated)
820 mg sodium

Buffalo Shrimp

Deep-fried chicken wings coated in butter and dipped in blue cheese can be a bit of a one-note affair: fat on fat on fat. By trading lean shrimp for the wings, using a yogurt-based blue cheese sauce in lieu of the blue cheese, and, most importantly, turning to the grill instead of a vat of bubbling oil, we've trimmed 75 percent of the calories from the classic bar food while adding new dimensions to its enduring appeal. We think you'll approve.

You'll Need:

- ¼ **cup plain Greek yogurt**
- ¼ **cup olive oil mayonnaise**
- 2 **Tbsp crumbled blue cheese**
- **Juice of ½ lemon**
- 1 **lb medium shrimp, peeled and deveined**
- **Salt and black pepper to taste**
- **Metal skewers, or wooden skewers soaked in water for 30 minutes**
- 2 **Tbsp butter**
- 1 **Tbsp hot sauce (we like Frank's RedHot)**

How to Make It:

- Combine the yogurt, mayonnaise, blue cheese, and half the lemon juice in a small bowl. Reserve.

- Preheat a grill or grill pan over high heat. Season the shrimp with salt and pepper and thread on the skewers. Grill the shrimp for 1 to 2 minutes per side, until pink and just firm.

- Melt the butter in a large sauté pan. Stir in the hot sauce and remaining lemon juice and remove from the heat. Strip the shrimp from the skewers and add to the pan, tossing until evenly coated with the sauce. Serve with the blue cheese sauce for dipping.

Makes 4 servings

Per Serving:
$2.42

230 calories
12 g fat (5 g saturated)
230 mg sodium

Grilled Scallop Ceviche

All signs point to Peruvian food being one of the next big international cuisines to make an impression on North American eating. At the heart of the Peruvian kitchen is ceviche, a simple dish of raw seafood marinated in lime juice and onion until the citric acid effectively "cooks" the fish. This isn't a traditional ceviche since the scallops are cooked first, but the grilling adds a new dimension to the original formula, while the lime juice, onions, and cilantro help retain the classic ceviche flavors. If there is a healthier dish anywhere in the world, we haven't found it.

You'll Need:

1 lb medium sea scallops

Salt and black pepper to taste

2 medium oranges (preferably blood oranges), peeled and segmented

½ English cucumber, thinly sliced

1 small avocado, peeled, pitted, and cubed

1 small red onion, thinly sliced

½ jalapeño pepper, minced

2 Tbsp olive oil, plus more for coating the scallops

Juice of 2 limes

½ cup chopped cilantro

Grilled bread or grilled corn tortillas

If you can't get your hands on scallops, shrimp make for a fine substitute.

How to Make It:

● Preheat a grill or grill pan over high heat. Drizzle the scallops with just enough olive oil to coat, then season on both sides with salt and pepper. When the grill is very hot, add the scallops and grill for about 2 minutes, until nice grill marks have developed and the flesh easily pulls away from the grill. Flip and cook for another 2 minutes, until the scallops are firm but gently yielding to the touch.

● Slice the scallops in half horizontally, then combine with the oranges, cucumber, avocado, onion, and jalapeño. Drizzle in the 2 tablespoons olive oil, the lime juice, and cilantro, and season with salt and pepper. Serve with grilled bread or corn tortillas.

Makes 4 servings

Per Serving:
$3.93

340 calories
16 g fat (2 g saturated)
390 mg sodium

Vietnamese-Style Chicken Wings

Down a small side street in downtown Ho Chi Minh City, an open-air restaurant called Ban Xeo 46A houses hungry revelers who line up until the early hours of the morning to eat crispy crepes, spring rolls, and what may be the greatest chicken wings on the planet. No, they're not doused in Texas Pete and drowned in blue cheese dressing, but rather gently coated with a perfectly balanced sweet-salty mix of sugar and fish sauce. This recipe is, we hope, a faithful interpretation of the original, but with the smoke of the grill standing in for the oil of the fryer.

You'll Need:

- 2 lb chicken wings
- ½ cup fish sauce
- ¼ cup sugar
- 2 cloves garlic, minced

Black pepper to taste

- ½ cup chopped fresh cilantro or mint

How to Make It:

- Combine the wings, fish sauce, sugar, garlic, and black pepper in a sealable plastic bag. Seal and refrigerate to marinate for at least 2 hours (or up to 8 hours).

- Preheat a grill over medium heat. Remove the wings from the bag, reserving the marinade. Grill the wings for about 5 minutes per side, until the skin is nicely browned and crispy and the meat pulls easily away from the bone.

- While the wings cook, place the marinade in a saucepan over medium heat and bring to a simmer. Cook for about 10 minutes, until reduced by half. When the wings are done, toss with the sauce and garnish with the fresh herbs.

Makes 6 servings

Per Serving:

$1.80

340 calories
24 g fat (7 g saturated)
670 mg sodium

SECRET WEAPON

Fish Sauce

Made from fermented oily fish, fish sauce tends to pack a stiff aroma. But this funky condiment forms the backbone of much of Southeast Asian cuisine and, despite it's strong nose, adds a pleasantly salty, sweet punch of flavor to a variety of dishes and sauces. Try marinating steak or vegetables in a 50-50 mix of fish sauce and olive oil and you'll be won over instantly. Find a bottle in large grocery stores or Asian markets.

Smoking Gazpacho

It's tough to improve on a dish that's been around for hundreds of years. Gazpacho was invented by Spaniards as a way to cool off and nourish during the oppressive heat of the Andalusian summer. But the heat of the grill brings out the best in the vegetables that compose this cold soup, making for a more intensely flavorful gazpacho than those made with raw vegetables alone. Like most soups, this one is best made at least a few hours ahead, giving the flavors time to make friends while they chill out in the refrigerator.

You'll Need:

- 3 large tomatoes (about 1½ pounds)
- 1 medium onion, halved
- 1 green bell pepper, stemmed, seeded, and quartered
- 1 small hothouse cucumber, roughly chopped
- 1½ cups low-sodium tomato juice
- ¼ cup olive oil, plus more for drizzling
- 2 Tbsp sherry vinegar
- 2 cloves garlic, peeled
- A few shakes Tabasco sauce
- Salt to taste
- Garlic Croutons

How to Make It:

- Preheat a grill over high heat. When hot, grill the tomatoes, onion, and bell pepper, turning, for about 12 minutes, until their skins are lightly blistered and their flesh very soft.

- Combine the grilled vegetables with the cucumber, tomato juice, olive oil, vinegar, garlic, Tabasco, and salt in a blender and puree until mostly smooth (a few light chunks in gazpacho is a good thing). Place the gazpacho in the refrigerator to chill for at least 1 hour before serving.

- Serve each bowl of gazpacho with a crouton and an extra drizzle of olive oil.

Makes 4 servings

Per Serving: **$1.46**

200 calories
14 g fat (2 g saturated)
560 mg sodium

Garlic Croutons

You'll Need:

- 1 baguette
- Olive oil for drizzling
- 2 cloves garlic, halved

How to Make It:

- Preheat a grill over medium heat. Use a bread knife to slice the baguette on the diagonal into ¼"-thick slices. Drizzle the bread with olive oil and place on the grill. Cook for about 3 minutes per side, until brown and crunchy. Rub one side of each slice with a piece of garlic and serve. Keeps for up to 1 week, covered, in the pantry.

Makes about 20 croutons

SALADS

CHAPTER 9

You Can Grill
THAT?

Grills were made for more than steaks and burgers. These unusual ingredients also benefit from the smoke-and-fire treatment.

Spinach

Both full-grown spinach and arugula can be cooked directly on the grill grate. Thoroughly clean the leaves and leave the stems intact (it will make them easier to handle on the grill). Place over a medium fire and grill for 3 to 5 minutes, until the leaves begin to wilt and crisp around the edges. Dress the greens with a drizzle of olive oil, the juice of a lemon, some shaved Parmesan cheese.

Lettuce

Firm heads of lettuce like iceberg, cabbage, or—our favorite—radicchio, take well to the transformative powers of the grill. Halve or quarter the heads and drizzle with olive oil. Grill over high heat until the outer leaves are blackened and wilted and the center is softened. Serve radicchio drizzled with balsamic, dress cabbage with Honey-Dijon Vinaigrette (page 49), and anoint iceberg wedges with crumbled bacon, fresh tomatoes, and blue cheese dressing.

Edamame

Most people only know edamame as those green little pods they pick at before their sushi arrives, but tossed onto the grill and cooked until nicely charred, they become a whole different animal. Grill them over medium heat directly on the grate or in a grill basket for about 10 minutes, until the pods begin to blacken. Toss with coarse sea salt, sesame seeds, chili powder, or any other spice that gets you going.

Avocado

Grilled guacamole? Absolutely. Halve the avocado lengthwise and remove the pit. Place directly on the grate of a hot grill, cut side down, and grill for about 5 minutes, until nice grill marks have developed. From here, you can cube the avocado for salad, mash it for a smoky guacamole, or fill each half with tuna or chicken salad for an incredible twist on the classic.

Watermelon

Nothing wrong with a hunk of juicy watermelon as is, but like with all fruit, the grill helps to concentrate its sweetness and intensity. Cut thick watermelon steaks, drizzle with a bit of olive oil, and grill over high heat, turning once. Your mission is to sear the outside while keeping the center close to raw, creating a lovely hot-cold contrast. This should take about 8 minutes. Grilled watermelon can be eaten as is right off the grill (sprinkled with a bit of coarse sea salt), or put to use in a salad of arugula, goat cheese or feta, and toasted almonds.

Cake

Angel food cake, biscuits, and banana bread all benefit from a turn on the grill, not just because they come off hot, but also because the grill crisps the surface while keeping the interior warm and moist. Grill slices of banana bread over medium-high heat, turning, for 8 minutes, until crisp. While the bread grills, make a sauce by simmering ½ cup butter with ½ cup brown sugar. When sticky and dark, stir in ½ cup coffee. Top the banana bread with a scoop of cool Greek yogurt and a few spoons of the coffee caramel.

Cheese

Halloumi is a Middle Eastern cheese famous for its ability to stand up to high heat, but plenty of other cheeses can also take the heat. Provolone, mozzarella, and even a wheel of brie can be grilled until hot and gloriously gooey. Keep the cheese cold until the grill is ready to go, then place it on the grate and grill for 6 to 8 minutes, turning, just until the surface of the cheese browns and begins to melt. You can use grilled cheese to top a sandwich or anchor a salad, but the best move is to serve it as is, with slices of grilled bread rubbed with garlic for scooping.

Bacon

Yes, grilled bacon. It's best to use thick-cut bacon, as it stands up better to the heat than the scrawny stuff produced by most national brands. Grill over a low flame, turning, for about 12 minutes, until the fat renders and the meat crisps up. Use grilled bacon in a BLT or as a burger topping, or turn it into pig candy: Rub the bacon with brown sugar and a bit of cayenne before going on the grill; during the final 5 minutes of cooking, brush on thin coats of maple syrup. Mmmm, candied bacon.

Sizzling Caesar Salad

This is no gimmick: Grilled Caesar salad is a revelation. Standard Caesar qualifies as one of those faux-healthy foods we implore people to avoid ordering in restaurants, but when grilled at home, it's a whole different story.

You'll Need:

DRESSING

Juice of 1 lemon

2 Tbsp red wine vinegar

1 Tbsp olive oil mayonnaise

1 clove garlic, minced

2 anchovies (soak in milk for 10 minutes if you want to mellow the flavor)

1 tsp Worcestershire sauce

6–8 turns of a black-pepper mill

½ cup olive oil

2 heads romaine lettuce

Olive oil for coating the lettuce

¼ cup finely grated Parmesan

Garlic Croutons (page 280)

How to Make It:

- To make the dressing, combine the lemon juice, vinegar, mayonnaise, garlic, anchovies, Worcestershire, and pepper in a food processor or blender. With the motor running, slowly drizzle in the olive oil until a thick, creamy dressing is formed.

- Preheat a grill over high heat. Peel off the dark outer leaves of the romaine (if using hearts of romaine, no peeling necessary). Halve each head vertically, leaving the stems intact to hold the lettuce together. Drizzle with just enough olive oil to coat the cut sides. Place the lettuce, cut side down, on the hottest part of grill and cook for 3 to 5 minutes, until the leaves have begun to wilt and char.

- Divide the lettuce among 4 plates, drizzle with enough dressing to lightly coat, and top with the Parmesan and a few croutons.

Makes 4 servings

Most grocery stores now sell bags of romaine hearts, which are ideal for this recipe.

| Per Serving:
$1.66 | 310 calories
26 g fat (4 g saturated)
460 mg sodium |

Upgrade

NUTRITIONAL

The main nutritional knock against Caesar salad is that, beyond the lettuce itself, there's nothing particularly healthy about it. In the worst hands, that's true, but there are many ways to bolster a Caesar, making it both more substantial and more nutritious. Here are three tasty additions that will boost the basic grilled Caesar recipe:

ı Grilled or shredded rotisserie chicken and sundried tomatoes

ı Chopped olives, marinated artichoke hearts, and roasted red peppers

ı Grilled shrimp, grilled corn kernels, and grilled strips of poblano peppers

Grilled Peach Salad

No fruit can take the heat quite like a peach can. The sear of the flame does something magical to stone fruit, concentrating its sweetness and acidity, transforming its flesh into something creamy and luxurious. A perfect summer peach hot off the grill is a special enough on its own, but when paired with crunchy almonds, salty prosciutto, and tangy crumbles of goat cheese, it makes for one of the greatest salads you can eat.

You'll Need:

- 1 shallot, minced
- 2 Tbsp balsamic vinegar
- ½ Tbsp chopped fresh rosemary leaves (optional)
- ½ Tbsp honey
- 3 Tbsp olive oil
- Salt and black pepper to taste
- 2 peaches, halved and pitted
- 16 cups mixed baby greens
- 4 slices prosciutto, torn into strips
- ½ cup fresh goat cheese
- ¼ cup chopped almonds

How to Make It:

- Preheat a grill or grill pan over medium heat.

- In a mixing bowl, combine the shallot, balsamic, rosemary (if using), and honey. Let the shallot soften in the vinegar for at least 5 minutes. Slowly drizzle in the olive oil, whisking to incorporate. Season with salt and pepper and reserve.

- When the grill is hot, place the peaches directly on the grate, cut side down. Grill, rotating the fruit 45 degrees midway through, for 4 to 5 minutes, until the flesh is nicely caramelized. Flip the peaches and grill on the rounded sides for a few minutes, just until the bottoms begin to soften.

- Slice the peaches into ¼" pieces. Combine with the greens, prosciutto, goat cheese, and almonds in a large mixing bowl. Whisk the vinaigrette one last time, then add a few tablespoons at a time to the salad, tossing, until the ingredients are lightly coated.

Makes 4 servings

Per Serving:
$2.37

310 calories
21 g fat (6 g saturated)
530 mg sodium

Grilled Salmon Salad

For most people, the idea of a salad starts and stops with lettuce. But why confine yourself to leaves? Salads can be made from any combination of meat, fish, and vegetables bound together with dressing. This muscular salad brings together a full dinner's worth of protein and vegetables, playing tastes and textures off each other for the greater good of your taste buds.

You'll Need:

- 1 shallot, thinly sliced
- 2 Tbsp red wine vinegar
- 1 lb salmon fillet (preferably in a single piece)
- ½ lb green beans, tips removed
- ¼ cup olive oil, plus more for coating the fish and beans
- Salt and black pepper to taste
- ½ Tbsp Dijon mustard
- 20 cherry tomatoes, halved
- 2 Tbsp capers, rinsed

How to Make It:

- Preheat a grill over medium heat. Combine the shallot and red wine vinegar in a bowl and set aside.

- Coat the salmon and the green beans with olive oil and season with salt and pepper. Place the salmon on the grill, skin side down. Grill for 5 to 6 minutes, until the skin firms up and pulls away from the grill. Flip and continue grilling for 2 to 3 minutes longer, until the thickest part of the fish flakes with gentle pressure from your finger. While the salmon grills, cook the green beans in a grill basket or directly on the grill grate, turning, for 7 to 8 minutes, until soft.

- Stir the mustard into the reserved vinegar mixture. Slowly whisk in the ¼ cup olive oil. Break the salmon into large flakes. In a bowl, combine the salmon with the green beans, tomatoes, and capers. Pour the vinaigrette over the top, season with salt and pepper, and toss to thoroughly combine.

Makes 4 servings

Per Serving:

$3.53

310 calories
21 g fat (3 g saturated)
400 mg sodium

Master THE TECHNIQUE

Protein-based salads

This style of salad works especially well with left-over meat or fish, such as an extra rotisserie chicken from the market, leftover Thanksgiving turkey, or a neglected tuna steak from last night's dinner.

ı Shredded chicken or turkey, mandarin slices, almonds, and broccoli florets

ı Sliced pork tenderloin, peaches, green beans, pecans, and crumbled blue cheese

ı Grilled tuna, roasted red peppers, olives, sundried tomatoes, and pine nuts

Asian Beef Salad
with Sriracha-Honey Dressing

Restaurant salads suffer from a double dose of shamefulness: They are not only boring and sloppily executed, they also come with more calories and fat than your average bacon cheeseburger. A frightening example: You'd be better off eating three full orders of Applebee's Asiago Peppercorn Steak than tussling with the tame-sounding Oriental Grilled Chicken Salad. Disgraceful. Here, we harbor the big flavors of the East—sweet, spicy, tart, cool—but leave all the excessive calories out of the equation. A generous portion of lean flank steak and creamy cubes of avocado make sure this salad truly satisfies.

You'll Need:

1 lb flank steak

Salt and ground black pepper to taste

1 tsp sriracha or other hot sauce

2 tsp honey

½ Tbsp low-sodium soy sauce

Juice of 1 lime

¼ cup canola oil

1 bag watercress (if your market doesn't stock watercress, a head of Bibb lettuce will work fine)

1 pint cherry tomatoes, sliced in half

1 small red onion, thinly sliced

½ English cucumber, thinly sliced

1 avocado, peeled, pitted, and chopped

Handful of fresh cilantro leaves

How to Make It:

● Preheat a grill or grill pan over medium-high heat. Season the flank steak all over with salt and pepper and cook until medium rare, about 3 to 4 minutes per side. Allow the steak to rest for at least 5 minutes before slicing thinly across the natural grain of the meat.

● While the meat rests, combine the sriracha, honey, soy sauce, and lime juice with a pinch of pepper in a mixing bowl. Slowly drizzle in the oil, whisking to combine.

● In a large salad bowl, combine the watercress, tomatoes, onion, cucumber, avocado, cilantro, and sliced steak and slowly drizzle in the dressing, tossing the ingredients gently with each addition, until everything is lightly coated.

Makes 4 servings

Per Serving:
$4.39

430 calories
31 g fat (6 g saturated)
475 mg sodium

Panzanella

This salad, a staple throughout Tuscany, is a powerful example of the importance of eating foods in their proper season. Make this bread-and-tomato salad in the winter and it might fail to win you over. But try it in August, when tomatoes are juicy and peppers and cucumbers crisp and sweet, and it's a revelation. Serve it next to a hunk of juicy grilled chicken and it will become one of your backyard standbys.

You'll Need:

- 1 loaf ciabatta or country bread, sliced into ½"-thick pieces
- 2 cloves garlic, halved
- 2 large tomatoes (preferably heirloom), chopped
- 1 medium cucumber, seeded and sliced
- 1 large red or yellow bell pepper, stemmed, seeded, and chopped
- ½ medium red onion, thinly sliced
- 15–20 fresh basil leaves, roughly chopped
- 3 Tbsp olive oil, plus more for drizzling
- 2 Tbsp red wine vinegar
- Salt and black pepper to taste

How to Make It:

- Preheat a grill or grill pan over high heat. Lightly drizzle the bread with olive oil and grill for about 3 minutes per side, until nicely browned and crisp. Rub both sides of the bread lightly with a garlic clove half, then cut the bread into cubes.

- Toss the toasted bread with the tomatoes, cucumbers, bell peppers, onion, and basil in a large bowl. Drizzle in the olive oil and vinegar. Season with salt and pepper.

Makes 4 servings

Per Serving:
$2.86

260 calories
11 g fat (2 g saturated)
500 mg sodium

$$(\text{¶} + \text{|})^2$$

MEAL MULTIPLIER

Panzanella may traditionally be a summertime salad, but the idea of tossing grilled bread with vegetables can be carried through all four seasons. Simply replace the tomato, cucumber, and peppers with any of the following combinations and proceed with the recipe.

ı Fall: Brussels sprouts and butternut squash
ı Winter: Carrots and cauliflower
ı Spring: Asparagus, radish, and cubes of avocado

Grilled Halloumi & Strawberry Salad

Halloumi, a firm sheep and goat's milk cheese with a lightly salty bite, is popular in the kitchens of the Middle East. More than anything, halloumi is known for its ability to stand up to high heat without melting, making it a killer weapon in the grill master's arsenal. It works best when paired with something sweet, like these strawberries, which helps cut through the richness of the cheese.

You'll Need:

- 2 cups sliced strawberries
- 3 Tbsp balsamic vinegar
- 1 medium shallot, thinly sliced

Freshly cracked black pepper

- ½ lb halloumi, cut into 4 rectangles
- 3 Tbsp olive oil, plus more for coating the cheese
- 16 cups baby spinach, arugula, or mixed baby greens
- ¼ cup smoked almonds

How to Make It:

- Preheat a grill or grill pan over medium-high heat. Combine the strawberries, vinegar, shallot, and pepper in a large mixing bowl. Let the shallots and strawberries macerate in the vinegar for at least 10 minutes.

- Coat the cheese with a light film of olive oil. Grill for 2 minutes, until grill marks have developed, then rotate 45 degrees and grill for another 2 minutes. Flip the cheese and repeat the process until the cheese is lightly charred and warm throughout.

- Drizzle the 3 tablespoons of olive oil into the bowl with the strawberries. Add the spinach and almonds and toss. Divide the salad among 4 plates and top each with a piece of grilled cheese.

Makes 4 servings

Per Serving:
$2.94

420 calories
28 g fat (9 g saturated)
970 mg sodium

SECRET WEAPON

Halloumi

For those looking to cut carbohydrates from their diet, halloumi serves as a protein-packed replacement for quick-burning starches. Try it in place of grilled bread for any of the crostini recipes in Chapter 8, as a stand-in for croutons in salads, or even as a pancake surrogate in the morning: Sauté in a pan until crispy, then top with fresh fruit and a light drizzle of maple syrup. Find halloumi at Middle Eastern grocers, Whole Foods Markets, or online at Igourmet.com.

Blackened Chicken & Mango Salad

Calorie for calorie, there is not a more nutrient-dense recipe in this book. This salad has it all: fiber, healthy fat, lean protein. Oh, and it's delicious!

You'll Need:

- 1 lb boneless, skinless chicken breasts
- 1 Tbsp chili powder
- Salt and black pepper to taste
- 1 ear corn, shucked and blanched in boiling water for 5 minutes
- 1 Tbsp honey
- ½ Tbsp chipotle pepper puree
- Juice of 1 lime
- 1 clove garlic, minced
- 3 Tbsp canola oil, plus more for coating the chicken
- 1 head Bibb lettuce
- 1 mango, peeled, pitted, and chopped
- 1 avocado, peeled, pitted, and chopped
- 1 cup black beans
- 1 small red onion, thinly sliced

How to Make It:

- Preheat a grill or grill pan over high heat. Coat the chicken breasts with canola oil then season with the chili powder and salt and pepper.

- Grill the chicken for about 5 minutes per side, until nicely charred, firm to the touch, and cooked through. At the same time, grill the ear of corn, turning, for 8 to 10 minutes, until the kernels are nicely browned. Let the chicken rest for 5 minutes before slicing into thin strips. Use a knife to separate the toasted corn kernels from the cob.

- Combine the honey, chipotle, lime juice, and garlic in a bowl. Slowly add the oil, whisking constantly to incorporate. Season with a few pinches of salt and pepper.

- In a large mixing bowl, combine the chicken, corn, lettuce, mango, avocado, black beans, and onion. Slowly add the dressing a tablespoon at a time, tossing, until it lightly coats all ingredients.

Makes 4 servings

SAVE-MONEY STRATEGY

Chicken breasts are excellent sources of lean protein and take well to the grill, but they typically cost up to twice as much as less-popular chicken thighs. Considering that a 4-ounce serving of thigh has just 6 calories more than the breast and is usually a good deal juicier, it's a perfect substitute for those looking to save a few dollars on dinner.

Per Serving:	
$3.69	440 calories 22 g fat (2.5 g saturated) 490 mg sodium

Grilled Calamari Salad

Squid is one of the most abundant forms of seafood in the global market, yet few Americans have ever enjoyed it in any other way than deep-fried. This recipe is proof positive that the grill produces better calamari than the fryer.

You'll Need:

- 1 lb squid, cleaned, tentacles reserved for another use
- ½ Tbsp peanut or canola oil
- Salt and black pepper to taste
- Juice of 1 lime
- 1 Tbsp fish sauce
- 1 Tbsp sugar
- ½ Tbsp chili garlic sauce (preferably sambal oelek)
- 4 cups watercress

- 1 small cucumber, peeled, seeded, and cut into matchsticks
- 1 medium tomato, chopped
- ½ red onion, very thinly sliced
- ¼ cup roasted peanuts

Watercress isn't always easy to find. Baby arugula, or even a few big handfuls of fresh basil leaves, can easily take its place here.

How to Make It:

- Preheat a grill over high heat. Toss the squid bodies with the oil and generously season with salt and lots of black pepper. When the grill is very hot, add the squid and grill for about 5 minutes, until lightly charred all over.

- Combine the lime juice, fish sauce, sugar, and chili sauce in a mixing bowl and whisk to blend. Slice the grilled squid into ½" rings. In a salad bowl, toss the squid, watercress, cucumber, tomato, onion, and peanuts with the dressing. Divide the salad among 4 plates.

Makes 4 servings

Master THE TECHNIQUE

Cooking calamari

Grilling squid ranks right up there next to tying your shoes and making your bed in the difficulty category, yet most people are terrified of the prospect. Purchase whole squid bodies (available fully cleaned, fresh or frozen, at any decent fish market or quality grocery store) and either grill them whole over high heat for no more than 5 minutes, or cut them into rings and sauté in olive oil for the same amount of time. When the calamari turns taught and firm, it's done.

Per Serving:
$3.04

220 calories
8 g fat (1.5 g saturated)
590 mg sodium

Tuna Niçoise

Tuna salad is a food industry euphemism for fish awash in a sea of mayo. But this French-inspired tuna salad is the real deal. Tucked within the leaves are vitamin-dense green beans, lycopene-loaded cherry tomatoes, and omega-3-packed tuna, providing a perfect balance of protein, fiber, and healthy fat.

You'll Need:

- 4 eggs
- Salt and black pepper to taste
- 1 lb red potatoes, quartered into ½" chunks
- ½ lb green beans, ends removed
- 2 tuna steaks (6 oz each)
- 16 cups baby mixed greens (8-oz bag)
- ¼ cup Honey-Dijon Vinaigrette (page 49)
- 1 pint cherry tomatoes, sliced in half
- ¼ cup chopped black or green olives (kalamata and Niçoise are best)

How to Make It:

- Bring a large pot of water to a gentle simmer. Carefully lower in the eggs. Cook for 8 minutes (this should yield creamy, not chalky, yolks) and remove with a slotted spoon. Transfer to a bowl of cold water.

- Salt the same pot of water and add the potatoes. Cook for 15 to 20 minutes, until tender but not mushy. Right before the potatoes are done, toss in the green beans and cook for 3 to 5 minutes, until crisp-tender. (You can cook the green beans in their own pot, but why waste the water and the energy?)Drain both vegetables together.

- Heat a grill or grill pan over high heat. Season the tuna with salt and pepper. When the grill is very hot, cook the tuna for 2 minutes per side, until browned on the outside but still pink in the middle. Remove, rest for a few minutes, then slice into thin strips.

- Peel the eggs and slice in half. Toss the greens with enough vinaigrette to just lightly cover. Divide among 4 chilled plates or bowls. In individual piles around the lettuce, arrange the potatoes, tomatoes, olives, green beans, and eggs. Top with slices of tuna and drizzle with extra vinaigrette, if you like.

Makes 4 servings

Per Serving:	
$5.17	350 calories 11 g fat (3 g saturated) 370 mg sodium

SAVE-MONEY STRATEGY

Fresh tuna is an amazing product that takes well to quick pan-searing and high-heat grilling. Trouble is, it can set you back up to $20 a pound. If you're looking to cut the cost of this dinner by about 60 percent (and speed things up a bit), ditch the fresh fish and reach for a high-quality can of tuna instead (our favorite brand is Ortiz from Spain). If you'd like to cut costs but still want to fire up the grill, use chicken breasts, thighs, or pork tenderloin in place of the tuna.

Watermelon-Tomato Salad

Nothing to grill here at all. In fact, this recipe is only marginally more challenging than pouring yourself a bowl of cereal. But the results speak for themselves: sweet, refreshing watermelon made all the better when paired with the acidity of tomato, the saltiness of feta, and the bite of basil. A lovely summer salad meant to go with anything you pull off the grill.

You'll Need:

- 8 cups cubed watermelon
- 2 lbs tomatoes, chopped into ½" chunks
- ½ cup feta cheese
- 1 cup chopped fresh basil
- 3 Tbsp olive oil
- 2 Tbsp balsamic vinegar
- Salt and black pepper to taste

How to Make It:

- In a large mixing bowl, combine the watermelon, tomatoes, feta, and basil. Drizzle in just enough olive oil and balsamic to lightly coat the ingredients and season with salt and pepper.

Makes 6 servings

This salad tastes—and looks—best with a mixture of heirloom tomatoes: red, yellow, green.

Upgrade

NUTRITIONAL

Watermelon might taste like dessert, but it's no nutritional slouch. Beyond containing a healthy dose of vitamins A and C, watermelon is also one of the produce world's greatest sources of lycopene. This potent antioxidant, found commonly in red foods like tomatoes and strawberries, has been found to provide a strong defense against a variety of cancers, including breast, prostate, lung, and others.

Per Serving:
$2.60

180 calories
10 g fat (3 g saturated)
375 mg sodium

CHAPTER **10**

VEGETABLES

How to GRILL any Vegetable

To maximize flavor and texture, every vegetable demands its own specific treatment. Here's your grilling game plan for getting the most out of everything veggie, from asparagus to zucchini.

Asparagus

HEAT: High
TIME: 10 minutes

Trim the bottom inch off the spears and toss in a good amount of olive oil, salt, and black pepper. To prevent asparagus from rolling and slipping through the cracks, line up groups of 6 to 8 spears and run skewers through the top and bottom ends. Grill over high heat, turning once, for 3 to 4 minutes per side, until lightly browned and just tender all the way through. Asparagus turns from tender to mushy very quickly, so watch them carefully.

Broccoli/ Cauliflower

HEAT: Low
TIME: 10 to 15 minutes

If you like your broccoli or cauliflower al dente, then simply break the heads into smaller florets, rub them with oil, skewer them, and grill over low heat for 15 minutes. But if you want the florets tender from head to stem, you'll need to blanch them first. Bring a pot of water to a boil, drop in large pieces of either (or both), and boil for 3 minutes. Drain and

rinse with cold water for 30 seconds. Grill over low heat on skewers, in a grilling basket, or directly on the grate until lightly charred and tender, about 10 minutes. Cauliflower is incredible rubbed in curry powder, while broccoli just needs olive oil before, grated Parmesan and lemon juice after.

Carrots

HEAT: Low
TIME: 20 minutes
Wash and peel the carrots; if the carrots are thick, halve them lengthwise. Toss with olive oil, salt, and pepper (cumin and coriander are also excellent carrot spices). Place directly on the grate and grill over low heat for about 20 minutes. Grilled carrots take well to sauces: Try Barbecued Carrots (page 334), or brush on bottled teriyaki or hoisin at the end of grilling. Save brushing with sauce for the last 10 minutes of cooking,

otherwise a sugary sauce will burn before the carrots are tender.

Eggplant

HEAT: High
TIME: 8 to 10 minutes for slices, 15 minutes for whole eggplant
Whether using smaller Japanese eggplant or darker, larger Italian eggplant, slice the vegetable into ½"-thick rounds, coat with a light film of oil, and season with salt and pepper. Grill over high heat for 4 to 5 minutes per side, until lightly charred and softened. For dips and purees, grill eggplant whole for about 15 minutes, until the skin is charred and the flesh is very soft.

Mushrooms

HEAT: Medium-high
TIME: 8 to 12 minutes
While mushrooms have a high water content, they can dry out if grilled too long, so it's best to grill

them over a medium-high flame until lightly charred and just cooked through, about 8 minutes for shiitake caps, 12 minutes for whole portobellos. If you want to grill smaller button or cremini mushrooms, run a skewer lengthwise through the caps. Or make individual mushroom packets by seasoning ½" chunks of mushrooms with olive oil, chopped garlic, salt, and pepper and enclosing in foil packets, then grilling for 10 minutes.

Onions

HEAT: Medium
TIME: 6 to 10 minutes
Onion rings can go directly on the grill, but you're bound to lose at least a quarter of your product to the fire. Instead, peel the onions and slice into ¼"-thick pieces. Skewer with toothpicks to secure the slices and grill over medium heat for 3 to

4 minutes per side, until soft and browned. If you want a deeply caramelized onion, turn the heat down and grill the onions for up to 10 minutes per side.

Peppers

HEAT: Medium
TIME: 10 minutes for quarters, 25 minutes for whole peppers

If you plan on peeling the peppers, it's best to place whole peppers on the grill and close the lid. If you want chunks of grilled peppers for sandwiches or fajitas, cut whole peppers into quarters, removing the stem, seeds, and white, flavorless ribs inside. Grill whole peppers in a covered grill over medium heat, turning once or twice, for about 25 minutes, until the skin is black and blistered (peel off the skin before eating). Grill pepper quarters or pieces, turning, for about 5 minutes per side.

Potatoes

HEAT: Medium
TIME: 15 minutes for wedges or slices, 30 to 40 minutes for whole potatoes

Grilled potatoes are best when parboiled, then finished on the grate. Cook them in a large pot of boiling water until just tender, about 10 minutes, then drain. Cut into slices or wedges and rub with oil, salt, and pepper. Grill over medium heat, turning, for about 15 minutes, until brown and crispy all over. For an incredible "baked" grilled potato, prick whole russet potatoes with a fork, wrap in foil, and place directly in the hot embers of a charcoal fire (or on the grate of a gas grill). Grill, rotating them 45 degrees every 10 minutes or so, for 40 minutes, until very tender.

Tomatoes

HEAT: High
TIME: 5 to 10 minutes

The sweet and smoky intensity of a grilled tomato plays great as a side dish to meat, just as it forms a powerful base for sauces, soups, and salsas. Halve the tomatoes, rub with oil, and place cut side down on the grate. Grill over high heat for 5 minutes, until caramelized. Serve as is, or, if building a sauce or salsa, flip the tomatoes and continue grilling for another 5 minutes, until the skins blister. Peel off the skins and pulverize.

Zucchini

HEAT: High
TIME: 6 to 8 minutes

You'll lose tiny rounds through the grates, so it's best to slice zucchini lengthwise into ¼"-thick planks. Lay them at a 45-degree angle across the grate to maximize caramelization. Grill over high heat, turning, for 6 to 8 minutes. The same rules apply for summer squash.

Spicy Steak Fries

The number one most consumed vegetable in America is the french fry, a woeful reality for a populace already starved for something green in its diet. But the potatoes themselves (a vegetable rife with powerful antioxidants) aren't to blame; it's the cauldron of bubbling fat. We should call this recipe Freedom Fries, since these spicy, crispy grilled potatoes liberate you from the nutritional tyranny of the oil-soaked spud. Serve these next to a juicy steak and a glass of red wine for an all-world dinner.

You'll Need:

- **2** large russet potatoes, thoroughly washed

Salt to taste

- **1** Tbsp canola oil
- **1** tsp smoked paprika
- **1** tsp chili powder
- **½** tsp garlic powder
- **⅛** tsp cayenne pepper
- **¾** tsp salt
- **½** tsp black pepper

How to Make It:

- Place the potatoes in a pot, cover with water, and season with salt. Cook over high heat for 12 to 15 minutes, until tender but still firm. Drain.

- Preheat a grill over medium heat. When the potatoes are cool enough to handle, cut each lengthwise into 8 wedges. Toss with the oil and all the spices. Place the potato wedges on the grill and cook, turning once, for about 12 minutes, until brown and crispy.

SAUCE *selector*

What's a fry without something to dunk it in? Here are five quick DIY sauces you can serve alongside these grilled spuds:

- Ketchup spiked with curry powder, smoked paprika, or chipotle peppers
- Olive oil mayonnaise cut with lemon, minced garlic, and chopped fresh parsley
- Greek yogurt mixed with sriracha hot sauce, garlic, and lime juice
- Peanut Sauce (page 48)
- Chimichurri (page 47)

Per Serving:
$0.53

180 calories
4 g fat (0.5 g saturated)
450 mg sodium

Grilled Corn
with Miso Butter

One of the great pleasures of summer is eating candy-sweet fresh corn any way you can get it. That pleasure is intensified threefold by the transformative powers of the grill, which teases out every last milligram of natural sugars locked inside those kernels. Remember: Just like meat or fish, corn can be overcooked, turning from sweet and juicy to dry and chewy in a flash. Allowing the corn to steam inside the husks first helps cut the risk substantially.

You'll Need:

4 ears corn

¼ cup (½ stick) butter, softened at room temperature

¼ cup white (shiro) miso

How to Make It:

- Peel the corn husks back, being careful so they remain attached to the base of the cobs, and remove the silk inside. Re-cover the ears with the husks and soak in cold water for 5 minutes.

- Mix together the butter and miso until they form a uniform spread. Set aside.

- Preheat a grill or grill pan over medium heat. Grill the corn for 10 minutes, turning a quarter-turn every few minutes. Peel back the husks and place the corn back on the grill. Cook, turning occasionally, for about 5 minutes, until the kernels are nicely browned. Slather each cob with the miso butter.

Makes 4 servings

MEAL MULTIPLIER

Other delicious ways to anoint a cob of grilled corn:

- Drizzle with Chimichurri (page 47).
- Brush with mayonnaise thinned with lime juice, then top with chili powder and grated Parmesan.
- Brush with softened butter mixed with chopped cilantro, garlic, and minced jalapeño.

Per Serving:
$0.78

190 calories
11 g fat (5 g saturated)
340 mg sodium

Grilled Asparagus
with Romesco

Grilled asparagus with a drizzle of olive oil, a shake of salt, and a squeeze of lemon represents one of the simplest and most delicious expressions of a vegetable's potential, especially when done in the early months of spring when asparagus is sweet and tender. But we thought we'd take it one small step further, adding to the mix the Spanish sauce called romesco. Made from roasted peppers and toasted almonds, it brings a sweet and smoky dimension to asparagus—and, for that matter, anything savory you pull from the grill. One dip and you'll be slayed.

You'll Need:

1 bunch asparagus, woody ends removed

2 Tbsp olive oil

Salt and black pepper to taste

Romesco (page 50)

How to Make It:

• Preheat a grill or grill pan over medium heat. Toss the asparagus with the olive oil and salt and pepper. Grill, turning once midway through, for about 8 minutes, until lightly charred and just tender (but not mushy!). If you're serving this as an appetizer, place the asparagus on a large platter with the romesco in the center for dipping. If intended as a side with dinner, divide the asparagus among 4 plates and pass the romesco at the table.

Makes 4 servings

Per Serving:	180 calories
$1.49	11 g fat (1.5 g saturated)
	380 mg sodium

Blackened Cauliflower Steaks
with Worcestershire Aioli

We're unabashed fanatics of blackened food, since the quick and easy blackening technique brings huge flavors to meat and fish without tacking on calories (in fact, if anything, the antioxidant-rich spices boost the overall nutritional value of blackened food). But why limit the fun to fish and fowl? Hearty vegetables like portobello caps, zucchini planks, and, above all, cauliflower, are perfect for the blackening treatment.

You'll Need:

- 2 Tbsp olive oil mayonnaise
- Juice of ½ lemon
- 2 tsp Worcestershire sauce
- 1 clove garlic, minced
- 1 head cauliflower
- ½ Tbsp canola oil
- 1 Tbsp Magic Blackening Rub (page 51, or store-bought blackening seasoning)

How to Make It:

- Preheat a grill or grill pan over medium heat. For the aioli, combine the mayonnaise, lemon juice, Worcestershire, and garlic and reserve.

- Cut away the green branches from the cauliflower, but leave the stem fully intact (it will help hold the steaks together). Remove the last inch from each side of the cauliflower head so that you're working with only the most substantial part (save those florets for another use). Cut the cauliflower into four ½"-thick steaks. Drizzle the steaks lightly with the oil, and cover both sides of each with the blackening seasoning.

- Grill the steaks for 4 to 5 minutes per side, until the spices blacken and the cauliflower is tender all the way through. Serve with the aioli drizzled on top.

Makes 4 servings

Per Serving:
$0.56

100 calories
5 g fat (0.5 g saturated)
290 mg sodium

Brussels & Bacon

Brussels sprouts used to be the vegetable that nobody wanted to eat, the one kids and adults alike pushed around on their plates until fate or a hungry animal under the table intervened. But recent years have seen brussels become one of the best-selling vegetables in the restaurant world, an easy way for chefs at trendy restaurants to stretch profit margins. Why the big change? Smart cooks stopped boiling and steaming brussels and started using high-heat cooking techniques to bring out the best in the vegetable. They also discovered pork fat does a lot to make a sprout more sexy. This recipe honors both advancements.

You'll Need:

1 lb brussels sprouts, bottoms removed

Olive oil for coating

Salt and black pepper to taste

4 strips thick-cut bacon, cut into ¾" pieces

4 metal skewers, or wooden skewers soaked in water for 30 minutes

1 Tbsp maple syrup

How to Make It:

- Bring a pot of water to a boil. Add the brussels sprouts and cook for about 7 minutes, until barely tender. Drain. Toss with enough olive oil to lightly coat and season with salt and pepper.

- Preheat a grill or grill pan over medium heat. Thread the brussels and bacon onto the skewers, alternating between the two. Grill, turning once, for about 5 minutes per side, until the sprouts have browned and the bacon is cooked through and crispy. Use a spoon to drizzle a very light stream of maple syrup over each skewer before serving.

Makes 4 servings

Per Serving:
$1.18

260 calories
21 g fat (6 g saturated)
340 mg sodium

Miso Tofu Bowls

Sometimes the best way to approach cooking tofu and vegetables is to think, "What would a carnivore do?" That's why we cut tofu into thick steaks and marinate it in a powerful miso sauce that doubles as a dressing for the finished product. This is tofu for vegetarians and meateaters alike.

You'll Need:

- ¼ cup white miso
- ¼ cup sugar
- 2 Tbsp soy sauce
- 2 Tbsp rice wine vinegar
- ¼ cup water
- 2 cloves garlic, minced
- 2 Tbsp minced ginger
- 1 block firm tofu (12 oz), sliced into ¼"-thick steaks
- 1 head broccoli, florets broken into 1" pieces
- Oil for coating
- Salt and black pepper to taste
- Metal skewers, or wooden skewers soaked in water for 30 minutes
- 4 cups cooked brown rice
- Toasted sesame seeds for garnish

How to Make It:

- Combine the miso, sugar, soy sauce, vinegar, water, garlic, and ginger in a mixing bowl and whisk until smooth. Place the tofu steaks in a sealable plastic bag and pour the miso marinade over the top. Seal the bag and marinate in the refrigerator for at least 1 hour (or up to 1 day).

- Preheat a grill or grill pan over medium heat. Toss the broccoli with the oil and season with salt and pepper. Thread the broccoli onto the skewers, running the sharp point through each stalk to hold it in place.

- Remove the tofu from the bag, reserving the marinade. Grill the tofu, turning once, for about 10 minutes, until caramelized and lightly crisp on the outside. Cook the broccoli, turning, for about 12 minutes, until the florets are browned and the stalks have softened.

- Divide the rice among 4 bowls. Top with the tofu and broccoli, then drizzle some of the leftover marinade over the top. Garnish with sesame seeds.

Makes 4 servings

Per Serving:
$1.74

390 calories
7 g fat (1 g saturated)
820 mg sodium

Tackling tofu

Grilled tofu, when done properly, can satisfy even the most relentless carnivore. That means cooking it over a medium flame until the outside is crispy and the center warm and creamy. It also means starting with a powerful marinade, which can be brushed on during or after cooking as well. Try one of these other options as an alternative to the miso:

- Equal parts Asian-style chili sauce such as sriracha, lime juice, and honey
- Horseradish Steak Sauce (page 198)
- Rub with Blackening Rub (page 51) and top with Smoky Aioli (page 242)

Grilled Portobellos
with Tomato and Mozzarella

Ah, the portobello mushroom, the one vegetable nearly every backyard chef has turned to at least once in his career. It can be a satisfying alternative to a steak, but it nearly always emerges from the grill as an overcooked afterthought, a half-hearted attempt to appease the meatless crowd. With a bit of finesse, though, the portobello's potential is limitless, especially when that finesse involves filling its generous cap with one of the culinary world's greatest triumvirates: tomatoes, basil, and mozzarella.

You'll Need:

- 4 portobello mushrooms, cleaned, stems removed
- 1 Tbsp olive oil
- 2 Tbsp balsamic vinegar
- Salt and black pepper to taste
- 2 medium tomatoes, chopped
- ¾ cup chopped fresh mozzarella
- 2 Tbsp prepared pesto

How to Make It:

- Preheat a grill over medium-low heat. Use a spoon to lightly scrape away some of the gills on the underside of the mushroom caps (this will create extra space for the filling). Place the mushrooms in a shallow baking dish, drizzle with the olive oil and balsamic vinegar, and season with salt and pepper. Combine the tomatoes, mozzarella, and pesto in a mixing bowl.

- Grill the portobellos, gill side down, for 2 minutes, then flip and fill each cap with the tomato mixture. Close the grill and grill for another 8 to 10 minutes, until the mushrooms are soft and lightly charred and the mozzarella has melted.

Makes 4 servings

MEAL MULTIPLIER

Three more fillings to reinvent the stuffed mushroom:

- Toasted fresh bread crumbs mixed with fresh rosemary, garlic, and crumbled goat cheese
- Fresh chicken or turkey sausage sautéed with onions, minced garlic, and a ladle of your favorite bottled tomato sauce
- Grilled shrimp or chicken tossed with olives, capers, roasted red peppers, and feta cheese

Per Serving:
$1.92

270 calories
17 g fat (7 g saturated)
345 mg sodium

Stuffed Peppers

Oven-baked stuffed peppers have long been a simple, healthy solution to the dinner dilemma. But why use an oven when you can get better results with a grill? With the top closed, the peppers soften and caramelize and absorb those toasty notes of a real fire. No empty carb fillers here, just the pure flavors of sautéed spinach, sundried tomatoes, and chicken sausage.

You'll Need:

- 1 Tbsp olive oil
- ½ medium onion, minced
- 2 cloves garlic, minced
- 2 links uncooked chicken sausage, casings removed
- 1 bag (10 oz) frozen spinach, thawed
- 2 Tbsp chopped oil-packed sundried tomatoes
- ½ cup crumbled feta cheese
- Salt and black pepper to taste
- 4 large red, yellow, or green bell peppers

Dry sundried tomatoes are considerably cheaper, but they need to be reconstituted in warm water for 15 minutes before chopping.

How to Make It:

- Heat the olive oil in a large skillet or sauté pan over medium heat. Add the onion and garlic and cook until soft, about 3 minutes. Add the sausage and continue cooking for about 5 minutes, until the fat has rendered out and the meat is cooked through. Drain any excess fat. Stir in the spinach and sundried tomatoes and cook for another 3 minutes, until the tomatoes are softened and the spinach is wilted. Remove from heat, stir in the feta, and season with salt and pepper.

- Preheat a grill over medium-low heat. Carefully remove the tops of the peppers so the stems are still intact. Remove the seeds from inside. Distribute the stuffing among the peppers, packing them tight so that the stuffing doesn't fall out during cooking. Place the tops of the peppers back on, securing them with toothpicks.

- Place the peppers on the grill, cut side up. Close the grill and cook for about 10 minutes, until the bottoms are lightly charred and softened. Carefully place the peppers on their sides and cook, turning occasionally, for another 10 minutes, until the flesh is tender but the peppers still hold their shape.

Makes 4 servings

Per Serving:
$3.38

240 calories
11 g fat (4.5 g saturated)
620 mg sodium

Onion-Stuffed Onions

No vegetable is more vital to everyday cooking than the onion, the base of countless sauces, stocks, roasts, and stir-fries. For all the work the onion puts in as a selfless supporting actor, it rarely takes on a leading role. This recipe is all about the onion, a tribute to its versatility and overall deliciousness. Slow-cooked onions are combined with mushrooms, stock, and cheese, then stuffed into an onion and grilled. It's like eating French onion soup infused with the smoke of the grill and served inside a caramelized-onion bowl.

You'll Need:

- **6 medium red onions**
- **1 Tbsp butter**
- **Salt and black pepper to taste**
- **¼ lb button mushrooms, chopped**
- **¾ cup red wine**
- **¾ cup chicken stock**
- **1 cup shredded reduced-fat Swiss cheese**
- **1 tsp chopped fresh rosemary**
- **4 Tbsp dried bread crumbs**

How to Make It:

- Use a paring knife and a spoon to scoop out the centers of 4 of the 6 onions, leaving the base and a few outer layers of onion intact. Dice the scooped-out onions and the remaining 2 onions.

- Heat the butter in a saucepan over medium heat. Add the diced onions and a pinch of salt and cook, stirring occasionally, for 5 minutes, until softened and translucent. Add the mushrooms and continue cooking for another 5 minutes. Stir in the wine and stock and simmer for about 15 minutes, until the liquid has thickened around the onions. Remove the pan from the heat and stir in the cheese, rosemary, and a generous amount of pepper.

- Preheat a grill over medium-low heat. Fill the 4 onion shells with the onion mixture and top with the bread crumbs. Place on the grill, close the lid, and grill for about 20 minutes, until the onion shells are very soft but still hold their shape.

Makes 4 servings

Per Serving:	
$1.66	270 calories 11 g fat (7 g saturated) 350 mg sodium

Baby Artichokes
with Mint Vinaigrette

Regular artichokes require more prep work than some cooks at home are willing to do. Baby artichokes, on the other hand, are tender enough that they can basically be cooked as is, with minimal peeling and trimming. That makes them perfect candidates for the grill, where a steady medium flame turns the artichoke hearts soft and sweet and the outer petals beautifully crisp. The dressing here works like a marinade in reverse, suffusing the artichokes with friendly flavors *after* the cooking process.

You'll Need:

- 12 baby artichokes
- 3 Tbsp olive oil, plus more for coating the artichokes
- Salt and black pepper to taste
- Juice of 1 lemon
- ¼ cup chopped fresh mint
- 2 cloves garlic, finely minced
- ¼ tsp red pepper flakes

How to Make It:

- Preheat a grill over medium heat. Split the artichokes in half and peel off the first layer of tough outer layers of leaves. Drizzle with enough olive oil to coat, then season with salt and black pepper. Grill the artichokes, cut side down, for about 10 minutes, until lightly charred and soft. Flip and grill for another 8 to 10 minutes, until tender all the way through.

- Peel off any burnt dark outer leaves. Combine the artichokes with the 3 tablespoons olive oil, lemon juice, mint, garlic, and red pepper in a large mixing bowl. Serve immediately, or allow to sit and marinate for an hour or two before serving.

Makes 4 servings

Master
THE
TECHNIQUE

Prepping artichokes

Can't find baby artichokes in your local market? You can follow the recipe with normal artichokes, only you'll need to prep them more carefully. This means trimming the spiky half-inch top of the vegetable, removing a few outside layers of leaves, then splitting them in half and scooping out the purple choke with a spoon. Grill them for 25 to 30 minutes, using low heat to ensure they'll cook all the way through before burning.

Per Serving:
$1.56

170 calories
10 g fat (1.5 g saturated)
320 mg sodium

Crispy Polenta

Unless you use a stick of butter to fatten it up, boiled cornmeal can make for a drab side dish. But polenta has a second life as a firm, grilled triangle that can be flavored or topped however you like. Pour soft, cooked polenta into a shallow dish, allow it to firm up, then cut it into triangles. Cooked on the grill until hot and crisp, polenta makes a great side to Grilled Whole Fish (page 220) and Chicken Under a Brick (page 158), but it also works beautifully as a substitute for bread in crostini and bruschetta recipes.

You'll Need:

1 cup dried polenta

2 Tbsp butter

¼ cup grated Parmesan

2 tsp chopped fresh rosemary

Salt and black pepper to taste

How to Make It:

- Prepare the polenta according to package instructions, stirring in the butter, Parmesan, and rosemary at the last moment. Season with salt and pepper.

- Pour the polenta into a shallow 8" x 8" square or 11" x 7" rectangular dish, using a spatula to spread it out evenly, as if making a cake. The polenta should come about ½" up the sides of the dish. Leave on the countertop or in the refrigerator until it cools and hardens, at least 30 minutes. (This step can be done a day or two ahead of time.)

- Preheat a grill or grill pan over medium heat. Remove the polenta from the dish in one piece. Cut into triangles, squares, or whatever shape you prefer. Grill the polenta pieces, turning, for about 5 minutes per side, until crisp and grill marks have developed on both sides.

Makes 6 servings

$$(\text{\Pisymbol{}}+\text{I})^2$$

MEAL MULTIPLIER

Use one of these toppings to punch up the potential of grilled polenta.

- Chopped tomatoes, garlic, basil, and olive oil
- Grilled Japanese eggplant tossed with mint, red pepper flakes, olive oil, and vinegar
- Ricotta cheese and roasted red peppers
- Any of the crostini recipes in Chapter 8

Per Serving:
$0.37

150 calories
6 g fat (3 g saturated)
380 mg sodium

140 calories
6 g fat
(1.5 g saturated)
415 mg sodium

Barbecued Carrots

Sometimes it's best to pretend your vegetables are meat. This recipe treats the orange root vegetable just like a pork shoulder or a chicken drumstick: First, you coat the carrots in a spice rub, then you glaze them with a sweet-spicy barbecue sauce until the centers are soft and the edges crisp and caramelized. Beats boiling, steaming, or sautéing any day. Test out the same treatment on any firm root vegetables: turnips, parsnips, sweet potatoes.

You'll Need:

8 medium carrots, peeled and cut in half lengthwise

1 Tbsp olive oil

½ Tbsp All-Purpose Barbecue Rub (page 50)

½ cup Classic Barbecue Sauce (page 45)

How to Make It:

● Preheat a grill over medium heat. Toss the carrots with the olive oil and the rub. When the grill is hot, add the carrots and grill, turning occasionally, for 10 to 15 minutes (depending on the size of your carrots), until the outsides are deeply browned and the flesh is tender throughout. In the final 5 minutes of cooking, use a brush to continuously glaze the carrots with the sauce.

Makes 4 servings

130 calories
8 g fat
(1 g saturated)
260 mg sodium

Crack Kale

If you're wondering why it's called Crack Kale, you won't be by the time you finish making this recipe. Cooked slow over a low flame, the water inside the kale evaporates as the stems and leaves turn crispy like potato chips.

You'll Need:

1 bunch kale, bottom 2" of stems removed

2 Tbsp olive oil

Coarse sea salt and black pepper to taste

How to Make It:

- Preheat a grill over low heat. Toss the kale with the olive oil, salt, and pepper. Spread out over the grill grate, being sure that the kale doesn't overlap. Cook, turning once midway through, until the kale darkens and turns very crispy, about 15 minutes total. Sprinkle with more sea salt.

Makes 4 servings

110 calories
3 g fat
(0.5 g saturated)
340 mg sodium

Miso-Glazed Eggplant

Eggplant handled the wrong way can turn into a sponge for salt and oil, but when cooked over high heat on a roaring grill, the flesh turns sweet and smoky without absorbing excess fat or salt. Slender, light purple Japanese eggplant (smaller and less bitter than the dark Italian orbs more commonly available in American supermarkets) can be found in markets like Whole Foods or Asian markets (though regular eggplant will work in a pinch). The sweet-salty miso paste, a traditional sauce used in Japanese kitchens, caramelizes on the surface of the eggplant slices, turning them into little coins of vegetable candy.

You'll Need:

- 2 Tbsp white (shiro) miso
- 1 Tbsp honey
- 1 Tbsp peanut, vegetable, or canola oil
- ½ Tbsp rice wine vinegar
- ½ Tbsp soy sauce
- 2 medium Japanese eggplant, cut into ⅓"-thick slices

How to Make It:

- Preheat a grill or grill pan over medium heat.

- Combine the miso, honey, oil, vinegar, and soy sauce in a small bowl. Lay the eggplant slices on a baking sheet and brush the tops with the miso mixture. Place on the grill, miso side down, and grill for 3 to 4 minutes, until nicely caramelized. Brush the tops with the miso mixture, flip, and cook for another 3 to 4 minutes, until the miso has formed a deep brown crust on the eggplant. Brush one last time with the mixture before serving.

Makes 4 servings

Cole Slaw

130 calories
8 g fat
(1 g saturated)
200 mg sodium

Crunchy, cool, and suffused with vinegar tang, this slaw has nothing to do with those soupy, mayo-drenched, oversweetened versions you find in most supermarket deli cases. Great as a side, but also perfect for topping sandwiches.

You'll Need:

- 2 Tbsp Dijon mustard
- 2 Tbsp mayonnaise
- 2 Tbsp vinegar (red wine, white wine, or cider)
- 2 Tbsp canola oil

Salt and black pepper to taste

- ½ head green cabbage, very thinly sliced
- ½ head red cabbage, very thinly sliced
- 3 carrots, cut into thin strips
- 1 tsp fennel seeds

Pickled Jalapeños

How to Make It:

- Mix the mustard, mayonnaise and vinegar in a bowl. Slowly whisk in the oil. Season with salt and pepper.

- Combine the cabbages, carrots, fennel seeds, jalapeños (if using), and dressing in a large bowl. Toss so that everything is evenly coated and season with more salt and pepper.

Makes 6 servings

Grilled Potato Salad

250 calories
12 g fat
(2.5 g saturated)
460 mg sodium

There will always be a time for a mayo-heavy potato salad, calories be damned, but we're firm believers that the standard formula could use some readjustment. As rich as it sounds, the use of an olive oil dressing makes this salad a good deal healthier than the standard.

You'll Need:

- 2 lb medium Yukon gold potatoes
- 2 medium yellow onions, sliced into ¼"-thick rings and skewered with toothpicks
- ¼ cup white or red wine vinegar
- 1 Tbsp Dijon mustard
- ½ Tbsp sugar

- ¼ cup olive oil, plus more for coating the potatoes and onions

Salt and black pepper to taste

- 4 strips bacon, cooked and crumbled
- ½ cup crumbled blue cheese
- ½ cup chopped fresh parsley

Cut 75 calories per serving by eliminating the bacon and blue cheese. Even without these two, it's still a superlative potato salad.

How to Make It:

- Place the potatoes in a large saucepan of water and season with a few pinches of salt. Bring to a boil over high heat and cook for about 15 minutes, until the potatoes are just tender. Drain and slice into ¼"-thick disks.

- Preheat a grill over medium-high heat. Drizzle the potatoes and the onion slices with enough olive oil to coat. Grill the potatoes for about 5 minutes per side, until the surface is browned and crisp. At the same time, grill the onions for about 4 minutes per side, until lightly caramelized and soft.

- Combine the vinegar, mustard, and sugar. Whisk in the ¼ cup olive oil. Season with salt and pepper. Combine the potatoes, onions, bacon, blue cheese, and parsley in a large mixing bowl. Toss with the dressing.

Makes 6 servings

140 calories
3 g fat
(0.5 g saturated)
210 mg sodium

Sweet & Sour Butternut Squash

"Sweet and sour" conjures images of mediocre Chinese takeout, but most food cultures across the world play with the combination in some way or another. This particular version comes from the Italian love of agrodolce: the sweetness from honey, the sour from red wine vinegar, plus a bit of garlic, rosemary, and red pepper to liven it all up. Tossed with hot, caramelized pieces of butternut squash, it creates an incredible side dish.

You'll Need:

¼ cup red wine vinegar

2 Tbsp honey

2 cloves garlic, minced

1 tsp chopped fresh rosemary

Pinch red pepper flakes

1 medium butternut squash, peeled and cut into ⅓"-thick slices

Olive oil for coating the squash

Salt and black pepper to taste

How to Make It:

● Preheat a grill or grill pan over medium heat. Bring the vinegar, honey, garlic, rosemary, and red pepper flakes to a simmer in a small saucepan. Simmer for 5 minutes, until the mixture is thick and syrupy.

● Toss the squash with enough olive oil to coat and season with salt and black pepper. Grill the squash, turning, for 12 to 15 minutes, until lightly browned on both sides and soft and tender throughout. Toss with the vinegar-honey syrup.

Makes 4 to 6 servings

Grilled Vegetable Salad

This amazingly simple, satisfying grilled salad (called escalivada) hails from Catalonia, where eggplant, onion, and red pepper are the most common faces in vegetable stands and supermarkets. But the idea can work with any combination of vegetables: zucchini, asparagus, fennel, carrots, squash, and more. It's about the interplay of smoke and the different types of natural sweetness found in slow-cooked vegetables. Cook them until soft, dress with a bit of vinegar, good olive oil, and coarse salt, and eat with gusto.

You'll Need:

- 1 **medium eggplant**
- 2 **medium yellow onions, halved**
- 2 **red bell peppers**
- 2 **Tbsp olive oil, plus more for coating the vegetables**
- 1 **Tbsp sherry vinegar or red wine vinegar**
- 2 **cloves garlic, minced**

Coarse sea salt

How to Make It:

- Preheat a grill over medium heat. Drizzle the eggplant, onions, and bell peppers with enough olive oil to lightly coat. Grill, turning the vegetables occasionally, for about 20 minutes, until the outsides of the vegetables pick up a deep char and the insides are completely soft.

- Place the eggplant and peppers in a large bowl and cover with plastic wrap. Let steam for 5 minutes, which will help when stripping off the charred skin. Remove any of the heavily charred exterior pieces of the onions. Peel the eggplant and bell peppers. Cut the vegetables into thin strips (for the onions, separating the individual petals should suffice). On a large serving plate, organize each vegetable into individual piles so that they look like the stripes on a flag. Sprinkle with the 2 tablespoons olive oil, the vinegar, garlic, and salt.

Makes 4 servings

Asian Slaw

Most coleslaws turn out to be a bowl of mayonnaise dressed with a bit of cabbage, a formula for a nutrition disaster—not to mention a tide of drab, palate-numbing fat. Our Eastern-inspired take on the Western classic uses the big flavors of lime, sesame, and chili sauce to phase out the reliance on mayo, making for both a lighter and more flavorful slaw that goes as well on sandwiches as it does by itself.

You'll Need:

Juice of 1 lime

1 Tbsp olive oil
mayonnaise

1 Tbsp sugar

1 tsp Asian-style chili
sauce like sriracha

1 tsp sesame oil

8 cups shredded
cabbage (preferably
a mix of purple and
napa cabbage)

1 large carrot, peeled
and grated

1 Tbsp sesame seeds

How to Make It:

- In a large salad bowl, mix together the lime juice, mayonnaise, sugar, chili sauce, and sesame oil. Add the cabbage, carrots, and sesame seeds and toss to combine. Season with salt and pepper.

Makes 4 to 6 servings

Cowboy Beans

170 calories
3 g fat
(1 g saturated)
570 mg sodium

Baked beans, both the type that come in cans and those that come from the kitchens of barbecue shacks, are usually one step away from candy, bombed as they are with brown sugar, molasses, and honey. Too bad, since beans really are A-list eats. To preserve their health status and maximize deliciousness, we mitigate the sugar surge and build flavor instead with a few of our all-time favorite foods: cayenne, beer, and bacon.

You'll Need:

- 4 **strips bacon, chopped into small pieces**
- 1 **medium onion, minced**
- 2 **cloves garlic, minced**
- 1 **cup dark beer**
- 2 **cans (16 oz each) pinto beans, rinsed and drained**
- ¼ **cup ketchup**
- 1 **Tbsp chili powder**
- 1 **Tbsp brown sugar**

Pinch of cayenne pepper

How to Make It:

- Heat a large pot or saucepan over medium heat. Add the bacon and cook until it's just turning crispy, 3 to 5 minutes. Add the onion and garlic and sauté until translucent, another 3 minutes. Stir in the beer, beans, ketchup, chili powder, brown sugar, and cayenne. Simmer until the sauce thickens and clings to the beans, about 15 minutes.

Makes 6 servings

Grilled Cauliflower with Fish Sauce Vinaigrette

100 calories
3 g fat
(0.5 g saturated)
435 mg sodium

In most American households, cauliflower is eaten in one of two ways: steamed or boiled. Too bad, since besides being boring ways to eat most vegetables, both methods actually concentrate cauliflower's sulfurous undertones. Grilling mellows the gases and teases out cauliflower's natural sugars, creating something infinitely more enjoyable than the soggy florets most people are accustomed to. Tack on a punchy dressing and suddenly the prospect of eating your veggies is looking a whole lot more enjoyable.

You'll Need:

- ¼ **cup warm water**
- 1 **Tbsp sugar**
- ¼ **cup fish sauce**
- **Juice of 1 lime**
- **12–15 fresh mint leaves, chopped**
- 1 **small red chile pepper, minced**
- 1 **head cauliflower, cut into large pieces**
- 1 **Tbsp canola, vegetable, or peanut oil**
- **Salt and black pepper to taste**

How to Make It:

- Combine the water and sugar in a small mixing bowl and stir to dissolve the sugar. Add the fish sauce, lime juice, mint, and minced chile. Reserve.

- Preheat a grill or grill pan over medium heat. Toss the cauliflower with the oil and season with salt and pepper.

Place the florets in a vegetable grill basket (or directly on the grate) and grill, turning occasionally, for 12 to 15 minutes, until the cauliflower is browned on the outside and just tender all the way through. Toss in a large mixing bowl with the vinaigrette.

Makes 4 servings

GRILL
THIS
~~NOT~~
THAT!

DESSERTS

Sundae Matrix

The grill does magical things to fruit, softening its flesh, concentrating its natural sweetness, and transforming it into something that feels like dessert on its own. Trick it out with ice cream and a few toppings and you have a world-class sundae on your hands. As decadent as it may seem, a scoop of ice cream combined with fresh fruit and a few toppings comes in under 300 calories—pretty impressive considering how indulgent these sundaes taste.

CHOOSE A FRUIT

Other stone fruits like apricots and plums work just as well on the grill.

PINEAPPLE

PEACHES

CHOOSE AN ICE CREAM

As always, our ice cream brand of choice is Breyers, which makes low-calorie products with a minimum number of ingredients. Using Breyers instead of a "premium" brand like Häagen-Dazs or Ben & Jerry's will save you nearly 150 calories per scoop.

VANILLA

BUTTER PECAN

CHOOSE A TOPPING

A hot shot of concentrated espresso is best, but even a pour of good strong coffee can be an excellent—and unexpected—addition to a sundae. Both provide a huge rush of virtually calorie-free antioxidants.

CHOCOLATE SYRUP

ESPRESSO

Four Quick Recipes

Mix and match fruit, ice cream, and add-ons however you like; there are literally hundreds of different paths to deliciousness. These four here just happen to be among our favorites.

ADD SOME CRUNCH

CHOPPED ROASTED PEANUTS

CRUSHED WALNUTS

AFFOGATO
Grilled figs + vanilla ice cream + espresso + chocolate-covered espresso beans

PEACHES AND CREAM
Grilled peaches + butter pecan ice cream + Sauternes + granola

BANANA

Figs should be ripe, but firm. Too soft and they won't hold their shape on the grill.

FIGS

Any flavor of ice cream will work, as long as it matches well with the fruit you're grilling. Chocolate and banana? Perfect!

CHOCOLATE

COCONUT

A splash of Vin Santo, port, or Sauternes adds a sophisticated touch to a sundae.

DULCE DE LECHE

SWEET WINE

CHOCOLATE-COVERED ESPRESSO BEANS

GRANOLA

PIÑA COLADA
Pineapple + coconut ice cream + dulce de leche + coconut flakes

THE ELVIS
Grilled banana + peanut butter ice cream + chocolate sauce + crushed peanuts

Sundae Basics

Rule 1
Grill fruit with the same attentiveness with which you grill steak. You don't want to blast the fruit so the heat melts it into mush. You want fruit that is caramelized and soft on the outside, but with a bit of bite in the center. For most fruit, that means 10 minutes tops on the grill.

Rule 2
The interplay of hot and cold is what makes this dessert so special. Have the ice cream at the table, slightly softened, ready to be scooped shortly after the fruit comes off the grill.

Rule 3
Use salty (roasted peanuts, granola) and bitter (espresso, a drizzle of olive oil) ingredients to cut through the sugar of the fruit and ice cream; it makes for a more interesting dessert.

Rule 4
Use small bowls and spoons. A study from Cornell University found that people who used both ate 30 percent less ice cream than people who used big bowls and spoons.

345

Grilled Banana Splits

This isn't just some gimmicky way to cram a popular dessert into a book about grilling: There truly is something transformative about the way the banana emerges from the grill grate. The warm caramelized fruit adds a layer of sexiness to the classic split, especially in the way the heat of the banana plays off the chill of the ice cream. Salted peanuts add crunch and contrast while chocolate doubles down on the decadence. And yet all of this can be yours for the low, low price of just 320 calories!

You'll Need:

- 2 **bananas, unpeeled**
- 2 **Tbsp light brown sugar**
- 4 **scoops vanilla ice cream**
- 4 **Tbsp chocolate sauce, heated**
- 4 **Tbsp roasted and salted peanuts, roughly chopped**

For the best possible splits, the bananas should be ripe, but not soft.

How to Make It:

- Preheat a grill or grill pan over medium-high heat. Cut the bananas in half horizontally, being sure to leave each half in the peel. Coat the cut sides of the bananas with the brown sugar, using your fingers to press the sugar into the flesh of the fruit. Place the bananas on the grill, cut side down, and grill for about 3 minutes, until the sugar caramelizes and forms a deep-brown. Flip and grill for another 2 to 3 minutes, until the bananas are warmed all the way through but not mushy.

- Remove the peels from the bananas and place each half in the bottom of a bowl. Top with a scoop of ice cream, a good drizzle of hot chocolate sauce, and a handful of crushed peanuts.

Makes 4 servings

Per Serving:
$0.96

320 calories
12 g fat (5 g saturated)
38 g sugars

Stone Fruit Pizzas

After graduating from college, one of us (we won't say who) decided to go into the grilled pizza business. The plan was to set up shop in the farmers' markets of Southern California. At a final tasting to decide which vendors won a slot and which were sent packing, this dessert pizza won over the panel of judges and caused a small riot among passing pedestrians.

You'll Need:

- ½ cup balsamic vinegar
- 1 Tbsp honey

Pizza Dough (page 110)

- 2 lbs mixed stone fruits (peaches, plums, apricots), halved and pitted

Olive oil, for brushing

- 1 cup low-fat ricotta or mascarpone cheese

Mascarpone, a creamy, spreadable Italian cheese, makes for a great dessert pizza. It's more caloric than ricotta, so be mindful of the portion size if using.

If making the dough expressly for these pizzas, cut the salt by half and triple the amount of sugar.

How to Make It:

- Preheat a grill using a two-zone fire (see "Go High and Low," page 40), one zone high and the other low. Close the lid so that the heat can effectively build up. While the grill heats up, simmer the balsamic and honey in a small saucepan set over medium-low heat for about 10 minutes, until the liquid has reduced by about three-fourths.

- Cook the fruit on the hottest part of the grill, flesh sides down, for about 5 minutes, until caramelized and soft. Flip and grill for another 2 to 3 minutes, until the bottoms are soft. Remove and slice into ¼" pieces.

- Divide the dough into two equal balls. On a well-floured surface, use a rolling pin to stretch each ball into 12" circles.

- Place one of the dough circles on a lightly floured pizza peel. Brush the top with oil and slide it directly onto the hot part of the grill. Cook for about 30 seconds, until the dough begins to brown, then use a pair of tongs to rotate it 45 degrees. Grill for another 30 seconds, creating diamond-shaped grill marks on the crust. Flip the dough and place, raw side down, on the cooler side of the grill. Working quickly, spread half of the cheese on the pizza, then top with half of the grilled fruit slices. Close the grill top and let the pizza grill for 2 to 3 minutes. Use your tongs to rotate the pizza 45 degrees and continue grilling for another minute or two, until the crust is crisp beneath. Repeat with the other pizza. Drizzle the balsamic over the tops of the pizzas.

Makes 6 servings

Per Serving:	350 calories
$1.81	4.5 g fat (2 g saturated)
	16 g sugars

Banana-Nutella Panini

Sandwiches have always been defined as savory affairs, but there's no reason you can't bookend your dessert with two slices of bread the same way you would your lunch. Toast those pieces of bread until the sandwich is crispy on the outside and hot on the inside, and the appeal of a handheld dessert is all the more obvious. There are few better partnerships on the planet than banana and chocolate—so, really, there's no way this recipe could go wrong.

You'll Need:

- 4 Tbsp chocolate-hazelnut spread
- 8 slices whole-wheat bread
- 2 very ripe bananas, sliced
- 2 Tbsp butter, melted

The most widely available version is Nutella, but we prefer Nocciolata, which has a much more respectable ingredient list.

How to Make It:

- Preheat a grill or grill pan over medium heat. Divide the chocolate spread among 4 slices of the bread, pave completely with the banana slices, and top with the remaining pieces of bread. Brush both sides of each sandwich with a light coating of melted butter (which will help the sandwiches brown and crisp easily).

- Place the sandwiches on the grill and top with a light object—a clean pot or pan works great—that applies just enough pressure to weigh down the sandwiches and help them crisp. Grill for 3 to 4 minutes, until the bottoms are nicely toasted; flip and repeat. Cut the sandwiches in half on the diagonal and serve.

Makes 4 servings

MEAL MULTIPLIER

More additions to your dessert-sandwich repertoire:

- Peanut butter, banana, and honey
- Mascarpone or ricotta cheese and strawberries
- Marshmallow spread and dark chocolate chips (think s'mores)

Per Serving: **$1.12**

340 calories
13 g fat (5 g saturated)
20 g sugars

Grilled Apples à la Mode

When it comes to grilling fruit, peaches and pineapples tend to get most of the love. But if pie-eating has taught us anything, it's that apples become exponentially more delicious when cooked. We like to skip the fussy, calorie-dense crust in favor of a crunchy, sweet stuffing baked directly inside the apple. The heat of the grill softens and sweetens the fruit from the outside while it melts the butter and toasts the pecans within. Hot off the grill, with a scoop of vanilla ice cream melting over the top, this apple rivals a slice of warm homemade apple pie à la mode any day.

You'll Need:

- 4 **medium baking apples (Golden Delicious, Roma, etc.)**
- ¼ **cup brown sugar**
- 2 **Tbsp cold butter, chopped into small pieces**
- ¼ **cup chopped pecans or walnuts**
- ¼ **cup raisins**
- ¼ **tsp cinnamon**
- 4 **scoops vanilla ice cream**

How to Make It:

- Preheat a grill over medium-low heat. Using a paring knife and spoon, and working from the top of the apple, scoop out the core and center part of the fruit, leaving a firm base and a ½" shell of apple around the middle section.

- Combine the brown sugar, butter, pecans, raisins, and cinnamon in a mixing bowl. Pack each apple full with the mixture. Place the apples directly on the grill grate and close the lid. Grill for about 25 minutes, until the fruit is soft all the way through. Serve each apple with a scoop of ice cream over the top.

Makes 4 servings

Per Serving:

$1.70

390 calories
17 g fat (8 g saturated)
51 g sugars

Strawberry Shortcake

Why take a classic—one as basic and beloved as strawberry shortcake—and mess with it on the grill? The short answer: Why not? The long answer: The grill helps caramelize sugars, amplify texture, and gives the dish a hot-cold component that makes it more compelling—and delicious—than the original. This version is special for other reasons, as well. Strawberries come alive in a marinade of balsamic and cracked pepper (a classic Italian pairing that is hard not to love once you try it), and the fresh whipped cream is laced with a shot of balsamic, giving it an addictive tang that brings the whole dessert together.

You'll Need:

- 1 cup whipping cream
- 4 Tbsp balsamic vinegar
- 1 small carton strawberries, stemmed and sliced
- A few pinches of black pepper
- 4 (1½"-thick) slices angel food cake

How to Make It:

- Preheat a grill or grill pan over medium heat. Use an electric beater to beat the cream until it forms soft peaks (it should cling to the beaters, but not get stuck inside them). Add 2 tablespoons of the balsamic and continue beating until the whipped cream has a uniform color. (Alternatively, this can be done by hand with a whisk and a cold metal bowl. Makes for a good workout.)

- Combine the remaining 2 tablespoons balsamic with the strawberries and pepper in a bowl. Allow them to marinate while you grill the angel food cake.

- Grill the cake slices for 3 to 4 minutes per side, until well browned and crispy on the outside. Divide among 4 plates or bowls, top with the strawberries and spoon the whipped cream over the top.

Makes 4 servings

Per Serving:

$2.16

220 calories
12 g fat (7 g saturated)
6 g sugars

S'mores
Chocolate–Peanut Butter & Chocolate-Caramel

In the 80-odd years since the first known recipe for s'mores surfaced in an obscure Girl Scout publication, very little has changed with the campfire classic; it had the same three ingredients back then as it does now: graham crackers, chocolate, marshmallow. Admittedly, it's tough to improve upon the time-tested formula, but with the original as our inspiration and the grill as our muse, we think these two new iterations would do the Girl Scouts proud.

You'll Need:

- 8 large marshmallows
- 8 metal skewers, or wooden skewers soaked in water for 30 minutes
- 2 Tbsp dulce de leche
- 16 chocolate wafer cookies (like Nabisco Famous Chocolate Wafers)
- 2 Tbsp smooth peanut butter

Dulce de leche is a special type of caramel popular in Latin America. It's now widely available in the states, but if you can't find it, standard caramel sauce will do.

How to Make It:

- Preheat a grill over medium heat. Place a marshmallow at the end of each skewer. (If everyone wants to toast their own marshmallows, pass them around to guests.) Grill the marshmallows, turning, for about 3 minutes, until lightly brown and toasted all over. If using a charcoal grill, remove the grate and roast the marshmallows close to the coals; if using a gas grill, you can place directly on the hot grate.

- Spread ½ tablespoon of dulce de leche on each of 4 cookies and spread ½ tablespoon of peanut butter on each of another 4 cookies. Top each with a toasted marshmallow and another cookie. If you like, place the s'mores directly on the grill just long enough to warm, 1 to 2 minutes.

Makes 4 servings

Per Serving:	330 calories
$1.02	13 g fat (3 g saturated)
	29 g sugars

Upgrade

NUTRITIONAL

While swapping in peanut butter for chocolate in this recipe constitutes a step up in the nutrition status of the s'more, there are even greater strides that can be made while not sacrificing the overall feeling of decadence. Try pairing slices of banana with the peanut butter, slices of apple or pear with dulce de leche, or, in a riff on the classic s'mores construction, thick slices of strawberry with antioxidant-rich dark chocolate.

Index

Boldface page references indicate photographs.
Underscored references indicate boxed text and tables.